*This book is dedicated
to those who seek
the Truth*

Contents

vii

W HY ARE you reading this? What prompted you to pick up this book and start reading these words? Take a moment, even as you are holding this book in your hands now, and think about the underlying motive which brought you to the experience which is now occurring.

Within all human consciousness there is a guiding force which is seeking the Truth; an aspect of yourself which needs to be fulfilled, or realized. Deep inside, you know there is something more to life...some purpose to your existence. There is no "coincidence" in the fact that you happen to be reading this book at this particular time in your life. You are drawn to these words because you are ready to take the next step; you are continuing to read on because you are ready to go beyond to a higher level of awareness.

The *SPIRITUAL SEEKER'S GUIDE* is my attempt to provide others the resource that I had always looked for in my spiritual development: A guidebook which would provide an unbiased synopsis of the world's spiritual teachings. This book is divided into Eastern and Western Religions and their denominations, Spiritual Paths, Metaphysical Teachings, and Masters and Movements of the Twentieth Century. Each subject description includes a summary of the group's history, its ideology and its practices. Addresses and phone numbers of each representative group are provided, when available, so that you can make further enquiries about the organization. Also included at the end of each section is a recommended reading list. I have limited the span of my research to those teachings which are currently active and accessible, and have omitted other groups which are either relatively small, isolated, or did not want to be listed. If there is a group you feel has a place in this book, please send information on it to the address mentioned at the end of the book. In the conclusion, I have provided a summary of common spiritual practices such as meditation, contemplation and prayer; and I have provided some simple techniques for you to formulate and develop your own spiritual practices.

Being human, I cannot be completely unbiased. My vantage is that no one path is the path for everyone, and that all spiritual paths and religions provide what is needed for the consciousness that adheres to its doctrines and practices. Moreover, the Truth is not something which can be directly spoken or written about, or understood or experienced per se, but rather it is what you innately ARE and you will realize it when you are ready to. Scriptures and sutras can direct a seeker to Truth, but ultimately individuals must come to realize it for themselves. We are all here to learn lessons which will guide us to the Truth, and each individual will have unique circumstances in their lives which will guide them in different directions. All paths ultimately lead to the Truth. Rather than trying to convince another which one is best, I suggest we all work on realizing the Truth for ourselves and teach through our example. As you flip through these pages, allow your curiosity to be your guide and trust your intuition.

Throughout the book the words "mankind" or "man" are used to refer to the human race, including women and men equally, in order to make the book more readable (as opposed to wo/man, humankind, etc.). I herein acknowledge women as equally important members of "mankind," and personally feel their contribution is greatly needed in the spiritual community to counterbalance the inequities of male dominated religions.

THE MAKING OF THE BOOK

In one sense, the research for this book began over seventeen years ago (in the early 1970's) as I began, consciously, to question the purpose of existence and the true nature of my Self. As a child I intuitively started meditating on my own, and began learning yoga from a T.V. program which was on after school. As a teenager, I started exploring different kinds of churches, enrolled in a raja yoga class, took initiation into Transcendental Meditation and read all the spiritual books that I could get my hands on. The more I read and heard, the more engrossed I became in learning about myself and about God. None of the ministers, spiritualists, monks or teachers were able to answer the great questions of life to my satisfaction. So every year I just kept digging deeper, asking more questions, and looking into other spiritual paths. There are so many different opinions and beliefs about God, so many facets to our perception of reality. It seems that the deeper you go in your search for the Truth, the more invigorated with life you become. Although studying different spiritual ideologies often creates confusion, it's all part of a learning process which sows the seeds of wisdom. The growth takes place as you work out the answers for yourself. Hopefully, my leg work will make your journey a little easier, at least as far as accessing resources is concerned.

I was inspired to write this book during a backpacking trip in 1985, while sitting on top of a mountain peak meditating (kinda corny isn't it). On that day and every day since I prayed for guidance, and an amazing thing happened: I was given that guidance. Whenever I started researching a particular group or teaching, information about that organization would just fall into my lap. Literature about a group that I was investigating would mysteriously arrive in the mail, or I would "just happen" to bump into someone who was involved in that group. Spiritual leaders would come to the area, just as I began my research on them. On several occasions I arrived unannounced at the door of a Spiritual Master, to find that I had been expected and that the Master knew who I was and why I had come. Opportunities to travel to Asia, the Middle East and Europe also materialized, just as needed to complete the sections that I was writing on relevant to those cultures and teachings. The "co-incidences" and uncanny timing of events that took place to facilitate the writing of this book are innumerable. This book was guided by an "invisible hand."

In order to gain first hand experience with each spiritual teaching, I personally involved myself in the worship, rituals and rites of each path that I could; taking classes, workshops, and lectures whenever possible. In the course of my research I have taken over a dozen initiations from spiritual masters from numerous disciplines, and have studied yoga and meditation extensively with several of the world's most renowned Saints and Yogis (see acknowledgements). Whenever possible I would meet with the spiritual leaders, or at least listen to their lectures live or on tape, and would interview group members in order to get their feelings and perspectives. Literally hundreds of books were consumed over the years.

After writing about a group, I would send them a copy of what I had written so that they could make any changes THEY felt were necessary. Every attempt was made to represent each path from the perspective of the group leader and/or organization (rather than my opinion). In the case of large religions this was particularly difficult, for the broader the category of teaching the greater the diffusion of views and beliefs. I am NOT recommending any one particular path; trust how you feel inside.

WARNING AND DISCLAIMER

Many of the organizations mentioned in this book are subject to criticism by ex-members, the press, the law or other religious organizations. The reader should take care to look at any group which they are considering joining, and learn all they can about them before making any commitments. If you would like to get other perspectives about the group which you are considering joining, I suggest that you contact the Cult Awareness Network and ask them for information about the group that you are thinking about first.

The Cult Awareness Network compiles information about various spiritual organizations with questionable morals or ethics, and provides direction for those involved in what THEY consider destructive cults or mind control. Many religious organizations also offer counseling. Please consider that all groups have their own biases, opinions and judgments of each other, so you must always consider the source of your information.

The Cult Awareness Network
2421 West Pratt Blvd., Suite 1173
Chicago, IL 60645
Phone: (312) 267-7777

ACKNOWLEDGEMENTS

This book was made possible through the constructive guidance of the leaders and representatives from each of the respective paths which I have written about; without your help, this book would not have been possible. May all of you who teach, serve the Seeker for the benefit of all mankind.

I would like to express a special thanks to the following people who I was able to personally see, or speak with, and/ or who provided personal guidance to me while writing this book (from Eastern to Western): Yogiraj Vethathiri Maharishi, Sri Sri Sri Shivabalayogi Maharaj, Satya Sai Baba, Mata Amritanandamayi, Sri Chinmoy, Gurumayi Chidvalasananda, Baba Hari Dass, Osho Rajneesh, Sant Thakar Singh, Swami Chetanananda, Swami Laksmana Joo, Swami Vishudevananda, Swami Shantinand, Swami Sahajananda, Swami Hariharananda Giri, Bhattacharya Swami, Yogi Bhajan, Yogi Sidhoji, B.K.S. Iyengar, H.H. Tenzin Gyatso the XIVth Dalai Lama, H.E. Kalu Rinpoche, H.E. Jamgon Kongtrul Rinpoche, Roshi Suzuki, Master Ho, Sindari, Pir Vilayat Inayat Khan, Rabbi Dr. Philip S. Berg, Dr. Robert S. Schuller, Rev. Artivas Manasian, Rev. James Keck, Rev. Peggie Basset, Sri Harold Klemp, Jach Purcel/ Lazaris, Lady Janet, Wallace Black Elk, Bear Heart Williams, Danny Ravenwing, Kahiliopua and Usha Baul. I would also like to express my appreciation to the many other teachers who provided valuable assistance to the writing and to my personal growth. To all of you, I am grateful beyond words; may my thoughts, words and actions reflect the wisdom which you imparted.

Several resources were invaluable in my research, which the readers may want to take note of: The Abingdon Dictionary of Living Religions, by Abingdon in Nashville; *Hinduism Today*, a monthly newspaper published by the Himalayan Academy. I drew heavily from these resources, and they may provide you assistance in pursuing a more in-depth study. Most organizations mentioned in this book had published information which I used to describe their history and beliefs; and whenever possible I tried to quote or paraphrase from their own literature in order to insure an accurate representation.

Special thanks to Robert Leathers, the President of Allwon Publishing, for his support at a spiritual, personal and professional level, and to Dr. Robert Ellwood, professor of Religion at the University of Southern California, for his valuable feedback. I thank my parents and family for accepting me the way I am (a bit out of the norm perhaps), and I am grateful to Grandma and Grandpa Sadleir for introducing me to Jesus. Great love and appreciation is extended to my students and friends at the Self Awareness Institute for hearing me out, and encouraging me to push on with the book in the midst of innumerable obstacles, and to Swamiji for his support and guidance. And from the depths of my soul I thank God for making it all possible.

*T*HROUGHOUT RECORDED history human beings have sought to know God, to know themselves, and to understand the relationship between themselves and God. All cultures throughout history show signs that they understood there to be some greater being, or force, that set forth into motion this Divine Play that we know as our existence. Yet so few beings have been able to discover, and convey to us, who our Creator is, or what our purpose is in creation. Developing a relationship with the Divine is a central theme in the creation and development of all societies, and discovering purpose to this life experience is at the core of our very existence. Man's eternal quest is to discover meaning in his existence, to seek out the Truth of who we essentially are, and who, or what, "God" is.

Man's perspectives and opinions of the Divine are as varied as the multitude of cultures and peoples that have inhabited the planet. In areas where man lives closest with nature, he sees God expressed through nature—animism. As societies begin to see the divergent nature of natural laws, they have attributed what they experienced to Divine intervention and gave each expression a name to identify and explain it—polytheism. Historically, great thinkers came to realize that there was one underlying and unifying force in the Universe, and that force was characterized as having attributes that man could identify with—monotheism. And there are those few throughout history who so devoted themselves to the attainment of the Divine, that they came to know God through their own personal experience—realization. All are perceiving the Divine through their own perspective, and each can validate their Truth given the angle from which they choose to see it. Whatever God is, just is, and it is only our perspective of what God is that ever changes.

Most people belong to one of the world's great religions, and accept its belief, or concept of God, on faith. Of the 5.5 billion people of this world, the vast majority are either Christian, Islamic, Buddhist or Hindu. Christianity is the largest religion in the world with approximately 1.5 billion members, 1 billion of which are Catholic or Orthodox, and .5 billion are Protestant. There are also around 1 billion members of the Islamic faith, making it the world's second largest religion. They, incidently, believe in the same God as the Jews and Christians, but refer to God as "Allah." Buddhism comprises the world's third largest religion, and if the Chinese government hadn't banned the practice of religion in China, Buddhism may well have become the world's largest religion. There are some 1 billion Chinese who are now culturally communist, which officially does not recognize any religion, but who traditionally are aligned with Buddhist, Taoist and Confucian teachings. Hinduism, the world's next largest religion, is actually a number of religious systems originating from India. Buddhist teachings are akin to Hindu theology, and together practicing Buddhists and Hindus make up about 1 billion of the world's population. The remaining 1 billion people of the world's population belong to numerous other smaller religions, spiritual paths and teachings, or they are atheists.

Interestingly enough, all the world's great teachings tend to have very similar messages and advice: That God is the unifying force in the Universe, and that we should love "him" and obey "his" laws. The differences are primarily cultural and depend upon man's interpretation of the laws that were given by God. Of course every religion maintains that its interpretation is the correct one; but as all societies have evolved, their interpretations of their own laws have also changed. All religions have adapted their theologies to accomodate changes in society and science. Ultimately each individual has a unique understanding of, and relationship with, the Divine, and each follows his or her own path.

Recent history has documented radical changes in the spiritual development of mankind. Churches, temples and mosques are having to adapt to the new free thinking ways of an educated population. In the past, religious leaders proclaimed dictates for their constituents to live by, and those dictates were rarely challenged. Now, the role of the governing religious bodies is to provide guidelines for living, based on their interpretation of the laws of their Faith. These days more and more people are taking it upon themselves to live by their own interpretation or understanding of God's law, and they are basing their convictions upon their own experiences, rather than purely on faith. The more educated a society becomes, the more they question, and the better basis they have to evaluate the Truth for themselves.

In the Western Civilization, the trend has been to strike out for independent investigation of the Truth. Church attendances are down, and many new movements are forming to reflect the changing values and beliefs of the society. A "New Age" movement was forming during the turn of the century, with independent thinkers like Emerson, Whitman and Thoreau developing a "transcendentalist" movement, which appears to now be in full swing with a plethora of new spiritual groups espousing transcendental doctrines. Indeed, meditation has come out of the occult closet, and is starting to become not only a household word, but practice. Interestingly enough, meditation, introspective studies and rituals are re-entering many religious organizations, in an effort to add sustenance to ailing dogmas. In our societies' drive to know the Truth, many people have delved into ancient esoteric teaching and traditional paths in an effort to uncover the secrets that would enliven their spirituality. Still others have looked to the East to gain an understanding from a preserved history, or are consulting with the Masters who have realized the Truth for themselves. One thing is constant throughout all spiritual circles these days, and that is change. Mankind is in a fervor for the Truth.

The purpose of this book is to assist YOU to evolve your own understanding by becoming familiar with what others have said, and then use that wisdom to inspire you to discover the Truth for yourself. No matter what path you follow, and no matter if you even follow a path, your relationship with God is personal and your awareness of who you are is experientially based. The spiritual paths described in this book provide a forum for you to develop an awareness of Truth for yourself. That which we come to know is expressed through our thoughts, feelings and actions, and is conveyed, usually quite inadequately, through the very limited form of expression, as words. As you read these words, realize that they are only being used to provoke a response that will help awaken within you something that you already knew, deep inside, was True. Allow your personal direct experience to be your guide.

This book is designed so you can either read it through cover to cover for a complete overview of the world's spiritual teachings, or flip through it leisurely to provide insight into areas that you are curious about. Each section is condensed into the essentials in an effort to make the book more readable, and is only intended to provide a brief overview. After getting the gist of the teachings, hopefully you will be inspired to investigate one or more of these teachings independently. I could not possibly do any of these spiritual paths justice in such short space. Please determine the qualities of these vehicles for learning through your own research and understanding. The responsibility for really understanding the messages of these teachings rests with you.

The search for Truth is an adventure, an exploration into the very meaning and purpose in your life. Look around you, most people don't really live, they merely exist. Those who make the effort to discover their own spiritual identity, begin to wake up to a new exciting life. They add sustenance to their lives. Imagine living a life with an understanding of who you really are, and what your purpose in life is. Imagine a life with real meaning. There IS a purpose and meaning to your existence, and if you don't know it, then you haven't looked deep enough. When you begin to feel invigorated with life, when you are just naturally happy for no apparent reason, and when you understand why certain events in your life are occurring and can deal with life's tests and trials, then you have begun to awaken your inner spiritual nature. Why settle for anything less? Ask for direction and guidance and it will be given; seek out the Truth for yourself and you will find it. There is no reason that you cannot know the Truth for yourself, it just takes making the effort to discover it. Don't believe anyone, including me. Find out for yourself. It starts by turning the page.

EASTERN RELIGIONS

EASTERN RELIGIONS

*B*E LEERY of writers who make broad generalizations about Eastern thought or religion—including me. Those teachings that originated in the East are quite divergent and encompassing. Moreover, trying to understand Eastern philosophies from a Western perspective is in itself distorting. The broad, holistic, Eastern perspective of the Divine just doesn't fit into the narrow analytical boundaries of Western thought. Western religions (Judaism, Christianity, and Islam) evolved from one source, the patriarch Abraham, and from the common belief that there is only one God and that "He" has set laws which we must obey. In the East, "universal Truths" were revealed to various enlightened individuals at different times and places in history, and no one particular philosophy or belief was adopted by Asia as a whole. In the West, we tend to make judgments about which philosophies and beliefs are "right" or "wrong," whereas in the East there is generally more freedom to evaluate the Truth for yourself, and each can come to a different conclusion within the multifaceted expression of the divine.

Eastern religions are eclectic, drawing upon the insights of various learned seers and saints. The predominant strains of Eastern thought evolved on the Indian subcontinent, first from the Vedic wisdom of the *rishis* (seers) dating back several thousand years, and later from the Buddha, who lived approximately 2,500 years ago, as well as from many other enlightened beings since then. The Chinese influences of Taoism and Confucianism have also melded in the cauldron of Eastern philosophy, as we tend to clump it together in the West. Shamanistic elements have also contributed to Eastern teachings, particularly in Tibetan Buddhism and Japanese Shinto. So Eastern religion is a vast body of philosophy that provides for flexibility in spiritual thought and practice.

This section begins with Hinduism, which is so involved that individual components within Hinduism—such as the Vedic religion (scriptural); the Brahmanic religion (societal); and the Bhakti religion (devotional), including Vaishnavism and Shaivism—are explained in a special supplement at the back of the book. The summary of Hinduism is followed by those spiritual practices that evolved within the Hindu culture, such as Yoga, Tantrism, Sikhism, Jainism, and Buddhism. This section closes with an explanation of the Chinese contributions to Eastern religion, including Taoism and Confucianism, and the Japanese religion of Shinto. So my context of Eastern religion extends from India to Japan, and those religions that originated in the Middle East are categorized under Western religions, as they have had their greatest influence in the West. Zoroastrianism and Sufism are discussed in the section "Spiritual Paths" for the convenience of explanation. Smaller spiritual orders and spiritual masters from the East are discussed in the section "Masters and Movements."

HINDUISM

*H*INDUISM IS not a religion per se, but rather a variety of religious beliefs and practices making up the major religious traditions of the Indian subcontinent. *Hindu* is a Persian word for the people and culture of the Indus River region (northwest India), hence the synonym *Indian*. Unlike other world religions, Hinduism was not founded by any particular person, and it is not based on any one set of beliefs, or dogma. Hinduism is based on the *Sanatana Dharma*, the Eternal Truths, or Law, that have been realized and expounded by the *rishis*, or great seers, dating back to well over ten thousand years ago. Thus Hinduism is the oldest living religion in the world.[1]

During the second millennium B.C., nomadic Aryan tribes invaded the northern part of India, bringing a culture and theology that became integrated with the beliefs of the various indigenous agrarian communities that existed throughout India at that time. For many years the spiritual traditions of this ancient civilization were passed on orally, but eventually these sacred teachings were compiled into the world's oldest collection of spiritual texts, known as the Vedas. The Vedas were written down over a period of thousands of years, and evolved different theologies over time.

The Vedas consist of over 1,000 hymns, which describe the various relationships God has with man. No one theology is adopted in the Vedas, but rather a cosmology and philosophy that developed out of animistic, polytheistic, and pantheistic mythologies and evolved into a monotheistic relationship. The oldest Vedic text is the *Rig Veda*, which in its written form dates back to 1400 B.C. The Vedic theology evolved through a collection of writings called the Upanishads, which were compiled between 500 B.C. and A.D. 200, and then concludes with the Vedantic writings, also known as Vedanta ("End of the Vedas"), which were written between

---

[1] Ruins of a Dravidian civilization (ca. 3000-2000 B.C.) that worshiped Shiva were found at Mohenjo-Daro in western Punjab, India.

A.D. 200 and 800 (See the section "Vedic Religion" in the special supplement.) Another important set of spiritual texts that influenced the Hindu culture are the Sutras and the Sastras, which were written from 500 B.C. to 200 B.C. The Sutras consist of various instructions for the Brahman priests as to how to conduct various religious acts and ceremonies, and serve as a guide for human conduct. The Sastras are primarily concerned with matters of personal conduct and a code of ethics. (See the section "Brahmanic Religion" in the special supplement.)

With the advent of the teachings of Buddha around the year 500 B.C. (see also the section "Buddhism"), a trend developed in India. Rather than relying on a Brahman priest or rigorous austerities to relate or commune with the divine, individuals were inspired to develop a personal relationship with God. This popular Hinduism began to spread throughout India, evolving into the devotional, or "Bhakti," form of worship that is most prevalent in India today. These devotional practices are outlined in a collection of writings known as the Puranas as well as in the Hindu epics, the *Mahabharata* and the *Ramayana*. (See the section "Bhakti Hinduism" in the special supplement.)

As the ancient wisdom was revealed and evolved through the different cultures that existed in different parts of India, various forms were adopted to depict the nature of God, and humanity's relationship with God. There are literally thousands of gods and goddesses that are revered in the Hindu traditions; all are generally accepted as personal forms of the divine. Hindus don't typically argue about which god is "The" god, but rather accept that God can represent itself through any and all forms, or through no form at all. There is a general underlying basic belief in a universal principal, or power, known as Brahma, which is omnipotent, omniscient, and beyond all the confines of time, space, and causation. This universal power is typically represented through three major principles: creation, preservation, and destruction. These three attributes are represented by the principal gods in the Hindu pantheon: Brahma, the creative aspect; Vishnu, the preserver; and Shiva (or Siva), the destroyer (of illusion). Thus, God incarnates into form, evolves through conscious-

ness, and transcends again, merging into Total Consciousness.

Although Brahma is represented as the creator, he is
revered but not really worshiped much today in India. The
most popular of the Hindu gods is Vishnu. Vishnu is often
depicted reclining on the seven-headed cobra Ananta. His
consort, or feminine aspect, is Lakshmi, the goddess of
wealth and prosperity. It is through a dream of Vishnu that
Brahma creates the universe. In times of great turmoil,
Vishnu incarnates into form to save the world. Vishnu's most
important incarnations include Rama and Krishna. Krishna
has developed a theology of his own, and is today the most
revered god in India, followed by Rama. (See the section
"Vaishnavism" in the special supplement.)

The oldest and most complex of the Hindu gods is Lord
Shiva. The archaeological ruins of Mohenjo-Daro and Harappa
in western Punjab, India, indicate that an advanced Dravidian
culture existed in 2,000 B.C., which worshiped a god identified as Lord Shiva. In these ancient ruins a pendant was
found that showed Lord An, or Shiva, seated in a yogic
posture with a trident (a symbol of Shiva). This makes
Shaivism the oldest living faith in the world. Shiva's present
personality is partly based on the attributes of (1) Rudra, the
wild god of the Vedas; (2) Agni, the god of fire and the first god
mentioned in the Vedas; and (3) Indra, giver of life. The
Puranas depict Shiva as the arch-yogi, who can deliver the
aspirant to the realization of God through his powers of
tapasya—the intense fire of inward-turned consciousness.

Shiva resides on the earth for mankind, and is often
represented by the lingam (a symbolic rounded column) that
represents his powers of transcendence. Shiva is often represented in the form of Nrttamurti (Nataraja), performing the
Cosmic Dance inside a mandala of fire, controlling the
interplay of creation and destruction. Shiva's consort, or
feminine aspect, is called Uma, or Parvati, who represents
the Divine Wisdom and Universal Energy (shakti). This
great mother goddess is known under many names, and
worshiped under many forms. The most prominent form
depicts her wrathful and terrifying aspects as Kali, or Durga,
whose powers destroy man's ego. Shiva's feminine aspects

7

represent the destruction of the illusion of physical existence, and the awakening of consciousness. The divine couple has two sons: Ganesha, the elephant-headed deity who provides access to the great gods, and Karikeya, the war god, who rides upon a peacock. (See the section "Shaivism" in the special supplement.)

For more information:

Hindu temples and centers can be found in many major Western cities. A listing of Hindu temples and information on visiting Hindu teachers or priests can be found in *Hinduism Today*. You can also check metaphysical bookstores and health-food stores for information on visiting Eastern spiritual masters. (See also the other Eastern religions and the "Masters and Movements" section of this book.)

Recommended Reading:

The Upanishads
(The Classics) *Bhagavad-Gita*
The Siva Sutras

Vedanta Catalog for other resources c/o:
Vedanta Society of Southern California
1946 Vedanta Place
Hollywood, CA 90068-3996
Phone:(213) 856-0322

Periodicals: *Hinduism Today* (a monthly newspaper)
1819 Second Street
Concord, CA 94519
Phone:(808) 822-7032

Yoga Journal
P.O. Box 3755
Escondido, CA 92033
Phone:(800) 334-8152

Clarion Call
815 Arnold Drive #124
Martinez, CA 94553-9849
Phone:(415) 372-6002

Meditation Magazine
17510 Sherman Way #212
Van Nuys, CA 91406
Phone:(818) 343-4998

EastWest
P.O. Box 57320
Boulder, CO 80322-7320
Phone:(617) 232-1000

YOGA

Y OGA IS the science of self awareness, and comprises various systems for attaining total consciousness. *Yoga* is a Sanskrit word that means "discipline" (literally: "to yoke" or "to harness"), and refers to the process of making a union with Divine Consciousness. The precise origin of Yoga has not been determined. A pendant found in the ruins of Mohenjo-Daro in western Punjab, India, depicts An (Shiva), the creator of the universe, sitting in a classical yoga posture. These ruins date back to around 2,000 B.C. The *Rig Veda* describes a spiritual ascetic (muni) with abilities attributed to yogis, and the *Atharva Veda* describes a group of ascetics who practice various postures and breathing exercises associated with yoga. Thus the concepts, at least, date back to the second millennium B.C. The term *yoga* was first recorded in the *Katha, Shvetashvatara,* and *Maitri* Upanishads, which were written sometime around 500 B.C.

Yoga as we know it today has its roots in the classical system called **Raja Yoga**, "The King of Yoga," which was delineated by the arch-yogi Patanjali, who lived around A.D. 300. In Patanjali's *Yoga Sutras* the methods of attaining enlightenment are established through eight limbs, or levels, known as **Ashtanga Yoga** (the eight-limbed path). Through yoga practice the aspirant evolves from "ordinary awareness" *(citta)* to becoming totally conscious *(purusha)*; from being aware "of" things (subject-object relationship) to becoming one with the consciousness. This transformation is achieved through various meditation techniques that quiet the mind and senses, allowing clear consciousness to naturally develop. By transcending the mind, the yogi is no longer limited by the constraints of maya (the illusion of separateness from the divine), and becomes liberated *(moksha)*.

Liberation is the purpose and goal of yoga practice.

The eight limbs of Ashtanga Yoga are as follows: (1) the restraint of mind and actions *(yama)*, (2) physical and moral purity *(niyama)*, (3) physical postures *(asana)*, (4) control of the breath *(pranayama)*, (5) detachment of the physical senses *(pratyahara)*, (6) the ability to focus the attention on the object of meditation *(dharana)*, (7) maintaining balanced concentration *(dhyana)*, and finally, (8) the attainment of a state in meditation in which the difference between "subject" and "object" disappears *(samadhi)*. *Samadhi* means "to hold together completely" and refers to the state of overcoming the mind and senses, and joining pure consciousness. Through this process the yogi makes union with the divine, *yoga*, and achieves enlightenment.

More familiar to the Westerner is the practice of the discipline of exertion, or **Hatha Yoga**. This discipline involves controlling the body and mind through various physical postures *(asana)*, breathing exercises *(pranayama)*, and a pure (usually vegetarian) diet. Sometimes various meditation techniques are also prescribed. These regimented practices act to purify the body and open up new sources of energy, called *shakti*, within special spiritual centers in the body, called *chakras*. Hatha Yoga provides a means of relaxation and physical and mental well-being, and is a foundation for both Tantric and Raja Yoga practices (generally the third and forth limbs of Ashtanga Yoga).

Kundalini Yoga is central to the awakening of consciousness, and is implicit in most forms of yoga. The body and mind operate on a life-force current called the *kundalini shakti*. It is this energy that allows the heart to beat, the lungs to expand and contract, and the mind to function. We draw in the Universal Magnetism, which is pervasive in the atmosphere, and convert it into biomagnetism through subtle channels that run down from our nose to the base of the spine. From the tip of the tailbone, the *kundalini* moves up the spine through the cerebrospinal fluid to the head, passing through a total of seven energy transformation centers, which are connected with the endocrine glands and are called *chakras*. By stimulating certain endocrine glands in the head through yogic meditation practices, the *kundalini shakti* is induced to move up into the head, stimulating dormant areas within the mind. As these dormant areas are "awakened" by the *kundalini*, the aspirants realize their true nature and remember who they really are. As the *kundalini* rises to the crown center at the top of the head (the

11

Thousand-Petalled Lotus), the yogi awakens his or her consciousness and achieves enlightenment.

In popular Hinduism, the *Bhagavad Gita* describes several types of yoga for the disciple to follow, these include: the discipline of knowledge, or **Jnana Yoga**, in which the seeker is instructed in reflective meditation, using the mind to transcend the mind; the discipline of action, or **Karma Yoga**, in which the practitioner is instructed in how to act without becoming attached to the fruits of the action; as well as the discipline of devotion, or **Bhakti Yoga**, in which the devotees are instructed in acting in continuing faith in God, or Krishna. It is believed that by following these disciplines, the devotee can transcend the embodied condition and become united in God consciousness.

For additional information:

Yoga is traditionally learned from a recognized yogi in an established lineage of instruction. (See the "Masters and Movements" section of this book.) *Yoga Journal* publishes a Yoga Teachers Directory for the entire world in each July/August issue (back issues may be ordered). Hatha yoga classes are often held in neighborhood centers, schools or colleges, and city recreation departments.

Recommended Reading:

Patanjali's *Yoga Sutra*
(various translations)

The Concise Yoga Vasistha
by Swami Venkatesananda

TANTRISM

*T*ANTRA IS the esoteric spiritual discipline that utilizes *shakti*, the creative power of the absolute, to attain self-realization. There is some evidence that proto-tantric elements existed as far back as 1000 B.C., when phallic lore was well established in India. Tantric elements appear in Hindu and particularly yogic disciplines, in Buddhism, and in Taoism. The first tantric written works appear around A.D. 300, through the Buddhist "radical institutions of Manjusri" and the "tantra of secret association" (Guhysamajatantra). The first authentic Hindu text was compiled in the eleventh century and was called "The Tantra of Great Liberation" *(Mahanirvanatantra)*. Tantrism peaked in India between the ninth and fourteenth centuries, and then as devotional (Bhakti) Hinduism began promoting its puritanical ideology, Tantrism was shunned and remains a relatively obscure practice. Most tantric practices have never been written down and are only passed on orally from guru to student when the student proves that he or she is ready.

Tantrism comes from a Sanskrit word meaning "that which extends, spreads." Tantrists assert that tantric teachings are essentially based on the Vedas, but Tantrism distinctly differs from traditional Hinduism in that it does not adhere to the caste system and is overtly anti-Brahmanical, allowing women and members of lower castes to practice its rites. Tantrists place their emphasis on yoga practices and meditation. Reliance is placed on a guru (spiritual teacher) rather than on written texts. Hindu tantric scriptures deal with the relationship between God (Shiva) and his Power (Shakti), with the aim of transcending the apparent duality of the spiritual (God) and the material (man) through realization of the union between Shiva and Shakti. Tantra takes what most people would consider obstacles and utilizes them as methods of self-realization. Tantra is considered a faster, but sometimes more dangerous, discipline for realization. It often utilizes extreme measures to achieve results more quickly, and if done incorrectly can hinder one's spiritual development.

The purpose of tantric practice is to achieve a rapid *moksha* or release of the human self *(atman)* from the cycle of birth and death *(samsara)*. The Tantrist achieves this liberation of the soul through *kundalini* awakening and through the union of male and female principles, where the male is characterized as Shiva (knowledge) and the female as Shakti (energy). The achievement of Brahman, or God realization, arises through the union of Shiva and Shakti, where the *kundalini* (life force energy) rises to the highest centers of awareness at the top of the head. Through the tantric techniques, the dualistic illusion *(maya)* of this world is dissolved, and the impersonal absolute is seen.

In tantric practices the aspirant typically must master a certain degree of control of the body, mind, and senses. Buddhist trantric practices tend to be more ritualistic and alchemical, while Hindu and Taoist practices tend to be yogic. Buddhist practices involve elaborate rituals, chanting, visualizations, and meditations. Hindu and Taoist practices are more physical, involving movement and breath control. In yogic practices the student learns to raise the "dormant power," or *kundalini*, from within. In *some* practices, after the student attains a prescribed degree of mastership in controlling the *kundalini*, male participants (Shivas) and female participants (Shaktis) work together to raise each other's *kundalini shakti*. Tantric practices usually involve some form of meditation in action. Sometimes various *mantras* are recited first, and certain *pujas*, or rituals of worship are observed. In some trantric practices in India, the participants imbibe generous quantities of Vijaya (a drink made with marijuana or other sacred substances and sweetened milk). Once a higher or altered state of consciousness is achieved, the Shivas initiate copulation with the Shaktis. The key in this technique is to keep the consciousness on the divine aspects of the male and female principles, and to refrain from ejaculating throughout the intercourse. The energy that is generated through the meditation and/or intercourse is raised to the centers of higher consciousness in the head. The achievement of simultaneous control of mind, breath, and semen is believed to be a shortcut to *moksha,* or spiritual liberation. Some tantric practices can be dangerous if improperly performed, particularly the retaining of semen.

There is also a special kind of tantric practice called Aghora, in which, in order to overcome attachments to sense perception, the Agori purposefully engages in activities that would otherwise repulse us due to our sociological and psychological conditioning. These practices can include practicing *mantras* or other *sadhana* on corpses, smearing feces all over themselves, or eating human flesh. Most Aghoris live in cremation grounds, do not wear clothes, and act like lunatics. Intoxicants are often used, and they are frequently assisted by spirits and other entities. Tantrists in general, and Aghoris in particular, tend toward the worship of the female aspect of the deity, such as Ma Kali or Durga. I am not familiar with any Aghora practice outside isolated parts of India.

For additional information:

Look under "Masters and Movements." Various yogis utilize tantric elements. Certain Tibetan Buddhist and Taoist teachers are also tantric in their practice.

Recommended Reading:

> *The Doctrine of Recognition*
> or *Spanda Karikas*
> by Jaideva Singh

> *The Book of the Secrets*
> *Tantra, Spirituality and Sex*
> or *Tantra: The Supreme Understanding*
> by Bhagawan Shree Rajneesh

> *Taoist Secrets of Love*
> (a version for men and for women)
> by Mantak Chia and Michael Winn

Aghora, At the Left Hand of God
by Robert E. Svoboda

see also: Books on Tibetan Buddhism

SIKHISM

*T*HE SIKH belief and line of Gurus started in northern India with the birth of Guru Nanak in A.D. 1469. It is believed by the Sikhs that at the age of thirty Nanak had gone to bathe in a nearby stream, disappeared in the water, and was supposed drowned. During this incident he was spoken to by God and given the mission to preach, after which he returned from the stream. This event is described in detail in his "Janam Sakhis" (birth stories).

During Nanak's life, Hinduism and Muslim Sufism were the dominant religions in northern India. Sikhism is an eclectic faith that includes the teachings of Bhakti Hinduism and the Muslim Sufis, as well as the teachings of Guru Nanak and the Gurus who followed. Nanak's followers were both Hindus and Muslims, and those who followed his teachings described themselves as "Nanakprasthas" (followers of Nanak's path), or his disciples—Sikhs. From Nanak came a succession of Sikh Gurus through to the present day. Before Nanak's death, he appointed a disciple, Angad, to carry on his mission. Angad was succeeded by another disciple, Amar Das, who then nominated his son-in-law, Ram Das Sodhi. From here on, guruship remained in the Sodhi family. Ram Das nominated his son, Arjun, who compiled the sacred scripture of the Sikhs, the *Granth Sahib (Adi Granth)*, which consists of hymns of the first four Gurus, his own compositions, and writings of Hindu and Muslim saints from northern India. Arjun then nominated his son, Hargobind, who was then succeeded by his grandson, Har Rai, who was in turn succeeded by his son Hari Krishen. Hari Krishen died as a child, so Hargobind's surviving son, Tegh Bahadur, was acclaimed by the Sikhs as their ninth Guru. Tegh Bahadur was beheaded by the Mogul court, which did not like, and were threatened by, his teachings; so his only son, Gobind Rai, became the tenth Sikh Guru.

On the Punjabi New Year's Day in A.D. 1699, Gobind Rai baptized the Khalsa (the Brotherhood of the Pure Ones), and gave them as well as himself the new family name of

Singh (lion), which has been carried on to present day by all Sikhs. He also made it obligatory for them to wear their hair and beards unshorn and to carry a saber *(kirpan)*. He also prescribed rules of conduct. Before his death, Gobind Singh proclaimed that the line of Gurus was at an end and thereafter the *Adi Granth* (Sikh Holy Scripture) would be regarded as the living Guru, and be known as SRI Guru Granth Sahib.

According to a 1971 census, there are approximately ten million Sikhs in India (slightly less than two percent of the population). Sikhism has also been accepted by many Westerners, and has spread around the world. The basis behind all Sikh beliefs comes from Guru Nanak's teachings, which as previously mentioned were influenced by both Hindu and Muslim teachings. Nanak thought that the aim of life was union with God, and that union could be achieved by blending our light with the eternal light. Meditation or the chanting of various names of God would bring about the inner light and sound, or word of God, which would then free one from the illusion *(maya)* of the physical world, whereupon one could then know God. In order to obtain true knowledge of God, one has to become detached from worldly things and "overcome the base desires and battle with the mind." Nanak thought that realization of truth comes from within the heart through the light and sound of God, and though one learns of God through inner experiences, one must be directed by a true Guru.

For more information contact:

Sikh *Dharma*
1620 Preuss Road
Los Angeles, CA 90035
Phone: (213) 552-3416

Recommended Reading:

The Gospel of the Guru-Granth Sahib
Tr. by the Theosophical Publishing House

The Jap-ji
by Guru Nanak

Sikh Gurus
by K.S. Duggal

JAINISM

*T*HE TERM *Jainism* comes from the Sanskrit word *Jaina*, which means "follower of a Jina." *Jina* is a Sanskrit word meaning "conqueror," or "victor." A Jina is one who conquers his inner enemies to bring out his highest qualities. Jainism is a system of asceticism and meditation that teaches *Jiva* (the soul of each person) how to conquer material existence and achieve liberation from it.

In Jain philosophy there was a series of twenty-four great teachers known as *tirthankaras*, or "crossing-makers," who have shown mankind the vehicle to freedom from the bondage of the material world. The founder of Jainism, the first *tirthankara*, was A-dina-than (or Rsabha). However, modern Jainism is based on the teachings of the twenty-fourth and last *tirthankara*, known as Mahavira, "the Great Hero," who was born in 598 B.C.[2] near the city of Patna in northeastern India. Mahavira was born into a warrior (Kshatriya) clan, and abandoned his home at age thirty to become an ascetic, wandering and begging and meditating. At age forty-two, Mahavira attained complete knowledge *(kaivalya)* and started spreading his teachings, and a following quickly grew. In 527 B.C. Mahavira died and the leadership passed on to the Ganadharas, "leaders of the assembly." The movement continued to grow throughout India, but not too much outside India, though there are several Jain Meditation Centers in the United States. There are about 500,000 Jains practicing throughout the world today. There are two Jain sects: the Digambaras and the Shvetambaras. The Digambaras completely renounce everything, including the wearing of clothes. The Shvetambaras wear only white clothes (as monastics), and propagate literature.

Jainism has traditionally been a very radical system of austere monasticism, but has recently offered to Western culture, ("lay persons,") Jain meditation techniques as a means of achieving liberation without adopting the severe

---

[2] A contemporary of Siddhartha Gautama

ascetic practices. Jainism is based on four main principles: *ahimsa,* nonviolence in its broadest sense, including nonviolence in action, speech and thought; Anekantwad, the belief that there is no "one Truth," but many truths that are represented by different viewpoints; Aparigraha, nonattachment to people and material things; and *karma,* responsibility for one's actions, words, and thoughts which shape our futures and involve reincarnation (repeated births on the earth in order to learn from our actions, or *karma*).

The thrust of Jainism lies in its meditation techniques. Emphasis is placed on the individual's inner experiences, and the development of a soul's consciousness. Key factors in Jain meditation are emptying the thoughts and energies of the mind and focusing attention on the inner. Through a process of controlled breathing, visualization, and chanting of *mantras* (power sounds or words), the aspirant directs spiritual energies upward through the body in order to connect with the real self (soul body, *jiva*). Developing this inner awareness liberates the soul/self from the bondage of the physical/material world with all its suffering. These meditation practices awaken the knowledge you already possess. Such practices also bring about peace of mind and tranquility in one's life.

For more information contact: ████████████

Jain Center of Southern California
8072 Commonwealth Avenue
Buena Park, CA 90621
Phone:(714) 994-2266

or   Jain Meditation Center
176 Ansonia Station
New York, NY 10023
Phone:(212) 362-6483

THE SPIRITUAL SEEKER'S GUIDE

Jain Philosophy
by Narendra Nath Bhattacharyya

*Realize What You Are: The Dynamics
of Jain Meditation*
by Gurudev Shree Chitrabhanu

BUDDHISM

*B*UDDHISM IS a religion based on the teachings of its founder, who was known as the Buddha. The term *buddha* is a participle of the Sanskrit verbal root *Budh*, "to awaken," and is employed as the title "the Awakened One," or "Enlightened One." The Buddha, whose personal name was Siddhartha Gautama, was born in Kapilavastu in Nepal near the Indian border, and is generally believed to have lived from 560 to 480 B.C.

Siddhartha was born a prince in the kingdom of the Sakyas, and lived in a palace with many luxuries. He is reported to have married a young princess named Yasodhara at the age of sixteen, and to have fathered a son, Rahula. During his time there was intense intellectual and spiritual ferment in the region, and while confronted with the reality of life and the suffering of mankind, he decided to find the solution to end universal suffering.

At the age of 29, Siddhartha left his family and kingdom to become an ascetic. He spent the next six years of his life wandering about the valley of the Ganges (India) meeting famous religious teachers such as Arada Kalama of Vaisali and Udraka Ramaputra of Magadha, studying various Hindu teachings, and practicing spiritual and yogic exercises and asceticism. Siddhartha gained a reputation for his severe ascetic practices, such as fasting and extensive meditation, and for his perseverance in trying to find Truth.

After undergoing many years of severe austerity without discovering the answers to liberation, Siddhartha abandoned his attachment to the religious systems that he had been following. It was while seated under a tree (since known as the Bodhi Tree, "Tree of Awakening") meditating along the bank of the river Neranjara at Bodhgaya (near Gaya in modern Bihar, India), at the age of thirty-five, that Siddhartha attained enlightenment. He was therefore known as the Buddha.

Upon his enlightenment, the Buddha began teaching his Middle Way to all who would listen, regardless of caste, race, or sex. His first sermon was to a group of five ascetics (his old colleagues) in Deer Park at Isipatana (modern Saranath) near Benares, India. For the next forty-five years, he and his disciples wandered throughout the larger Ganges River basin, proclaiming his teachings. Buddhism rapidly spread, as many were in search of truth and found this new teaching sensible and appealing. Today Buddhism is practiced around the world, with some 500 million adherents, primarily concentrated in the Asian countries.

Buddhist teachings center around the theme of liberation from suffering and repeated incarnations into a perfectly peaceful and enlightened state of transformed consciousness referred to as *nirvana*. The key to achieving this liberation *(moksha)*, lies in the cessation of selfish desires and attachments. Inherent in these beliefs are the Hindu principles of *karma* (the actions one takes in one's life on the planet). *Dharma* (righteousness) is considered the way to reach *nirvana*, and the Buddha's teachings focus on *dharma* as the means of acquiring liberation, or *nirvana*. *Dharma*, which he referred to as "the lovely" *(kalyana)*, denotes serene peace, in which the fires of self-centered desire and attachment are extinguished.

Buddha's insights into achieving *nirvana* by way of *dharma* came to be formulated as the Four Noble Truths. These truths comprise: *duhkha*—the universal fact of suffering; *samudaya*—the cause of suffering; *nirodha*—the overcoming of suffering; and *magga*—the way of overcoming suffering, or "the Noble Eightfold Path" or "Middle Way." This Noble Eightfold Path consists of practicing (1) right understanding, (2) right thought, (3) right speech, (4) right action, (5) right livelihood, (6) right effort, (7) right mindfulness, and (8) right concentration. Practice of this spiritual path is considered the method of acquiring *dharma* and achieving *nirvana* during one's life.

Buddhism has evolved into many different practices and beliefs, though the core teaching of the Buddha, such as the Four Noble Truths, is central to each religious practice within Buddhism. Within Buddhism lie two main streams of

thought and practice: Theravada-Hínayana or "small vehicle," which is now more commonly referred to as "the
School of Elders" (Theras); and Mahayana, or "great vehicle."
Theravada is generally considered orthodox Buddhism, and
is primarily practiced in Ceylon, Bangladesh, and Southeast
Asia. Mahayana, which developed later, is followed principally in China, Tibet, and Japan. It is more popularized and
embraces many sects, including Madhyamika, Vijnanavada,
T'ien-t'ai, Hua-Yen, and Ch'an, which is commonly referred
to as Zen Buddhism. The Theravada and Mahayana schools
are described more fully in the following pages.

For additional information: I highly recommend the
book *Buddhist America*, edited by Don Morreale (John Muir
Publications), for it describes the various centers, retreats,
and practices of Buddhists in North America. There are also
numerous Buddhist temples and centers throughout North
America, usually in Asian communities. Look up Buddhism
in your phone directory, or go to your metaphysical bookshop
or health-food store for more information.

Recommended Reading:

Buddhist America
by Don Morreale

What the Buddha Taught
by Walpola Rahula

*The Dhormapoda, Wisdom of the
Buddha*
Translation by Harischandra Kaviratna

(See also resources for Theravada, Mahayana, Tibetan,
and Zen Buddhism)

THERAVADA BUDDHISM

AFTER THE Buddha's Parinibbana (final liberation from the cycle of birth and death), his five hundred living disciples convened as the First Great Council of the Theras ("elders"— from which comes the word *Theravada*). All of the disciples were Arahants (fully enlightened beings) who met in an effort to preserve the entire body of Buddha's teachings for mankind. The entire body of knowledge preserved by the First Great Council of the Theras, plus its later commentary, comprises over twenty thousand pages known as the Pali Canon and serves as foundation and guide for the Theravadans.

The core of Buddhist discipline lies in the eradication of cravings, which is achieved through the practice of the Noble Eightfold Path. This path can be divided into three categories: (1) moral conduct, which includes right speech, right action, right livelihood; (2) mental discipline, which includes right effort, right mindfulness, right concentration; and (3) intuitive wisdom, which includes right views, right intentions. To summarize: One must not commit any harmful or negative action, deed, or thought; one should discipline the mind and gain control over it; and one should develop one's inner awareness through contemplation and introspection.

The Theravadans also believe that there is no permanent self or soul, and that an individual is only a combination of what they call the five aggregates *(skandhas)*: matter, sensation, perception, predisposition, and consciousness. Moreover, they believe that as we realize that the self is only a fluctuating state of physical and psychical phenomena, then we can eliminate our egotistical tendencies and attachment to worldly desires. It is through this eradication of ignorance, lustful cravings, and selfish thoughts that one can eliminate *karma* and repeated rebirths and achieve *nirvana*.

Theravada Buddhism is a discipline in which an individual is engaged in ascetic practices in order to achieve salvation or liberation *(moksha)* for himself by himself.

Buddha's teachings of Theravada are for both the monastics and lay persons, with renunciates and householders living in harmony and mutual support for one another. The monastics insure the continuity of the Vinaya, Buddha's teachings for the uprooting of all greed, aversion, and delusion, and provide spiritual services to the community. By supporting the renunciates and the monastic way of life, householders provide themselves with *dharma* and meditation teachers.

Recommended Reading:

> *The Heart of Buddhist Meditation*
> by Ven. Nyanaponika Thera
>
> *Buddhist Religion: A Historical Introduction*
> by R. H. Robinson & W. L. Johnson

MAHAYANA BUDDHISM

*E*LEMENTS OF the Mahayana tradition began developing one hundred years after Buddha's physical incarnation, as arguments occurred within the Sangha relevant to the interpretation and implementation of Buddha's words. The first group to split from the Theras were the Mahasanghikas, who were the forerunners of the Mahayana school. Five hundred years after Buddha's time, around the year A.D. 1, several major points of dissension had developed as the laity began to reject the "orthodox" and monastic forms of practice in favor of taking a more active role in the religion. Mahayanan adherents claimed that they were only revealing doctrines which had previously been considered too sacred to be shared with the laity.

The principal difference between Theravada and Mahayana Buddhism is that in Mahayana Buddhism it is believed that everyone possesses the Buddha nature and is capable of becoming a Buddha, an enlightened one. The Mahayana tradition is likened to a broad river that accommodates all manner of craft, and the religion has spread far and wide due to its willingness to assimilate cultural elements that were new and foreign to it. The main distinguishing characteristic in Mahayana Buddhism is the concept of the *bodhisattva*, one who combines compassion with wisdom. Rather than attaining individual enlightenment, the *bodhisattva* takes a vow to forgo the joy of *nirvana* until all beings have become enlightened. In the Mahayana tradition, the concept of Buddha developed into the idea that there is an eternal Buddha who embodies the absolute Truth. True reality is held to be knowledge experienced before the perception of duality, a predifferentiated state of *sunyata*, or "emptiness," which underlies the fundamental nature of all reality. Achieving this awareness of nonduality is enlightenment, and each person has the capacity to realize this true nature within himself or herself. Thus each individual has the Buddha nature within, and the goal is to reawaken this Buddhahood for the benefit of all mankind.

The **Madhyamika** school, founded by Nagarjuna in the second century A.D., contends that what is produced by causes does not in and of itself exist. Moreover, their belief is that nothing comes into being, and nothing disappears, nothing is eternal and nothing has an end, and nothing is identical or differentiated. It is believed that with these precepts, no attachment to thoughts can be created, and the inner awareness is freed. The best source from which to learn of Nagarjuna's thought is the Madhyamikakarika or "Stanzas on the Middle Path." The **Vijnanavada** (Yoga Cara) school, founded by Asanga and Vasubandhu around the fourth century A.D., contended that individuals have no direct perception of the external world. Therefore, the whole world is only a mental representation or "ideation." The **T'ien-t'ai** school purports that the absolute is one and undifferentiated, but is diverse and particular in its function. Therefore, the work of the layman is one with that of the Buddha, and strides should be made to realize that single beingness. Similarly, the **Hua-Yen** (Kegon in Japan) school follows that we are all sons of the Buddha and possess the Buddha-nature within us. The ***Ch'an*** (or **Zen**) school emphasizes a simple and direct method of meditation in order to realize the Buddha nature within. Because of its familiarity and popularity in the West, Zen Buddhism will be discussed at greater length as a separate religion later in the text. In Tibet, Mahayana first completely replaced the Theravada tradition, and then merged with the indigenous religion of Bon to become the esoteric branch of Buddhism called the **Vajrayana**.

Recommended Reading:

> *The Sutra on the Eight Realizations of the Great Beings*
> by Diem Thanh Truong, tr. by Carole Melkonian

A Treasury of Mahayana Sutras
ed. by Garma C. C. Chang

The Diamond Sutra
by Raghavan Iyer

TIBETAN BUDDHISM

*T*IBETAN BUDDHISM, often referred to as the **Vajrayana**, is a tantric form of Mahayana Buddhism indigenous to Tibet. Buddhism was introduced to Tibet during the reign of Srong-brtsan-sgam-po, the thirty-second king of Tibet, around A.D. 650. The king had married Chinese and Nepalese princesses who were both Buddhist and who swayed the king away from an animistic form of Shamanism called Bon, which had been the prevailing religion, toward Buddhist teaching. King Srong-brtsan-sgam-po had many Buddhist books from India translated into Tibetan and built several Buddhist temples.

By the seventh century, a form of Indian Tantrism called the Vajrayana, or "Diamond Vehicle," was established that taught formulas for sudden enlightenment ("the direct path"). In A.D. 747 a reform movement was spearheaded by the great teacher from India, Guru Padmasambhava, who re-established the ethical and intellectual heritage of older Buddhism and initiated the building of the first monastery in Tibet, the Samyas, which was completed in A.D. 787. In the following centuries, a vast amount of religious texts, such as the Kanjur and Tanjur, were compiled, and tension mounted between the ethical-intellectual and magical-ritualistic elements of Buddhism in Tibet. In the fourteenth and fifteenth centuries the Dalai Lama, who is the reincarnation of a *bodhisattva* (an enlightened being), was established as the spiritual and temporal head of Tibet. With the Communist revolt of 1959 in China, the Dalai Lama was forced to flee to India, awaiting a time to return to Tibet and re-establish Buddhist teachings there. Today Tibetan Buddhism is gaining interest in the West, with Lamas (monks) coming to the United States and Europe to teach the *dharma*, or spiritual law.

Tibetan Buddhism is founded on the Four Noble Truths established by the Buddha (see "Buddhism"). The object is to obtain the ultimate release of all sentient beings from the suffering of the endless cycle of reincarnations (*samsara*). In

Tibetan Buddhism, enlightenment, or *nirvana*, is found through the *bodhisattvas*, who are liberated themselves, but forgo *nirvana* in order to bring salvation to others. Tibetan Buddhism centers around a monastic way of living, though some of the teachings are available to the public through books and discourses.

Tibetan *dharma* is a sophisticated philosophy involving years of study. The meditations are highly intellectual, yet utilize magical formulas and cultic devotions. As a Tantric tradition, Tibetan Buddhism integrates the capacities of the mind with physical and emotional disciplines toward the search for salvation. There are four major orders of Tibetan Buddhism. These sects are the Nyingruapa, or "ancient ones," who trace their lineage back to Padmasambhava; the Kargyupa, which is an oral tradition founded by Marpa in the eleventh century and is based on the fundamental teachings of Naropa; the Saskyapa, which was founded in the eleventh century and was the first to establish a priestly monarchy; and the Gelugpa, or "merit system ones," which is headed by the Dalai Lama, and is perhaps the most widely recognized today.

For information contact: ▰▰▰▰▰▰▰▰▰▰

Tibet House
241 E. 32d Street
New York, NY 10016
Phone: (212) 213-5592

Recommended Reading:

The Opening of the Wisdom-Eye
by His Holiness Tenzin Gyatsho the XIV
Dalai Lama of Tibet

The Garland of Mahamudra Practices
by Khempo Konchog Gyaltsen

The Gem Ornament of Manifold Oral Instructions
by His Eminence Kalu Rinpoche

The Tibetan Book of the Dead
by Guru Rinpoche

The Hundred Thousand Songs of Milarepa
Tr. by Garma C.C. Chang

ZEN (CH'AN)

"ZEN" IS the Japanese pronunciation of the Chinese word *Ch'an*, which means "meditation." Zen is a highly refined form of Mahayana Buddhism, which emphasizes the aim of enlightenment. Zen, or Ch'an, is a Chinese synthesis and adaptation of two schools of Mahayana Buddhism that had their origins in India: The Madhyamika school, which emphasizes that all forms and thought are essentially empty in nature and utilizes the way of negation and intuitive thought; and the Yoga Cara school, which emphasizes that consciousness alone is real, and utilizes meditation as the principal discipline. As early as the fifth century A.D. the Indian teacher Kumarajiva and the meditation master Buddhabhadra were preparing the way for Zen. In fact one of Kumarajiva's disciples, Tao-sheng, is accredited by some as the actual founder of Zen. By tradition, Zen has its origin in the esoteric teachings of the Buddha, when the Buddha stood on Vulture Peak holding a lotus and remained silent before his disciples. Through the silence, the disciple Mahakasyapa achieved *nirvana*, or enlightenment, and from him the "lamp of enlightenment" was passed on to the twenty-eighth patriarch, Bodhidharma, who carried the "lamp" to China and founded the Ch'an (Zen) tradition.

Little is known about the patriarchs and about the evolution of Zen from Bodhidharma until the T'ang dynasty (618-906). During the T'ang dynasty, a revolutionary form of Ch'an (Zen) was developing that rejected sutra study, ritual, and the veneration of images, and preached the methods of "sudden enlightenment." Ch'an forms of Buddhism were introduced to Japan from Korea in A.D. 552, and flourished under the patronage of Prince Shotoku (d. 621). It was during the Kamakura period (1185-1333) that Zen was established in Japan, primarily through the efforts of two Japanese monks, Eisai and Dogen. Eisai (d. 1215) traveled to China and trained with Lin-Chi (Rinzai) masters, and brought the sect to Japan in 1191. The sect was readily accepted by the Shoguns and Samurai of Japan. Dogen (d. 1253) is credited

34

with the founding of the Soto sect in Japan, and with establishing the first Zen temple in Japan in 1236.

The Rinzai and Soto sects are the most influential forms of Buddhism in Japan today, with approximately 2.5 million and 7 million adherents, respectively. Zen has also impacted the West; with Zen Master Soyen Shaku's appearance at the World Parliament of Religions at the Chicago World's Fair of 1893, and decades of work by Dr. D. T. Suzuki (d. 1970), Zen practice has steadily grown—particularly in California and Hawaii.

Zen is fundamentally a school of Mahayana Buddhism, and shares traditions, *sutras*, rules, and rituals with other Mahayanists. However, the Zen tradition has veered away from scholasticism and emphasizes the direct personal experience of enlightenment, or "Satori." Fostering, deepening, and expressing the experience of the Buddha-mind is the primary focus of Zen Buddhism. The aim of enlightenment is the unfolding of the inner mind experience, as an inherent quality that lies within to be developed through meditation. Zen is characterized by the doctrines of *sunyata* (emptiness) and *bodhi* (enlightenment); and the direct experience of enlightenment, the Buddha-mind, is believed to express itself in every detail of nature and in every activity.

At the heart of Zen practice is monasticism. Monastic life combines simplicity and discipline, and involves the practices of seated meditation *(za-zen)* in a *zendo* (meditation hall); instruction from a *roshi*, or Zen master *(sanzen)*, manual labor *(samu)*; recitation of *sutras* and sometimes religious mendicancy. In **Rinzai** sects, emphasis is placed on seated meditation in which the student's concentration is intensified through the use of an "encouragement stick," which is applied to the student's back in order to rouse and deepen one's concentration during meditation. Another tool used in Rinzai is the *koan* exercises. An abstract thought, or riddle, is given to the student to contemplate, such as, "What is the sound of one hand clapping?" In Soto sects, emphasis is placed on identifying *zazen* itself with enlightenment and living in the present moment with mindfulness. In both disciplines meditation is the key to the practice, and understanding comes from a direct personal experience with Truth rather than from an intellectual understanding.

Recommended Reading:

The Awakening of Zen (or other books)
by Daisetz Teitaro Suzuki

Zen Essence
by Thomas Cleary

The Moon Bamboo
by Thich Nhat Hanh

The Three Pillars of Zen
by Roshi Kapleau

The Spirit of Zen
by Allen Watts

TAOISM

*T*AO IS the ancient Chinese word for "way" or "the way." Taoism is both a Chinese philosophical system and a religious teaching. The origin of Taoism is obscure, but it is generally believed to have evolved around 700-100 B.C. The earliest Taoist classic, the *Tao Te Ching*, was composed by Lao-tzu around the sixth century B.C. Lao-tzu was an older contemporary of Confucius who lived in the province of Honan, China. Both Confucianism and Taoism have played an integral part in forming Chinese (and other Eastern) thought and cultures. But whereas Confucianism is more concerned with day-to-day rules of conduct and ethics, Taoism is more concerned with the spiritual aspect of being. Taoism has evolved considerably since its inception, and will be explained herein in both its philosophical and religious contexts.

Taoist Philosophy. The Tao is "the way"; the source and essence of existence. Tao is the creator (Tsao-Wu Chu), impersonal and inseparable from creation. The Tao is viewed as both the source of creation, or "nonbeing" (*wu*, or "nothing"), and as creation itself manifested physically or mentally, or "being" (*yu*, or "to exist"). In this manner human beings and the rest of existence are inseparable. All aspects or manifestations of existence are part of the one, the Tao.

In Taoism, the life-giving or sustaining energy is manifested as the *Chi* (literally "breath," "vapor," or "air"). This force moves in cycles throughout nature, from a positive pole to a negative pole and back. This movement is known as "reversal" *(fan)*, and is characterized as the cycles of night and day, life and death, fortune and misfortune, and is responsible for the perceived chaos of existence. Later this belief evolved into the concept of Yin and Yang, with Yin representing the "nonbeing" and Yang representing the "being" aspects of creation. Lao-tzu taught that one could not transcend the cycle of creation, but by learning to flow with the tides of change one could find inner peace and tranquillity. The Tao is nonpurposeful, nondeliberate and continually changing. This should be the nature of human beings if they are to be at peace with themselves and with nature (which are one and the same).

The philosophy states that one should stop wanting, stop trying, stop thinking, or desiring things to be different than what they are, for nature provides everything without requiring payment; thus, we should work with and learn from nature. Moreover, truth comes naturally to a clear and open mind, and all is gained by giving up. In other words, one should simply be.

Taoist Religion. Tao-Chiao, "the teaching of the way," is a series of religious movements that worship the Tao (the way). These religious movements characteristically involve observing various ritual, alchemical, and meditative practices aiming at immortality. Taoist movements have involved frequent revelations based on direct communication with divine powers, and are often messianic, with visions of the ending of an old order and the coming of a new age.

The precepts of Taoism involve moral self-restraint, humility and unselfishness. As Taoists perceive spirit and matter as being a part of the whole (nonbeing and being), the goal is not to obtain liberation of the soul (spirit) from matter (as is characteristic in many other religions), but rather to conserve, harmonize, and transform the *chi* (body/mind energy). By nourishing the *chi* (vital life force), the cycle of progression from life to death, Yang to Yin, can be reversed and move back from death to life, Yin to Yang, in order to reach an eternal state of transcendent being called the Chen-Jen ("true human"). Thus the soul, not the physical body, achieves immortality, the goal in the Taoist religion.

In order to achieve this immortality, various techniques are used in the different Taoist movements. One means is to eat foods and herbs that contain energies for the various life-sustaining bodily organs. Hygiene and exercise are also regarded as part of the required discipline. Control of the *chi* (vital energy) through various deep and controlled breathing techniques is a common practice among Taoists as well as various meditative techniques usually done in conjunction with breath control. Sexual restraint is also often practiced by the Taoist. This discipline might include either celibacy or the retention of seminal fluids normally ejaculated and the suppression of orgasms during sexual intercourse in order to conceive the vital energies used to achieve spiritual immortality. Control over the worldly passions is seen as conserving vitality and is practiced in order to restore personal harmony with the Tao.

For additional information:

Best obtained through Chinese medical practitioners or healing centers (acupuncture, accupressure, herbalists, etc.), or through centers that practice the martial arts, such as Ta'i Chi and Kung Fu, or contact:

> Union of Tao and Man
> 117 Stonehaven Way
> Los Angeles, CA 90049
> Phone:(213) 472-9970

or   Taoist Esoteric Yoga Center and
> Foundation
> P.O. Box 1194
> Huntington, NY 11743
> Phone:(516) 367-2701

Recommended Reading:

> *The Tao Te Ching*
> by Lao-tzu
>
> *Tao-The Universal Subtle Law*
> by Ni Hua-Ching
>
> *Taoist Secrets of Love*
> by Mantak Chia
>
> *A Source Book in Chinese Philosophy*
> by Wing Tsit Chan

CONFUCIANISM

*C*ONFUCIANISM IS a system of thought based on the teachings of Confucius and his successors. Confucius is the Latinized form of the Chinese name K'ung Fu-tzu, which means "Great Master K'ung." He was born around 551 B.C. in the small feudal state of Lu, located in present-day Shantang, China. His family was of low-ranking nobility. His father died when he was young, which resulted in family hardships. As a young man he held various minor posts in government, married, and had a son and daughter. He later held higher posts in government and was recognized for his provocative ideas.

At around the age of fifty, Confucius left his native state of Lu and began wandering from state to state in an attempt to initiate political and social reforms. During this time he developed a considerable following. After thirteen years of teaching, Confucius returned to his state of Lu, where he was reported to have edited the Confucian classics: the *Book of Poetry (Shih Ching)*, 305 poems of the early Chou dynasty; the *Book of Rites (Li Ching)*, philosophical discussions of ritual; the *Book of History (Shu Ching)*, a documentary of Chinese history from the time of Emperor Yao (third millennium B.C.) to early the Chou dynasty (1122-249 B.C.), with discussions of kings Wen and *Wu* and the Duke of Chou, who served as paragons of his political ideologies; the *Spring and Autumn Annals (Ch'un Ch'iu)*, which discusses events that occurred during Confucius' time in his state of Lu; and the *Book of Changes (I Ching)* which is based on the ancient practices of divination and is used as a guide for taking the wisest course of action.

The teachings of Confucius emphasize moral and ethical standards within social, political, and religious thought. He did not preach a religious belief per se, but rather incorporated high spiritual values into a way of living. These concepts include   humaneness (Jen), where in order to achieve peace in this world men must practice benevolence with each other. Moreover, one should do good without expectation of recognition of that good. He believed heaven could best be understood through the study of history and of how the influences of heaven affected the world throughout its history. He taught that rites and music should fully express their potential to encourage virtuous behavior, and that one should act according to his position. This is the doctrine of rectification of names (Cheng-Ming)—a king acts within the ideals established for him, a father acts as an ideal father, etc. The bulk of Confucius' teachings center around the concept of "The Gentleman" (Chun-tzu); one should never lose sight of the virtuous or higher nature, and should take responsibility for one's actions. These teachings have been a cornerstone of Chinese philosophy and culture.

Confucianism has evolved into four classical schools, expressing variations of the Confucian perspective: Mencius, the Great Learning, the Doctrine of the Mean, and Hsun Tzu. Mencius (Meng-tzu, ca. 371-289 B.C.) held that man was initially good, and by recognizing his inner nature and his relation to heaven, man could realize his human potential for goodness. Great learning has its foundation in the *Book of Rites (Li Chi)*, and stresses personal moral cultivation as the means for achieving inner/personal and world peace. The Doctrine of the Mean, which was originally a chapter from the *Book of Rites*, stresses the metaphysical nature of human beings, or the heaven that is within us and how to realize it. Hsun-tzu (ca. 298-230 B.C.) believed that human nature was evil and that man could transcend his evil nature and realize the heaven within him through knowledge.

During the Han Dynasty (206 B.C.-A.D. 220), Confucianism was established as the state of orthodoxy, and other canons developed. Temples began to be erected, the concepts of Yin and Yang were introduced (see Taoism), and various cults formed. Confucianism continued to evolve, and now only two major schools exist: the School of Principal (Li-Hsueh), and the School of Mind (Hsin-Hsueh). Both are considered neo-Confucian, and emphasize more of an internal search for principle rather than the external intellectual investigation that was traditional in Confucianism. The School of Mind focuses on the internal experience of the self, and often utilizes meditation techniques. Religious rites are still performed for the layman; however, the influence of Confucianism has greatly diminished with the advent of the Communist government, which has subdued Confucianism's role in Chinese culture. The most informative source on the life and teachings of Confucius is in the *Analects* (Lun-*Yu*), or "Discourses." Compiled over a century after his death, the *Analects* contain the reputed sayings and conversations of Confucius and summarize his teachings.

I Ching. Of the Confucian classics, the *Book of Changes (I Ching)* is the most well-known and popular in the West. The *I Ching* evolved over a thousand years to its present form, which is presented by a Confucian editor from the first century A.D. This philosophy views changes in terms of cycles that move in opposites (e.g., expansion and contraction, rise and fall). The view incorporates the concept of Yin and Yang. The Yang refers to the active, male, hard, or expansive pole, and the Yin to the passive, female, soft, or contracting pole. Thus as changes occur in cycles, when one pole is reached (Yin or Yang), the movement invariably is directed to the opposite pole. Therefore, as changes occur in the individual, nature, and society, the attitude should be to accept the cosmic order and to flow with it.

The *I Ching* is used for the ancient practice of divination. Individuals consult the *I Ching* to determine which course of action to take in various instances. The book deals with eight "trigrams," which comprise solid and broken lines representing Yin (the female principal) as broken lines, and Yang (the male principal) as unbroken lines, and sixty-four hexagrams (each composed of two trigrams, in all possible combinations). Each hexagram is ascribed a particular action or judgment *(t'uan)* and archetype or image *(Hsiang)*. As stalks of the yarrow plant (typically) are manipulated, lines which represent the various hexagrams are formed. When the hexagram is identified, its corresponding judgment and image indicates the appropriate course of action to take.

For more information:

I am not familiar with any Confucian teachers or groups in North America. This wisdom is typically integrated into general Chinese philosophy.

Recommended Reading:

The Analects of Confucius
Translated by Arthur Waley

Confucius and Confucianism
by D. Howard Smith

T'AI CHI CH'UAN

T'AI CHI is the Chinese classical dance for health, self-defense and higher awareness. *T'ai Chi Ch'uan* literally means "Supreme Ultimate Boxing," and was used as a form of self-defense, but is now more popular as a form of active meditation. The study of T'ai Chi dates back to the founder Chang San-Feng, who wrote the "T'ai Chi Ch'uan Classic" during the Sung dynasty (A.D. 960-1279). This art (and science) was further developed during the Ming dynasty (A.D. 1368-1644), by the great master Wang Chung Yueh, who wrote both the "Treatise on T'ai Chi Ch'uan" and "Mental Elucidation of the Thirteen Postures." Within these three classics are the principles from which the techniques were derived. T'ai Chi was very popular up until the Cultural Revolution in China, when the government suppressed the practice of ancient Chinese traditions, but is again becoming increasingly popular in China. Moreover, T'ai Chi has become quite popular in many Western cultures, and is practiced by thousands throughout North America and Europe, some forms serving as a martial art for self-defense, and others as a practice for health, longevity, and higher awareness.

The classics from which T'ai Chi Ch'uan was founded were based upon the philosophy of Taoism and the principles of the *I Ching*. The underlying principle of T'ai Chi is becoming aware of, and cultivating, "*chi*," which is described as "The one through which the Tao manifests itself and then differentiates into two forces (Yin and Yang) that interact to produce the world phenomena." The belief is that this life force energy *Chi* can be generated in the area approximately two inches below the navel, known as the "Tan T'ien" or "Field of Cinnabar," and that this *chi* will then circulate throughout the body, providing increased vitality and intrinsic strength. The techniques of T'ai Chi cultivate this *chi* in the Tan T'ien, and the practice of the moving postures develops the ability to direct and utilize *chi* energy. This intensified energy can be used to neutralize aggressive actions, increase your body's vitality and stamina, and heighten your faculties of awareness.

The practice originally involved thirteen postures: Ward Off, Roll Back, Press, Push, Pull, Split, Elbow-Stroke, Shoulder-Stroke, Advance, Retreat, Gaze to Left, Look to Right, and Central Equilibrium. Now the complete "long style" sequence includes up to 150 postures (depending on how you count them), which are performed in slow, circular movements. The mind directs the *chi*, and the *chi* directs the muscles and bones; and through the practice of T'ai Chi one learns to control the mind and body. T'ai Chi consists of a system of rounded, fluid, balanced movements, which should be directed under the guidance of a qualified T'ai Chi Master. As the postures are performed, the practitioner becomes increasingly aware of the movement of *chi* with him or her and learns how to integrate the energies within himself, and between himself and others (such as an opponent).

For more information on T'ai Chi Ch'uan look in the phone directory for the nearest martial-arts studio or supply store and ask where classes are scheduled. Many city recreation departments, YMCAs and youth groups also offer classes in T'ai Chi, which are oriented toward the personal-growth aspects of the art.

Recommended Reading:

T'ai Chi Ch'uan
by Marshall Ho'o

T'ai Chi Ch'uan, for Health and Self-Defense
by Master T. T. Liang

Periodical: *T'ai Chi Magazine*
Wayfarer Publications
P.O. Box 26156
Los Angeles, CA 90026

SHINTOISM

SHINTO IS the indigenous religion of Japan. *Shinto* means "way of the *kami*, or gods." It is as old as the Japanese nation itself, evolving out of prehistoric religious practices as primarily a nature religion with tribal characteristics. As Japan evolved from a hunting-gathering culture into an agrarian culture, fertility rites were practiced and festivals commemorating the seasons and the harvest were integrated into the culture. By A.D. 500 Chinese culture and the organized religion of Buddhism began to influence the Japanese culture and Shinto practices. Shinto took on more structure as a religion and developed more theology regarding the veneration of ancestors and *kami*, or deities. During the Meiji period (1867-1912), Shinto developed into a form of national patriotism and ideology that is now referred to as "State Shinto," which was more naturalistic than religious. After 1945, with the defeat of the Japanese in World War II and the occupation of Japan by American forces, State Shinto was disestablished, although smaller sects of "Shrine Shinto" remain active to this day. Shinto is practiced primarily in Japan, and almost exclusively by people of Japanese descent.

To the ancient Japanese, each aspect of creation was a living being: The sun and moon, the rivers and ocean, the mountains, trees and herbs all had consciousness. Even the "Great-Eight-Island-Country" (Japan), was a supernatural being. The divine *kami* Izanagi (male) and Izanami (female), were responsible for creating the sun goddess Amaterasu Omikami, who is the ancestor of the emperor. In Shinto, ancestors are venerated, and the head (male) of each family clan is the priest. The emperor, or head of the imperial family, is the highest priest and was considered a *kami* incarnate. In Shinto the "gods are immortal men, and men are mortal gods." When a person dies, the soul leaves the body, and dead people are believed to have consciousness. Moreover, upon death a soul may either descend below the earth to the land of darkness "Yomi-no-Kuni," or ascend to the High Plain of Heaven "Takama-ga-Hara," which is the abode of the heavenly gods. Shinto has developed into more of an ethnic intellectual religion that emphasizes sincerity, truthfulness, uprightness, patriotism, and loyalty to the emperor.

Ancient Shinto practices involved the worship of spirits in nature and the physical representations of the *kami*, or deity, such as the sun, a mountain, or the wind itself. Offerings of rice, vegetables, or fish were offered to the *kami*, and later shared by the family members. As the nation became more agrarian, fertility rites and observances were held to assure a plentiful harvest and to give thanks for the assistance of the *kami* in the harvest. Early in Shinto history phalluses and fetishes representing *kami* were objects of veneration. Ancestors have traditionally been a principal source of veneration, and making contact with deceased souls (spiritualism) is a part of the shamanistic elements of Shinto. Veneration of the *kami* is a primary duty of the Shinto priests, and over 80,000 shrines have been erected throughout Japan for worship and contemplation.

In addition to observances at various shrines, several festivals are periodically held to mark such occasions as the enthronement of the Emperor. Shintoists pray for a rich harvest and present the new rice of the year to the ancestral Sun-Goddess. Other festivals commemorate various *kami*, seasons, and Shrines. However, emphasis is now placed more on physical and moral purity, and respect for tradition, family, and state.

For more information:

Visit cultural centers in the closest Japanese community. Some larger cities with a high percentage of people of Japanese descent have Shinto shrines, and universities that offer courses in Asian studies may offer helpful information.

Recommended Reading:

                A Study of Shinto
                by Genchi Kato

  or   *Shinto, The Kami Way*
                by Motonori Ono

                On Understanding the Japanese Religion
                by Joseph M. Kitagawa

WESTERN RELIGIONS

WESTERN RELIGIONS generally refer to the Judaic-Christian-Islamic heritages. The religions of Judaism, Christianity, and Islam all share common origins, and hold some similar beliefs, although their practices and other beliefs differ greatly. One commonality is the concept of monotheism, the belief in one almighty God. From the Western perspective, God is both omnipresent and omnipotent, and yet very personal, with apparent feelings and emotions such as love and compassion as well as jealousy and anger. Although this God is called by different names—Yahweh by the Jews, Jehovah or "God" by the Christians, and Allah by the Muslims—this God is considered to be the one, and the only, God.

Another common belief held by all three religions is that after creating the universe, God created man "in his own image" out of the dust from the ground (thus humans did not evolve from other, lower life forms). Then God breathed into man's nostrils the breath of life, and he became a living soul. Woman was later created out of the rib of man, and these first two humans are called Adam (man) and Eve (woman). Man and woman were created in the Garden of Eden, which is believed to have been Mesopotamia (modern Iraq), and their descendants populated the entire earth.

The story of the creation of mankind is told in the book of Genesis, which is the first book in the Torah (Jewish scripture) and in the Holy Bible (Christian scripture), and the second Sura of the Qur'an (Islamic scripture). In this account, God expressly tells Adam (man) that he can eat of all fruits in the Garden of Eden except for one, the fruit of the "tree of knowledge of good and evil," which is forbidden. However, a serpent in the Garden of Eden tempts Eve into trying the forbidden fruit, and then she convinces Adam to taste it as well. This serpent represents the evil force or "fallen angel" Satan (the Devil), whose influence has ever since tested and tainted mankind. Man's disobedience of God's laws, and his need to be forgiven for mistakes, or "sins," is a central theme in Western religion. In Western religions emphasis is placed on living in accordance with God's laws, as recounted by the prophets, whom God has sent to guide us. Thus all of mankind needs to be saved in order to live in God's grace, and live in peace.

The belief in salvation means that if you are saved, after the death of the physical body you will live with God eternally in Heaven, enjoying unimaginable pleasures. However, if you are not saved, then you are destined to an eternal existence in the hereafter in Hell, suffering unimaginable torture and pain. The principal differences among these three religions is in how they believe salvation will be obtained. Jewish prophecy holds that a Messiah (deliverer) will be sent by God to establish a Holy Kingdom upon the earth and to rule over the Jewish people and over the entire earth. Jews maintain that the Messiah has yet to come, and do not accept the belief that Jesus Christ was the Messiah, or that Muhammad is the prophet of God, because neither one fulfilled the Jewish prophecy.

Christians believe that Jesus of Nazareth did fulfill the prophecy, and he demonstrated that he was the Messiah, or Christ, by the miracles that he performed, and by the love and compassion that he exemplified. Christians believe that Christ will come again to rule on earth, and that one can be saved by believing in Jesus Christ as the Savior. Muslims believe that Jesus was a prophet of God (Allah), but as the people were still not obeying God's laws, God sent another prophet, Muhammad, to teach mankind. Muslims believe that Muhammad is God's last prophet, and that the Qur'an is a revision of God's law as directed through his prophet Muhammad. All three religions base their beliefs on faith, and maintain their convictions based on the scriptures that they believe to be the word of God.

Interpretations and beliefs about God and his laws vary considerably between, and within, each of the three great Western religions. Even fundamental generalizations about each of these religions can be challenged by sects within each faith, so keep in mind that every tenet interpreted here only represents the majority opinion and other opinions may be equally valid. The following serve as a brief overview of the those religions that have had the most influence on Western civilization.

JUDAISM

*J*UDAISM IS the religion of the Jewish people; its origins begin with the creation of mankind, and its foundation as a religion begins with a covenant between the patriarch Abraham and God, or Yahweh. Abraham lived in the city of Ur (in Mesopotamia—between the Tigris and Euphrates rivers), around 2000 B.C. Following God's call, Abraham left his home and led a life of wandering, believing that he would one day be the father of many people in a "Promised Land." Abraham was led by God to the Promised Land called Canaan, but was soon driven out again due to a severe drought. After traveling through Egypt during this difficult time, he returned to Canaan where, after proving his faith, he was given a son. To further test Abraham's faith, God asked Abraham to sacrifice his only son, Isaac, a task from which he was spared at the last moment. Having thus proven his loyalty to God, Abraham was assured by God that he would be the father of a great people in the land of Canaan, or Palestine (which is now the state of Israel). The people of this land and religion are collectively known as the Hebrews. Later, famine forced the Hebrew people to flee from the Holy Land into Egypt, where they become known as Israelites. They stayed in Egypt for several centuries under oppressive rule.

Around the year 1300 B.C. the Israelites were delivered from their oppression in Egypt by the noble leader and prophet Moses. In this exodus from Egypt, Moses led the Israelites southeast through the wilderness of what is now called the Sinai Peninsula. Suffering many hardships, the Israelites began to lose faith in their deliverance, whereupon Moses climbed up Mount Sinai and communed with God. It was then that the Lord gave Moses the famous Ten Commandments to guide his people; these commandments are as follows:

> *(1)   Do not worship any other Gods but me.*
> *(2)   Do not make any images or idols of God*

to worship.

(3)   Do not use the Lord's name in vain (dishonor God).

(4)   Keep the Sabbath day holy, and do not work on this day.

(5)   Honor your mother and your father.

(6)   Do not kill.

(7)   Do not commit adultery.

(8)   Do not steal.

(9)   Do not bear false witness against your neighbor.

(10)   Do not covet your neighbor's wife or property.[1]

The Israelites spent some forty years in the desert before entering again into the Promised Land of Canaan. After fighting for, and winning, the Holy Land back, the Israelites propagated and cultivated the land. However, the history of the Israelites, or Jews, is fraught with acts of war and persecution, even to the present day. The struggle to keep the Promised Land has persisted for over 3,000 years. Today a portion of the Holy Land has been reclaimed by the Jewish people as the state of Israel; and although the Jewish people are now spread throughout the world, they maintain a cohesive unity in faith and cultural heritage.

Judaism was instrumental in the Western acceptance of monotheism; the belief in one God. The sacred name for God was represented by the tetragrammaton (spelled in Hebrew without vowels) YHWH, which is generally believed to be pronounced "Yahweh," which means "I am that I am." This patriarchal God is both loved and feared; with absolute obedience to God's laws and conformity to his divine will being rewarded both spiritually and physically, and disobedience bringing the threat of spiritual and physical exile. The Jewish patriarchs made covenants with God, such as the sacred act of circumcision (cutting the male foreskin at birth), to remind God of his promise of genealogical continu-

---

[1] The Catholic and Lutheran churches combine the commandments prohibiting the worship of other gods with that of forbidding the making of images, and treat the coveting of neighbor's wife and property as two separate commandments.

ity and life in a sacred land. Also central to Judaic belief is the messianic ideal of a universal reintegration of mankind, and a spiritual monarchy headed by the Jews as "God's chosen people," followed by an era of peace and well-being on earth.

The primary source of revealing God's laws is the Torah, which comprises the books of Genesis, Exodus, Leviticus, Numbers, and Deuteronomy in the Bible (Hebrew or Christian). Also esteemed were the books of the Prophets and the Writings. Knowledge of God's will is further pursued in the study of the Midrash, the Mishnah, and the Talmud, whereas study of God's love is fostered in the Aggadah. The study of the mystical or esoteric aspects of Judaism is developed through disciplined contemplation of the Kabbalah, through the *Zohar*, or *Book of Splendor*. Jewish religious study encourages philosophical debate, which is believed to foster a greater understanding of God and his laws. Community prayers are emphasized in community synagogues and temples. Children are encouraged to study God's laws in Hebrew, and at the age of thirteen a boy's spiritual maturity is celebrated in what is called a Bar Mitzvah. The Sabbath is observed beginning on Fridays at sundown. Religious study is encouraged and work is forbidden for that day.

There are three major Jewish sects: Orthodox, Conservative, and Reform. Orthodox schools are the strictest in adhering to Mosaic laws, including dietary and Sabbath observances, whereas in Reform synagogues Mosaic laws have been modified to conform to circumstances in modern life, such as seating men and women together. Conservative Judaism is the centrist movement within contemporary Judaism, and is the largest of the sects in America. There is also a form of Judaism called Hasidism, which developed from two socio-religious movements in medieval and modern Jewish history, in Germany and Eastern Europe. This movement is more mystical, with a focus on the notion of "devekut," or communion with God's presence in all things, trying to sanctify the everyday.

Major holy observances include Passover, which is celebrated in gratitude for the Angel of Death "passing over" the Israelite boys during the plagues of Egypt in which firstborn Egyptian males were being slain. The celebration usually begins with a special dinner called a seder, held on the first night of Passover (in March or April). Rosh Hashanah is the celebration of the New Year (September-October), and is traditionally commenced with the blowing of ram's horns (nowadays trumpets). Yom Kippur is a day of solemn penitence observed on the tenth day of Tishri (September-October). On this day it is common for worshipers to spend the whole day in the synagogue praying, asking to be forgiven, and repenting. On this day it is forbidden to eat, drink, wash, wear leather, or have sexual relations. Another popular holiday is Hanukkah (December), which means "dedication." Lights are kindled for each of the successive eight days of the festival, and special prayers are used to commemorate each day. (See also Kabbalah.)

For more information...

...on Judaism, look in your local telephone book under synagogues or temples, or contact the local Chamber of Commerce. Also Judaic colleges and universities will have resources, and often offer classes.

Recommended Reading:

The Torah
(Jewish biblical translation)

To Be a Jew
by Rabbi Hayim Halevy Donin
(summary of beliefs and practices)

We Jews—Invitation to a Dialogue
by Efrain M. Rosenzweig
(an overview of Judaism)

The Jewish Book of Why
by Rabbi Alfred J. Kolatch
(Jewish customs and practices)

The Complete Works of Josephus
Trans. by Wm. Whiston
(ancient history of the Jews)

Periodical: *Commentary*
by the American Jewish Committee

CHRISTIANITY

*C*HRISTIANITY IS a religion based on the belief of the fulfillment of an ancient Jewish prophecy foretelling the coming of a Messiah—the expected deliverer and ruler of the Jewish people. Nearly two thousand years ago a special being was born in a manger outside the city of Bethlehem, who was recognized by many to be the Messiah, or Christ (Greek for "anointed one"). This man, who was named Yeshua ben Joseph, but is more commonly known by the Greek name of Jesus, is believed to have fulfilled the prophecy of the Messiah because foretold events occurred at his birth and because of the wisdom and love that he demonstrated and miracles that he performed. Those who believe in and follow the teachings of Jesus Christ are called Christians, and the source of Christ's teachings is the Holy Bible, which is believed to be the word of God.

Jesus was born a Jew sometime around 8-4 B.C. and died around A.D. 27-30 (the curious dates are the result of different calendar revisions). Jesus preached the word of God from his enlightened understanding of it, and exemplified it through selfless acts and unconditional love. Christianity developed when a small group of Jews gathered around the rabbi (teacher) Jesus, and began to follow his teachings. The central theme of his teachings was to turn to God in preparation for the coming "Kingdom of God." He preached repentance in order to prepare for the impending judgment, which was a motif in apocalpytic Judaism at that time. Jesus is thought of as both a reformer and a humanitarian. By representing himself as the Messiah and by calling for changes in the dogmas and commercialized practices in the synagogues (such as money changing), he incited the Jewish people and caused them to question many established beliefs and practices. Through numerous acts of selfless service and brotherly love, such as healing the sick, exorcising demons, and even raising the dead, Jesus gained a reputation as the messenger of God and the deliverer of the Jewish people.

Jesus's ministry lasted only about three years. As his teachings and his influence on the Jewish people were perceived as threatening by the Jewish priests, Jewish leaders pressured the Romans, who occupied the region, to condemn Jesus to death. Jesus was sentenced to death by the Roman procurator Pontius Pilate, who crucified him (nailed him on a wooden cross to die) at Calvary. After Christ's physical death on the cross, he was resurrected and appeared to several disciples, such as Mary Magdalene, before ascending to Heaven. According to the disciple Paul, Christians are assured that this ultimate sacrifice of love was an act of redemption for their sins. Christ's martyrdom compelled the disciples, and particularly Jesus' twelve Apostles, to preach the gospel throughout the world.

Most of the disciples traveled into the lands of the Gentiles, who were more receptive to the Christian theology than were the Jews. Most influential of the early Christian missionaries were the apostles: Paul (Saul), Peter, Barnabas, Philip, and Mark, who traveled north of the Holy Land into the areas now known as Syria, Turkey, Greece, Cyprus and Italy. The writings of Matthew, Luke, and John have also been tremendously influential in the development and acceptance of Christian theology. By the end of the first century Christianity was represented throughout southern Europe, North Africa, and the Middle East, and by the third century Christianity had spread and become the predominant religion throughout the Mediterranean. Through the strong missionary efforts of the Christian churches, Christianity has now spread to every corner of the globe and is currently the largest religion in the world, with over 1.5 billion believers. Christianity remains a strong evangelical movement to this day.

Christian theology is based on Christ's teachings as recorded in the Holy Bible; particularly in the New Testament, which is an account of Christ's life and the acts of the Apostles and the early Church. Interpretations of Scripture and perspectives of Christ and his teachings vary between churches. There are three principal branches of Christianity: Orthodox, Catholic, and Protestant churches. However, generally Christians share a common belief that Jesus Christ is the only Son of God, and that he is the Word of God made flesh. Moreover, as Lord, Christ preached the gospel of God, and the Bible is believed to be a pure representation of God's word. Generally Christians believe that Jesus died on the cross on our behalf as remission for our sins; and that if you believe in Jesus Christ, and accept him into your life (via his love and teachings), your sins will be forgiven and you will be given eternal life in Heaven after death. Most Christians also believe that if you do not ask for forgiveness of your sins and accept Jesus as Lord, then you will spend an eternity after death suffering in Hell. Central to Christ's teachings was to love God and to live by his laws, and to love your fellow man. Moreover, many Christians have faith in Christ's second coming, in which Christ is expected to return to this world during an apocalypse (the famous battle of Armageddon), in which the forces of good (God) and bad (Satan, or the Devil) come to a final confrontation, and God passes judgment over humanity, destroying evil, while the faithful will be saved by Christ and live in eternal peace beside the Lord in Heaven.

Christianity is practiced by adherence to God's word as preached in the Holy Bible, either through sermons from the clergy or by personal readings by the believers. Fundamental to Christianity is the personal relationship with Jesus Christ and God by way of prayer, in which individuals or groups communicate through an inner dialogue and emotional/ spiritual experiences. Central to Christian practice is attendance and participation in church services, which typically include a sermon, singing of hymns, blessings, and prayers. The Christian Sabbath is typically observed on Sunday, which is reserved for church attendance, rest, and contemplation of God. Several Christian festivals are also observed including Christmas (December)—the celebration of Jesus Christ's birth; Good Friday (March or April)— Christ's death on the cross; and Easter (March or April)— Christ's resurrection. A primary observance in Christianity is the Holy Eucharist, or the sacrament of Holy Communion, in which bread and wine are consecrated and consumed in recognition of Christ's sacrifice on Calvary. Common rites and sacraments include baptism—the ritual washing for initiation or a sign of remission of sin and spiritual rebirth;

confirmation—a ratification of vows by those baptized in infancy, often identified with the annointing immediately after baptism in the Eastern Orthodox Churches; penance—the sacramental reconciliation of sinners, often including confession of sins and sacramental acts performed to receive absolution.

As other beliefs and practices vary between churches, explanations of them will be provided in the following pages, where the various churches are described. (See also Gnosticism, Essenes, Christian Mysticism, and Swedenborgianism in the section "Spiritual Paths.")

EASTERN ORTHODOX CHURCHES

*T*HE WORD *Orthodox* is Greek for "straight opinion," or "right belief." Christian doctrine, liturgy, and spirituality were shaped in the eastern part of the Roman Empire, with its capital at Byzantium (Constantinople, or modern Istanbul). Since the reign of Constantine (A.D. 288-337), the first Roman Emperor to legalize Christianity, the Eastern church held official status in the empire and became the builder of the new Christian culture. For several centuries the Church was united in matters of faith and sacramental communion. Through a series of ecumenical councils, beginning with the one in Nicaea (now Iznik, Turkey) in A.D. 325, Church doctrines were officially established, the most important being the Nicene Creed, which affirmed the full deity of Jesus Christ as being *homoousios*, "of the same substance," as God the Father. (See also Christian Mysticism.)

After the eleventh century the Roman Catholic church split from the Eastern church, and both remain autonomous to this day. Eastern churches were established in Constantinople, Alexandria, Antioch, Jerusalem, Russia, Romania, Bulgaria, Serbia, and Georgia. Other Orthodox churches include those in Greece, Cyprus, Poland, Czechoslovakia, and Finland. As much of the east has converted to Islam or become Communist, the church has diminished in size, but it is still represented throughout the world, including the United States, Austrialia, and Western Europe.

The tradition of the Eastern church is transmitted through the Bible, in the creeds and cannons established in the ecumenical councils, and in local customs and attitudes. In the Eastern church, the purpose of worship and ritual is to achieve a mystical union with God. The aim of Christian life is to acquire the Holy Spirit, and to attune the individual human will with divine will. God became man so that man might become divine. This unity is realized in the holy sacrament of the Eucharist.

The Orthodox church observes seven sacraments: baptism, confirmation, penance, the Eucharist, holy orders, matrimony, and extreme unction. Baptism is administered by triple immersion in sanctified water, followed by a rite of confirmation called holy chrismation. The Orthodox church observes substantially the same holy days as the Catholic church, but these are calculated in a different manner, so they are observed on different days. There is also the widespread use in churches and homes of sacred images of Christ and the saints in such forms as paintings, mosaics, or other icons. The faithful do not worship icons, but venerate them as examples of the Holy Spirit within man.

Recommended Reading:

The History of the Church
by Eusebus

The Greek Orthodox Church
by Demetros J. Constanlelos

ROMAN CATHOLICISM

*C*ATHOLIC MEANS "universal," and "Roman Catholic" refers to the Latin western church. Since the sixteenth century "Roman Catholic" has meant the Christian religious body that acknowledges the pope, as head of the universal Church and the center of ecclesiastical unity. Papal authority is based on the doctrine of apostolic succession, which holds that the authority of the Church was given to the apostle Peter, the first bishop of Rome, by Jesus Christ, and this authority has been passed down through successive bishops of Rome to the current pope. The first Vatican Council, held in 1870, declared that the pope has primacy of jurisdiction over the whole Church and that under specific conditions he is infallible in proclaiming doctrines of faith and morals. In 1964, Vatican Council II further explained infallibility and set it in the context of the Church and the college of bishops.

After the emperor Constantine granted freedom of religion to Christians with the Edict of Milan in A.D. 313, the entire Roman Empire was converted to Christianity. Thus most of the Mediterranean and much of Europe became Christianized. From the fourth century on, the Church was identified with the Roman Empire. But as the fortunes of Rome declined, the power of the empire shifted eastward to Constantinople, which resulted in a split between the Eastern and Western churches in 1054. The Middle Ages were the classic period of Roman Catholicism. Numerous majestic cathedrals were constructed throughout Europe to glorify God, and religious orders such as the Franciscans and Dominicans were formed.

In the eleventh century a philosophical system known as scholasticism was introduced into the Church. Scholastics attempted to synthesize traditional faith and values with the logic and reason of the Greek philosopher Aristotle. The theologian Thomas Aquinas (d. 1274) was particularly influential in reconciling faith and reason, and his ideas dominated Catholic thought for seven centuries. As explorers from Europe discovered foreign lands and developed trade, missionaries were brought to convert the pagan people to the universal religion. Today Christianity is the largest religion in the world, and the Roman Catholic church is the largest branch of Christianity, with representation around the world, particularly in Southern Europe and Latin America.

The Roman Catholic church believes in the traditional Christian creeds and the Trinity of God as:

(1) *God the Father All Governing*
(2) *Jesus Christ, the Son of God, who was begotten by the Holy Spirit from the Virgin Mary and was crucified by Pontius Pilate, died and rose from the dead on the third day, ascended into Heaven, and sat at the right hand of the Father. At the end of the world, Christ will come to judge the living and the dead.*
(3) *The Holy Spirit, in the holy Church.*

Catholics also believe in the concept of "original sin," which states that mankind is inherently sinful due to the disobedient acts of Adam and Eve (the first man and woman), and thus needs to be saved. Although confession, repentance, and absolution are means of rectifying one's individual sins, salvation is achieved only through God's grace. As Jesus Christ died on the cross as atonement for our (humanity's) sins, the belief in and acceptance of Christ as Lord redeems us for our sins and assures us eternal life with God and Jesus in Heaven.

Roman Catholics observe the seven sacraments, venerate saints, particularly the Virgin Mary (Christ's mother), and acknowledge the presence of the Holy Spirit. The Eucharist, or Mass, is the center of church life, in which bread and wine are transformed into the body and blood of Christ (transubstantiation). The physical ingestion of the body and blood of Christ in Holy Communion confers grace upon the believers. Catholic beliefs and doctines are interpreted by the clergy, who are deemed properly prepared to interpret the word of God for the believers.

Recommended Reading:

Keepers of the Key
by Nicolas Cheetham

The Word Made Flesh
by Karol Wojtyla (Pope John Paul II)

Thomas Aquinas: His Personality and Thought (authorized translation)
by Virgil Michel

Mary's Way
by Peggy Tabor Millin
(on the Virgin Mary)

PROTESTANTISM

*P*ROTESTANTISM EMBRACES those churches where the emphasis is placed on personal interpretation of the Holy Bible. The English reformer John Wycliffe (d. 1384) protested against the power of the pope, and argued that believers are directly responsible to God. He placed emphasis on the Bible itself as the source of God's word rather than the Church. Later the teacher and priest John Huss (d. 1415), inspired by Wycliffe, lead a reform party in Bohemia that based its theology on Bible interpretation and called for church reforms. Huss was later burned as a heretic, which served as a catalyst for further rebellion against the Western church. The permanent Protestant reform began shortly after the invention of the printing press and the public availability of the Holy Bible. During a two-decade period Martin Luther in Germany, John Calvin and Huldrych Zwingli in Switzerland, and numerous reformers in the Netherlands, Scotland, and England broke away from Roman Catholicism. Within one century Protestantism spread throughout northern Europe, where it remains the dominant religion today. Later, Protestant churches entered North America, and today most churches in the West are Protestant.

Interpretation of the scripture may vary, but reliance on the written word rather than on papal dictates or religious doctrine is what separates Protestant churches from Catholic or Orthodox churches. Protestants generally recognize two of the seven sacraments that the Orthodox and Catholic churches recognize, namely: (1) baptism, through which a human spirit is cleansed of "original sin" and endowed with a new kind of life with Jesus Christ, and (2) Holy Communion (the Lord's Supper or the Eucharist) a representation of Christ's sacrifice on Calvary.

Protestantism is divided into three main groups, and there are many other secular and nondenominational churches. These three main branches are Lutherans, Presbyterians, and Anglicans (or Episcopalians, as they are known in America). Brief descriptions of these churches and other churches appear on the following pages.

Lutherans, named after Martin Luther, a German friar who is credited with starting the Reformation after nailing his Ninety-Five Theses (protests against the Catholic church) on the door of a church at Wittenberg, Germany, in 1517. Luther's reform movement quickly spread throughout Germany, then across northern Europe and eventually around the world. Lutheranism is today the oldest and largest Protestant denomination. Lutherans believe that in Holy Communion, Christ is "really present" in the bread and wine in a mystical and miraculous way, although not in the literal sense of the Catholic doctrine of transubstantiation.

Presbyterians (and members of reformed churches) are Protestants who trace their church to a reformer from France, John Calvin. In *The Institutes of the Christian Religion*, Calvin outlined a comprehensive system of Protestant doctrine. He moved to Geneva, Switzerland, where he preached his beliefs, which spread rapidly through Europe. One of his disciples, the Scottish reformer John Knox, brought Calvin's ideas to the British Isles. Calvinism then spread to America and the rest of the world. *Presbyterian* comes from the Greek word *presbuteros*, meaning "elder."

Calvin's theology, and the belief of the church, emphasized the distinctive theme of the absolute sovereignty of God and the importance of living an austere life. Presbyterians believe that in Holy Communion the consecrated bread and wine must be regarded as symbols, or "representations," of the Lord's body and blood. The Presbyterian and reform churches comprise the second largest and second oldest Protestant churches.

Anglicans. The Anglican church is composed of the Church of England and seventeen other autonomous national churches, including the Protestant Episcopal church. Two centuries before the Reformation began, the Oxford don John Wycliffe was translating the Bible into English, denying the supreme authority of the pope, and proclaiming the priesthood of all believers. When King Henry VIII was denied an annulment of his marriage to Catherine by Pope

Clement VII, Henry repudiated the authority of the pope, and proclaimed himself head of the Church of England, which eventually opened the door to reform in the British Isles.

Anglicans retain Catholic tradition while accepting the basic insights of the Protestant reform. The Anglican communion is a worldwide fellowship, and is the third oldest and third largest family of Protestant churches.

Episcopalians. Episcopalians are the American Anglicans. The name *Episcopal* comes from the Greek word *episkopos*, which means "bishop."

Other Christian Churches

Congregationalists were the Puritans. Originally from northwestern Europe, these Protestants wanted to reform the Reformation. A group of Puritans set off from England in a ship called the *Mayflower* to start a new life and church in America. They are known as the Pilgrims. Puritans set up colonies and churches in New England. The Congregational Christian churches merged with the Evangelical and Reform Church (Calvinist body) in 1957 to form the United Church of Christ. This church is now one of the progressive churches, which emphasizes the personal freedom of the individual to interpret Scripture and to worship God in their own way.

Baptists. Founded in 1609, the Baptists were a group of Puritans who fled from presecution in England to Holland under the leadership of John Smyth. This group of Protestants were influenced by the doctrine of another reforming church called the Anabaptists, who did not believe in infant baptism. Baptists place emphasis on adults confirming their faith in Christ by a baptism of total immersion of the body in water. This group of Protestants is fundamentalist, and emphasize the reading of Scripture and regular observance of the Lord's Supper. This group comprises the largest Protestant family of churches in America.

Methodists. The Methodist church was founded in England by John Wesley, a student at Oxford University preparing for the Anglican ministry. At Oxford, Wesley became a leader of a band of students who sought spiritual renewal through methodical diligence in study and worship. The term "Methodists" was originally a nickname given to the study group. Later, as an Anglican priest, Wesley traveled around England bringing a revival of the Church of England. The movement spread, but the Church of England would not ordain Wesley's priests, so he left for America in 1738 and formed his own church, which spread rapidly throughout the country. The Methodist church is now the second biggest Protestant denomination in the United States. Methodists are basically fundamentalists, with no clear doctrine but an emphasis on "living right."

Society of Friends. The Society of Friends is a relatively small church better known as the *Quakers.* This puritanical group is also descended from the Church of England. Its founder, George Fox, was considered a rebel because he did not believe in showing observance to anyone but God; he forbade his followers to doff their hats to the king. For maintaining such beliefs and attitudes, the Quakers were persecuted, so in 1671 Fox sailed to America and started settlements in Maryland, Rhode Island, and Pennsylvania. This church remains relatively small and concentrated in the eastern United States.

Fox developed the doctrine of the Inner Light, which holds that God is ever present within every human being, and that he can be approached and experienced directly by anyone who sincerely seeks him. The emphasis is placed on personal experience with God and not so much on theories or practices. Quakers live simple, ascetic lives and are extreme pacifists.

Mennonites. Mennonites are direct spiritual descendants of the Anabaptist movement, which was founded in Zurich, Switzerland, in 1535. These people were considered the left wing of the Reformation, and were persecuted by Catholics, Lutherans, and Calvinists for their extreme beliefs, such as that only adult believers could be baptized. Mennonites got their name from a former Roman Catholic priest named Menno Simons, who joined the movement. Many of these persecuted Protestants fled to America and settled there around 1683. Later, other Mennonite settlers

71

came to America, but these people have tended to keep to themselves.

Members of the Mennonites include the **Amish**, the **Hutterian Brethren**, and many smaller denominations. These people tend to interpret every word of the Bible literally. They live very austere lives and are complete pacifists.

Christians. The Christians are multi-denominational, but primarily fall within two main branches, namely the "Disciples of Christ," and the "Church of Christ," which are the oldest and largest of the religious movements indigenous to the United States. The Christian movement follows the principle that each man is free to read and interpret the Scriptures for himself; in other words, there is "no creed but Christ." In practice, any person who accepts Jesus Christ as his personal Lord and Savior is welcome as a member of the fellowship. Specific practices of worship vary between individual churches.

Unitarians. The Unitarian view was expounded as early as the fourth century by Arius of Alexandria, who taught that Jesus was sent from God, but was not actually God incarnate. Similar views continued to be manifested over the centuries by English and European intellectuals. The Unitarian movement first emerged as an organized denomination in 1819, under the leadership of William Ellery Channing. Later in the nineteenth century, Unitarian ideas were expressed by Ralph Waldo Emerson and Theodore Parker. Unitarians consider Jesus Christ to be one sent by God to lead men into the way, the truth, and the life, but do not regard him as divine. Unitarians place great emphasis on individual freedom of belief, and leave each member to "seek the truth for himself."

Universalists. The first Universalist congregation was established by a former Wesleyan minister named John Murray. In 1961 the Universalists merged with the Unitarians to form the **Unitarian Universalist Association**, which remains a relatively small group of churches. The Unitarian Universalist Association's stated purpose is "To cherish and spread the universal truths taught by the great prophets and teachers of humanity in every age and tradition, immemorially summarized in the Judaeo-Christian heritage as love to God and love to man."

Mormons. The Mormon church, formally known as the Church of Jesus Christ of Latter-Day Saints, was started by a man from Palmyra, New York, named Joseph Smith, Jr. At the age of fourteen, Smith had a series of visions and was visited by an angel named Moroni. Moroni directed Smith to a box of golden plates inscribed with hieroglyphics. Moroni also provided a pair of instruments—called Urim and Thummim—to enable Smith to read the hieroglyphics and to dictate an English translation. The result was the Book of Mormon, published in 1829, which tells of Christ visiting a lost tribe of Israelites who migrated to America in 600 B.C., and ends with a prophecy that the Church of Christ would be restored in America by a group of "Latter-Day Saints," to correct the errors of other churches and restore the communal life of the New Testament Christians.

The first Mormon church was established in 1831 in Kirtland, Ohio, and started spreading. The Mormons were persecuted for their "unorthodox" Christian views and practices. Later Brigham Young, Smith's successor, led a group of Mormon settlers to the valley of the Great Salt Lake in Utah (then a part of Mexico) and started a Mormon settlement. This settlement grew and other Mormons came and settled. This church is now represented around the world. In addition to the Holy Bible, Mormons regard the Book of Mormon as Scripture. One distinguishing difference from traditional Protestant doctrine is that Mormons believe that God is a flesh-and-bones person who became supreme by mastering universal knowledge, and that all human beings have an unremembered pre-existence in the spirit world. Mormons also observe strict rules of personal morality.

Seventh-Day Adventists. Early in the nineteenth century, in America and in Europe, a movement developed around the belief that the second coming of Christ was at hand. The church was formally organized in 1863 in Michigan by Mrs. Ellen White. Mrs. White was an advocate of good health, and emphasized the preparation of church members, and the world, for the second coming of Christ. This church is now represented around the world. Adventists are fundamentalists who emphasize the biblical prophecies found in the apocalyptic books of Daniel and Revelation. The Adventists are convinced that the promised "Second Advent" of Christ is near, but do not state or proffer to know exactly when. This church has a strong missionary program and maintains many medical facilities. Most Adventists are vegetarians, and the church promotes an austere and conservative lifestyle.

Christian Scientists. The Christian Science church was formally established in 1879 by Mrs. Mary Baker Eddy. Mrs. Eddy suffered a serious accident and she remained in critical condition for several days. After reading accounts of Christ's healing a man bedridden with palsy (Matthew, chapter 9) in the Bible, Mrs. Eddy said a prayer, then arose from bed, dressed herself, and walked out on her own. From this event grew one of America's major religious denominations, which is represented around the world.

Christian Scientists believe that God is "infinite good," and that all "reality" in the universe is necessarily good because God created it. The evil, sickness, and death that men think they see in the world could not have come from God; therefore, these things are essentially unreal. This church emphasizes spiritual healing. Mrs. Eddy's book *Science and Health* is typically read in addition to the Bible at Sunday services. The church also sponsors reading rooms containing Christian Science literature in most major cities.

Pentecostals. The Pentecostal movement was an outgrowth of the popular religious revivals that swept the world during the latter part of the nineteenth century. This movement comprises over twenty organized denominations plus thousands of independent local churches, predominantly within the United States. Pentecostals are Protestant fundamentalists who believe that authentic religious conversion is an ecstatic experience that should be accompanied by all the "signs" that attend the outpouring of God's Holy Spirit, as it did with the first Christian apostles. This experience may include "the gift of tongues," meaning that while filled with the Spirit, believers may be able to speak and understand many strange languages that they never learned. The common bond between various Pentecostal churches is their intensely emotional approach to religion.

Holiness Churches. The Holiness churches were founded in Pilot Point, Texas, in 1908, by the merger of two small regional Holiness Associations. Often referred to as **Nazarenes**, they are spread out across North America and several foreign countries. The commonality of all Holiness denominations is the strong emphasis on sanctification, which holds that the Holy Spirit can purify the hearts and motives of truly consecrated Christians, that they are freed from their natural human tendency to sin and are rendered capable of perfect holiness in this earthly life. Nazarenes are typically quite austere and place a great deal of emphasis on evangelism.

Jehovah's Witnesses. The Watchtower Bible and Tract Society, better known as Jehovah's Witnesses, was founded in Allegheny, Pennsylvania, in 1879 by Charles Taze Russell. Today this church is one of the fastest growing religious bodies in the United States, and is spreading throughout Europe, Latin America, and Africa. This church is character-ized by its zeal for evangelism and personal housecalls. Convert-winning is so important to them because of their conviction that the end of human history is imminent. They expect it to come any time now and feel it's their duty to convert as many people as they can because the only survi-vors of the Battle of Armageddon (the battle foretold in the Bible, in which the forces of God fight the forces of Satan) will be the members of Jehovah's Witnesses, who will live eternal and blissful lives right here on earth forever.

Unification Church. The official name of this church is The Holy Spirit Association for the Unification of World Christianity. People outside the church often refer to the members as Moonies, but this term is incorrect and is considered derogatory. The church was founded in Korea in 1954 by Reverend Sun Myung Moon. On Easter morning in 1936, Jesus appeared to Reverend Moon and asked him to take responsibility for establishing the Kingdom of God on earth. Rev. Moon also communicates with Moses and Bud-dha, among other spiritual masters, as he "travels in the spirit world." From Korea, the church has spread to over 120 countries, including Japan, Western Europe, and the United States.

Moon's lectures about the revelations that he has received are in his text *Won-li Kang Mon* (Lectures of Principle). The basic belief is that humanity is to be restored to its original perfect state by a principle of indemnity, by which all sin and wrong in the world must be put right at the proper time. Adam and Eve (in the Holy Bible) are considered the first parents, and because they sinned, a second set of parents came to indemnify the fall of mankind and establish the true family ideal lost by Adam and Eve. Jesus came as the second Adam. He was not God himself, but he was related to God "as the body is related to the mind" (Divine Principle, p. 211). Because Jesus' contemporaries did not support him, and therefore he did not marry, he could only complete a spiritual restoration through the Holy Spirit, who played the role of Eve. The material world has remained under the power of Satan (the Devil) to the present day, but Satan will soon be vanquished by the new Messiah.

Reverend Moon teaches that the coming of a new Messiah is near and will occur in Korea. This second coming will complete the restoration, and the Messiah will marry a new Eve, found a sinless humanity, and establish God's kingdom on earth. Members of this church are directed to follow puritanical sexual mores, since the misuse of love is believed to have been the original sin of the Archangel, Adam, and Eve. Reverend Moon takes responsibility for arranging marriages between members of the church and may unite hundreds of couples in matrimony in mass ceremonies in order to help create harmony among different nationalities, races, and religions of the world.

For additional information:

Unification Church
c/o Public Affairs
4 W. 43rd Street
New York, NY 10036
Phone:(212) 827-0463

RECOMMENDED READING

Each denomination will generally have its own reading material. Books by the denomination's founder are generally mentioned in the description of the organization. Other books and magazines (and other media) can be recommended by members of the congregation or by the ministers. The following suggested reading material is popular among a broad-based group of Christians:

Recommended Reading:

The Holy Bible
(various translations)

The Illustrated Bible Handbook
Ed. by Edward P. Blair (Abingdon)

Pilgrim's Progress
by John Bunyan
(a Christian Classic)

The Sermon on the Mount
by Emmet Fox

Mere Christianity
by C. S. Lewis

The Cost of Discipleship
by Dietrich Bonhoeffer

Inspiring Message for Daily Living
by Norman Vincent Peale

How to Be Born Again
by Billy Graham

The Meaning of Prayer
by Harry Emerson Fosdick

Move Ahead with Possibility Thinking
by Dr. Robert H. Schuller

Strength to Love
by Martin Luther King, Jr.

Periodicals: *Daily Word*
Unity Village, MO 64065
(816) 524-3550

Christianity Today
P.O. Box 11618
Des Moines, Iowa 50340
(800) 999-1704

ISLAM

*I*SLAM MEANS "Purity, by submission to Allah's will, and obedience to Allah's laws." Allah is the one God of infinite perfection and beauty. Islam is a religion based on the revelations and teachings of Allah to his prophet Muhammad (or Mohammed). Muhammad was born in the city of Mecca in Arabia, in the year A.D. 570. He was orphaned as a child, and was raised by his uncle in abject poverty. During this period, Mecca was a city where pagans made pilgrimages to worship idols at various shrines. After retreating to a cave near Mecca to pray and contemplate, Muhammad was visited by the angel Gabriel, who presented the message of Islam to confirm what the previous prophets of Judaism and Christianity had taught, and to correct adulterations that had perverted those teachings. Gabriel told Muhammad that he had been chosen to correct these errors, and he was told to complete the divine revelation that began with the older faiths, Judaism and Christianity.

Upon receiving the revelations, Muhammad went to the people of Mecca to proclaim the absolute unity of God (Allah) and denounce idolatry. But he was not at first well-received, so he moved to Medina, where he gradually gathered a large following. By A.D. 630 Muhammad was able to return to Mecca as a victorious leader of this new movement. Muhammad's words spread quickly throughout the Arab world. Within ten years, the whole of the Arabian Peninsula was conquered; within one generation, an area almost the size of the continental United States was converted to Islam; and within a century, Islam had spread as far as Spain and Morocco in the west and India and southeast Asia in the east. Today Islam is one of the world's largest religions (there are over a billion Muslims), and is represented around the world, with the largest followings in East Asia and the Middle East.

Islam is predicated upon the Six Articles of Belief, which are as follows: (1) Allah (God) is one; (2) the Qur'am (Koran) is Allah's truly revealed book; (3) God's angels are heavenly beings created to serve God, and they are opposed to evil; (4) God sends his prophets to earth at stated times for stated purposes. The last of these was Muhammad, and Allah makes no distinction between messengers; (5) the Day of Judgment will find good and evil weighed in the balance; (6) the lives and acts of people are foreordained by the all-knowing Allah. However, humans are the builders of their own destiny and are free to make or mar their future. Central to Islamic faith is submission to Allah's law and will, and a Muslim (Moslem) is one who adheres to the religion of Islam, or is "one who submits." The revelations of the Qur'an focus on the gifts or rewards that Allah will bestow upon the faithful in the hereafter and the severe punishments that will go to those who were unfaithful and disobedient. Muslims believe in the Law of Moses, the Psalms of David, and the Gospel of Jesus Christ (who is thought of as one of Allah's prophets), but believe that those Scriptures are superseded by the revelations given to Muhammad.

There are two primary sects of Muslims: Sunnites and Shi'ites. Over 90 percent of the world's Muslims are Sunnites. Sunnite Muslims accept four caliphs, or spiritual leaders, in direct succession from Muhammad and no others, and practice a moderate form of Islamic interpretation. Shi'ite Muslims are much more literal in their interpretation and application of the Qur'an, and they tend to be more militant. The highest concentration of Shi'ite Muslims is in Iran, where their spiritual leader is referred to as the Ayatollah. There is also a mystical sect called Tasawo, or Sufism, which is discussed in the section "Spiritual Paths." Central to the practice of Islam is the fulfillment of the "Five Pillars of Islam," namely: (1) Recitation of the Shahadah, or "confession," which states: "There is no God but Allah, and Muhammad is the prophet of Allah"; (2) Five daily prayers (Salat or Namaz) in Arabic, including genuflection and prostration in the direction of the holy city of Mecca; (3) Almsgiving (Zakat), regular charitable contributions; (4) Fasting (Saum or Ruzeh) during the entire month of Ramadan, when no food or drink is taken from sunrise to sunset for self-discipline and the atonement of sins; (5) A pilgrimage (Hajj) to Mecca (The holy city in Saudi Arabia) at least once in one's lifetime. Reading the Qur'an is also an important part of Islamic practice, as well as study of the Hadith, which is a collection of sayings and reported actions that provides guidance for the political and social structure of Islam. Muslims practice congregational prayers several times a day in mosques, which are found throughout the Islamic world, and they follow a strict moral and ethical code.

For more information...

...on Islam, look under mosques or Islamic centers in your local phone directory, or contact:

The Islamic Center of Southern
California
434 South Vermont
Los Angeles, CA 90020
Phone: (213) 384-5783

Recommended Reading:

The Holy Qur'an
The translation by A. Yusuf Ali

Islam
by Fredrich Denny

Message of the Qur'an
by M. Asad

The Life of Muhammad
by M. Haykal

*Islam and Revolution, The Writings and
Declarations of Imam Khomeini*
Tr. by Hamid Algar

SPIRITUAL PATHS

SPIRITUAL PATHS is a broad category that generally refers to the indigenous spiritual teachings of various cultures, and the esoteric teachings evolving from within established religions. These spiritual teachings either existed before the advent of one of the major Western religions, or developed within the established religious institutions as a subculture or movement. As many of these teachings were practiced privately to avoid chastisement by the predominant religious institution, they are sometimes considered "occult" or "esoteric," meaning the teachings contain a secret or hidden knowledge.

Kabbalism is the esoteric spiritual teachings of the Jews. It is recognized within Judaism as a legitimate and authoritative science, but has never been taught to the masses and has only recently been made available to the public. Many other spiritual teachings have drawn from the Kabbalah, such as the Freemasons and the Builders of the Adytum. The Kabbalah is also the source of Western astrology and numerology and tarot. Kabbalistic teachings may also have influenced the Essenes, Gnosticism, and Christian Mysticism.

Druidism was the spiritual practice of the people of Western Europe before the influx of, first, Roman culture, and later Christian missionaries. With the repression of Druidic (Celtic) culture by outside influences, the teachings went underground and have stayed there to the present day. The Druid teachings appear to have heavily influenced the Wiccan teachings and the practice of witchcraft in Europe

85

and abroad. With such dominant acceptance of Christianity in the Western world, which led to the persecution of followers of indigenous religions, the practice of Wicca and witchcraft has remained a secret science until recently. Pagans (or "heathens" as they are called by Christians), are those who believe in a form of god (or goddess) other than that which is believed in by Judaic-Christian religions. Paganism is becoming more accepted and more popular among a widely divergent group of people in the West.

The early Christian mystics, who were known as Gnostics (knowers of Truth), were eventually eradicated by the institutional Christian churches, but the element of mysticism gained a foothold from within the Church through individuals who, at great risk to themselves, shared their inner mystical experiences with their spiritual brothers and sisters. St. Augustine of HiPo, The Desert Fathers, St. Francis of Assisi, Meister Eckehart, St. Nicodemos, St. John of the Cross, St. Teresa of Avila, Jakob Boehme, Emanuel Swedenborg, and Thomas Merton, among others, played an important role in preserving the aspect of mysticism and personal gnosis (knowledge) within the context of Christian theology.

Zoroastrianism was the principal religion of Persia before the conversion to Islam. Although Zoroastrian theology appears to have influenced the monotheistic theology of the Western religions, it was considered a pagan religion, and was therefore shunned by the newly evangelized cultures. Most Zoroastrians migrated to other cultures that were more tolerant, with the heaviest concentration being in India, where they are known as Parsis. Within the Islamic culture, a group of mystics known as Sufis have maintained a tradition of knowing God through personal experience (gnosis), which has influenced both Western and Eastern theology and spiritual practice. Thus, within Jewish, Christian, and Islamic culture, a mystical element has been preserved for those who were inclined to know God through personal experience.

In other parts of the world, small groups have been able to preserve some of their own culture and spiritual practices; although most have been heavily influenced by the world's major religions, and have adapted to the cultural infusion. Shamanistic practices are common throughout Siberia and North America. Indigenous tribal groups, such as the Native Americans, have been able to preserve their rites and maintain their communion with the Earth Mother, despite strong resistance from orthodox "new" religions. In Hawaii a group of Shamanistic teachings known as Huna, has reemerged within public view to preserve the cultural and spiritual heritage of the Hawaiian Islands. In Africa, the Caribbean, and parts of South America, blacks have developed a spiritual practice which combines the essence of their native African spiritualism with the archetypes of Catholicism. This blended religion is generally referred to as Voodoo, Santeria or Macoumba. In Jamaica, the people have developed and adapted their spirituality to new circumstances that have affected them to create a new religion known as Rastafarianism. Thus each of these cultures appears to have been able to preserve some of their cultural heritage and maintain a personal relationship with their creator through mystical experiences.

It is human nature to be skeptical of anything that is new or not understood. People who have been brought up in theological belief systems often find mystical experiences frightening, and consider those things that they don't understand to be evil—like a fear of the dark. However, once the symbologies are interpreted, and the experiences explained, mystical traditions become easier to understand and accept. Each individual ultimately discovers the truth through their own independent investigation. The following traditional spiritual paths serve as alternatives to the generally accepted modes of understanding God, and provide a means of preserving cultural inheritances.

Recommended Periodicals:

*Gnosis, A Journal of the Western
Inner Traditions*
P.O. Box 14217
San Francisco, CA 94114-0217
Phone:(415) 255-0400

Circle Network News
(Wiccan/Pagan/Shaman newspaper)
Box 219
Mt. Horeb, WI 53572
Phone:(608) 924-2216

Magical Blend
(esoteric traditions)
Box 421130
San Francisco, CA 94142
Phone:(415) 673-1001

*The Quest, A Quarterly Journal of
Philosophy, Science, Religion & Arts*
P.O. Box 270
Wheaton, Il 60189-0270
Phone: (415) 548-1680

Shaman's Drum
(A Journal of Experimental Shamanism)
P.O. Box 430
Willits, CA 95490
Phone:(707) 459-0486

Wildfire
(Shamanistic/Naturalist)
P.O. Box 9167
Spokane, WA 99209
Phone:(509) 326-6561

DRUIDS AND PAGANS

*T*HE DRUIDS were the Magi, or philosopher-magicians, of the early Celtic civilization. The history of the Druids dates back to the migration of the Indo-European-speaking people in the second millennium B.C. (approximately 4,000 years ago), when nomadic tribes who occupied the area around the Caspian Sea in southern Russia began to migrate southeastward into the Indus Valley (India) and westward into Asia Minor, the Balkans, and the European plain. Around the tenth century B.C., a people recognizably Celtic began to emerge from Bohemia (in western Czechoslovakia). In the eighth to the sixth centuries B.C., they began to migrate down into Italy and Spain, and further west into France and Belgium, and eventually into the British Isles. These people were generally tall and were skilled horsemen, metalworkers, and warriors. The Welsh Triads or "Traditional Chronicles" hold that Hu Gadarn or "Hu the Mighty," who was a descendant of the patriarch Abraham, led a party of settlers from Asia Minor to the British Isles and established a religious practice among the Celts that we now refer to as Druidism. Several meanings are offered for the word *Druid*, including: "a servant of truth," "all knowing, or wise man," "an oak," or "equal in honor." Generally, a Druid is considered one with *gnosis*, or spiritual awareness.

Within the Celtic culture was a brotherhood, or perhaps a class of priests, known as the Druids, who served as the spiritual leaders and wise men of their day. As the Druids did not (apparently) keep a written record of their spiritual practices or culture, most of what is known about them comes from the records of their conquerors and the myths and legends of the Bards. The Romans considered the Druids to have been an established institution by the fourth century B.C. Posidonius, the philosopher-historian, had traveled throughout Gaul during the time of the Druids and had written about them in his *Histories*, written at the end of the second century B.C. Unfortunately, these writings were lost, but portions were later referred to by the historian Strabo

(63 B.C.-A.D. 21). The best records by people who lived during the time of the Druids were Caesar's *Conquest of Gaul* and *Natural History* by Pliny the Elder, who died in A.D. 79. By A.D. 37 Gaul and much of Britain were under Roman control, and Rome prohibited Druidic practices. However, Druidic beliefs and practices have been passed on though oral traditions within secret circles throughout Europe.

The influence of the Druids on the Celtic culture, and on Western civilization, has endured for thousands of years. Seasonal celebrations and festivals were adopted and adapted to the new Christianized cultures of Europe—such as Christmas at the winter solstice and the Druid festival of Samhain, or All Hallows Sabbath—which we now call Halloween. Moreover, Druid beliefs and customs, such as kissing under the mistletoe, have also been passed down to the present day. Wiccan groups appear to be heavily influenced by the Druids; however, as any form of "pagan" worship was repressed in Christian societies, such rituals were practiced very discreetly and little is known or available to the public. Thus, to this day many Druid practices remain a secret to the public.

In the latter part of the eighteen century, Druidic cults and societies appeared all over western Europe; one of the first was the Ancient Order of Druids, which was founded by an Englishman, Henry Hurle. Later the Ancient Order of Druids became more of a benefit society, and some of the members who were more interested in the esoteric side of Druidism formed other orders. Other noted orders include The British Circle of the Universal Bond; The Order of Bards, Ovates and Druids; and The Order of the Golden Dawn. Today there are numerous orders throughout Western societies; however, most of the older traditional ones do not solicit or even admit members unfamiliar to them.

Druids believed in the eternal nature of the Soul, and saw a living spirit in all forms of creation. There is an ancient saying attributed to the Druids, "Spirit sleeps in the mineral, breathes in the vegetable, dreams in the animal, and wakes in man." Druids held that souls could be contacted after death, and that souls reincarnate (are reborn). The universe is the Druid's living bible, written directly by the hand of

God. Moreover, mankind is seen as evolving and unfolding in its awareness of itself. Within the spiritual makeup of creation is a pantheon of gods and goddesses, as consciousness for the attributes in nature. Some of the most recognized are TARANIS—the father of the gods, associated with the oak tree; BELENOS—the god of the Sun, celebrated on Beltane, or May Day; CERNUNNOS—the horned god of the hunt, who rules the dark side of the year (winter); LUGH—the many-skilled; ESUS—the pastoral god and magician; TEUTATIS—the warrior god and ruler of the people; EPONA—the horse goddess, associated with fertility; MORRIGAN—the goddess of war; CARIDWEN—the mother goddess and triple goddess of fire, water, and air; RHEA—the mistress of life and sovereign of time; and DIANA—the huntress and goddess of the moon. The many gods and goddesses were known by many names, depending on the region and period of time.

Druids are the interpreters of the gods, the judges and teachers, astronomers and seers, as well as physicians and healers. Rites and rituals are generally held outdoors, typically in an oak grove or around a stone circle. Druids celebrate the four major Sabbaths: SAMHAIN—All Hallows, or Halloween; IMBOLC—The Feast of Lights, or Candlemas; BELTANE—May Day; and LAGHNASADH, or LAMMAS—the Feast of Bread; as well as the four lesser Sabbaths related to the changing of seasons, namely, the spring and autumn equinoxes, and the summer and winter solstices. Druid rites are generally merry occasions, with feasting, dancing, and singing, where feelings of love for the gods and goddesses are expressed and an appreciation for nature's abundance is celebrated. Druids are also, typically, homeopathic healers and astrologers. However, Druids are principally the teachers of Truth, who assist their aspirants in seeing the divine spirit within themselves, and indeed within all things. Druids use natural science and experience to verify truths, and spiritual development is an interactive process and not a faith. A triad of the three fundamental principles of wisdom is:

Obedience to the Laws of God:
Effort for the welfare of mankind:

And heroically enduring the unavoidable ills of life.

For more information...

... on Druid teachings, there is an excellent list of active organizations in *Drawing Down the Moon*, by Margot Adler (See the "Resources" section) or in the *Circle Network News*, a quarterly newspaper that has listings of Celtic and Druid organizations. As Druids typically do not write down their teachings, in keeping with a time-honored tradition, no books are available by a Druid that describe their teachings. My suggestion is that you either write to one of the groups listed in Margot Adler's book, or visit a metaphysical bookstore in your area and ask around to see if there are any Pagan groups nearby, and if there are, contact them. As you get to know people in Pagan circles, the Druids will observe you and judge your character. If they feel that you have the qualities and aptitude to become a Druid, then you will be invited to join their group.

Recommended Reading:

The Druids
by Ward Rutherford

Drawing Down the Moon
by Margot Adler

Mind of the Druids
by Dr. Graham Howe

Celtic Druids
by Godfrey Higgins

Resources: Circle Network News
Box 219
Mt. Horeb, WI 53572
Phone:(608) 924-2216

or   The 1990 Circle Guide to
Pagan Groups
c/o Circle Network News

The Divine Circle of the Sacred Grove
P.O. Box 2440
Fontana, CA 92334-2440

WICCA AND WITCHCRAFT

WICCA, OR witchcraft, is the old religion of Europe, which apparently evolved from Druidism. *Wiccan* is generally a term applied to a "wise one" or "magician," and Wicca is the practice of "magic," which is the application and utilization of natural laws. As witchcraft competed as a religion with Christianity (the "new" religion) in the Christianized Western world, witchcraft became repressed as a form of paganism (i.e., a primitive teaching) and was given an evil stigma, and therefore was not practiced openly. However, with the repeal of the English Witchcraft Act in 1951, many covens, or congregations, have opened up to the public and many new groups have formed. There are now dozens of Wiccan organizations in the United States and Europe, with perhaps thousands of active Wiccans and witches. Most witches practicing the craft publicly are considered white witches, that is, they use their knowledge for good ends and practice the Wiccan Creed: "Ye hurt none, do as ye will." Black witches (which have received the most notoriety, but are considered a minority), are generally not visible to the public and use their knowledge for selfish or evil means. Satanism is *not* considered a form of witchcraft, but was created by people who believe there is a Satan, or Devil.

Wicca/witchcraft generally involves some form of god or goddess worship, and many involve the invoking of spirits and guides as well. Wicca/witchcraft is a very individualized religion, and each person chooses his or her own deities to worship. Generally, the supreme being is considered genderless and is comprised of many aspects that may be identified as masculine or feminine in nature, and thus a god or a goddess. Originally, the horned God of hunting represented the masculine facet of the deity, whereas the female qualities were represented in the fertility goddess. The gods and goddesses form the personalities of the supreme being, and are a reflection of the attributes that the worshipers seek to emulate. Wiccans may draw upon the ancient civilizations of the Druids, Egyptians, Greeks, Romans, or other polytheistic cultures to commune with the particular aspect of the deity that they identify with. Some favorite gods include Osiris, Pan, Cennunnos, and Bacchus. Favorite goddesses include Isis, Caridwen, Rhea, Selene, and Diana.

Wiccans generally observe the four greater Sabbaths of Samhain, Imbolc, Beltane, and Laghnasadh; and the lesser Sabbaths—the spring and autumn equinoxes and the summer and winter solstices. These celebrations are typically free-spirited, and are sometimes held "sky clad" (naked) or in various styles of robes. Other services include handfasting (marriage), handparting (divorce), and wiccaning (birth rite). Regular meetings called Esbats are also held, at which magic and healing are performed. Wiccans/witches meet in small groups (up to twelve) called a coven, which typically join with other covens to form a "grove."

Rituals are typically held outside and consist of forming a circle and erecting the temple (consecrating the circle); invoking, praising, and soliciting assistance from gods, goddesses, and elementals; observing the change of seasons and the energies represented by the various seasons; singing; dancing; "cakes and ale" (sharing of bread and wine); and clearing the temple. Personal practice includes meditation and prayer, divination, development of personal will and psychic abilities through spells and various forms of healing. Most Wiccans/witches have altars where they burn candles and incense and practice their rites. To perform their rites, other tools of the craft are used, such as an athame, yag-disk or, seax (a handmade and consecrated knife), a sword, a wand, and sometimes special jewelry, amulets or talismans (magically empowered objects). Sometimes these objects are inscribed with magical writings. Joining a coven or grove typically involves an initiation, which is stylized by each individual group, but generally involves the confirmation that the initiate understands principles and an oath of secrecy.

For more information contact:

Metaphysical bookstores and herb shops. A very complete listing of Wiccan/witchcraft and Neo-Pagan groups is listed in Margot Adler's book *Drawing Down the Moon*, or you could get the *Circle Guide of Pagan Resources* by sending a self-addressed, stamped envelope to:

Circle
P.O. Box 219
Mt. Horeb, WI 53572
Phone:(608) 924-2216

(This guide lists over 500 Pagan organizations)

The Circle Network News also carries solicitations for memberships from different groups; look for a copy in metaphysical bookstores or send $3 to the above address for a sample copy.

Recommended Reading:

Buckland's Complete Book of Witchcraft
by Raymond Buckland

Helping Yourself with White Witchcraft
by Al G. Manning

Drawing Down the Moon
by Margot Adler

ZOROASTRIANISM

*T*HE ZOROASTRIANISM religion dates back to around the seventh century B.C. and was founded in south-central Asia (Iran) by the prophet Zoroaster, or Zarathustra, after whom the religion is named. The Zoroastrian religion has endured through the many conquests of Persia, and has had a profound influence upon the development of monotheistic ideology in world history. The religion first started to gain wide acceptance during the Achemaenid (Hakhamanian) Empire under Cyrus the Great (550-330 B.C.), the first emperor of Persia. The religion began to decline during the rule of the Seleucid Empire (330-250 B.C.) after Alexander the Great defeated Darius III and subsequently destroyed the NASKS—the sacred scriptures of the Zoroastrians.

The Zoroastrians gained strength again during the Parthian Dynasty (250-218 B.C.) and reached its height as a state religion during the rule of the Sassanid dynasty (226-641). However, in the seventh century the Arabs conquered Iran and gradually imposed their own religion of Islam. Early in the tenth century, a small group of Zoroastrians seeking freedom of worship left Iran and eventurally settled in India, where they are known as **Parsis**. Due to pressure and coercion from the Islamic government in Iran, many Zoroastrians have converted to the Islamic faith. The Zoroastrian population in Iran is now about 90,000, and some 13,000 now live in North America.

Zoroastrians believe in one God, known by the Avestan name Ahura Mazda (The Wise Lord). Zarathustra describes him more specifically as "The one Supreme God, Ahura-Mazda, who is All Wise, All Good, and Eternal conceived ideal creation in accordance with the principle identified with Asha (the truth). The truth represents the true order of the universe. Truth is also righteousness, because righteousness is action according to truth." The Zoroastrian God is a friend to all, not to be feared. The teachings about Ahura Mazda and the revelations of Zarathustra are expressed in poetic form in the **Gathas**. Zarathustra emphasized the virtue of righteousness, and his philosophy involves the practice of (1) good thoughts, (2) good words, and (3) good deeds. The events of this world are seen as a contest between the powers of good and evil. Upon death the soul is believed to cross a bridge, the Chinvat Bridge ("Bridge of the Separator"), which widens to permit easy passage to the righteous but shrinks to a knife-edge for the wicked, so that they fall into a life of hell below.

Zoroastrians worship in what are known as Fire Temples, where a fire always burns as the symbol of divine power, presence, and purity. Fires may also be burned in services in homes of the believers. Prayers are said in Avestan, rather than in modern vernaculars, since the pronunciation of these sounds has a Mantra-like or meditative quality to them. Zoroastrians receive a white undershirt called a sudreh and a hollow woven cord called a kusti, which are to be worn under their clothing the rest of their life (except while bathing). Several times a day the follower reties the kusti while saying certain fixed prayers. In addition to meditation and prayer, Zarathustra emphatically stated that "Those who served God best were those who rendered active service to God's creations which include fellow human beings." Service to others is therefore an integral part of Zoroastrian practice.

For more information:

California Zoroastrian Center
8952 Hazard Avenue
Westminister, CA 92683
Phone:(714) 893-4737

The Zoroastrian Association of
Greater New York
249 Weyman Avenue
New Rochelle, NY 10805

Recommended Reading:

The Gathas, Our Guide
Translated by Ali A. Jafarey

Zoroastrians, Their Religious Beliefs and Practices
by Mary Boyce

KABBALISM

*K*ABBALAH IS the esoteric doctrine of the Jewish faith. In Hebrew it is called QBLH, *qabalah*, which is derived from the root QBL, *qibel*, which means "to receive." The Kabbalistic teachings were kept secret, and were only passed down orally, so the exact date of the origin of the teachings cannot be pinned down. It is purported by some Kabbalists that the Kabbalah was first taught by God himself to a select company of angels, who imparted the sacred knowledge to Adam. From Adam the teachings were passed on to Noah, and then to Abraham, who emigrated to Egypt, where the Egyptians obtained some knowledge of it. From Egypt, other Eastern teachers introduced it into their philosophical systems.

Moses was initiated into the sacred Kabbalah and studied it throughout his life, and is said to have been instructed in it by one of the angels. Moreover, Moses is said to have covertly laid down the principles of this secret doctrine in the first four books of the Torah (Genesis, Exodus, Leviticus, and Numbers) but withheld it from Deuteronomy. These teachings were further passed down by way of an unbroken line of verbal tradition, until the time of the destruction of the second temple. During this period, Rabbi Simen Ben Jochai's treatises were collated after his death by his son Rabbi Eleazar and his disciples, and from these writings was composed the main and most significant written text of the Kabbalah, known as the *Zohar*, or the *Book of Splendor*. However, the bulk of the various strata and treatises that comprise the *Zohar* were written by Moses de Leon, and published in Spain around 1285.

The Kabbalah contains the keys that unlock the hidden meaning within the Bible (Torah), which has been withheld from those considered unworthy or unprepared to understand its significance. The Kabbalah discusses such topics as the hierarchy of being, mankind as a microcosm of the spiritual worlds, how moral purity is a precondition to spiritual enlightenment, and how one can purify himself and return to the Divine One. Kabbalah is the science of cause-and-effect relationships and the practice of developing one's awareness to understand, and commune with, the Holy One. Understanding Kabbalah requires going beyond mental constraints.

By using various contemplative and meditative techniques that alter the modes of perception, the aspirant can pierce the illusion of our reality and gain insight into, and reach harmony with, the source of all being. Moreover, the Kabbalah teaches that intuitive contact with spirit carries the divine power, or creative energy, and by developing this creative energy one can sustain a harmonious relationship with God. The Kabbalah places emphasis on symbology and numbers in relating to understanding the esoteric teaching in the Bible (Torah). Modern numerology and Western astrology were both developed through Kabbalistic practice, and were originally used as a means of understanding the process of evolving the consciousness and liberating the soul.

For more information contact:

> Research Center of Kabbalah
> 2376 Westwood Boulevard, Suite 1
> West Los Angeles, CA 90064
> Phone (213) 475-7079

> *or*　Research Center of Kabbalah
> P.O. Box 14168
> The Old City, Jerusalem, Israel and,

> *or*　The Research Center of Kabbalah
> 200 Park Avenue, Suite 303E
> New York, NY 10017

Other groups are mentioned in spiritual magazines such as Gnosis and Magical Blend.

Recommended Reading:

Kabbalah for the Layman
by Dr. Philip S. Berg

The Kabbalah, a Study of the Ten Luminous Emanations
by Rabbi Isaac Luria

The Zohar Parashat Pinhas
Transmitted by Dr. Philip S. Berg
(3 volumes)

The Mystical Qabalah
by Dion Fortune

Kabbalah, An Introduction and Illumination for the World Today
by Charles Ponce

The Kabbalah Unveiled
From the Latin 'Kabbala Denudata'
Trans. by S. L. MacGregor Mathers

ESSENES

*T*HE ESSENES were a society of ascetic Jews who lived throughout the Holy Land, but apparently concentrated around the area of the Dead Sea (in the modern state of Israel). Although opinions differ as to the origins and history of the Essenes, archaeological excavations at Khirbat Qumran provided documents known as the Dead Sea Scrolls, which support a date around the middle of the second century B.C. It is generally held that the Essene brotherhood evolved as early as the early part of the second century B.C., possibly as a countermovement to the Hellenization of Judaea; first by the Ptolemeys (Greek rulers of Egypt) and the Seleucids (Greek rulers of Syria), and then by Antiochus Epiphanes (d. 92 B.C.) who officially promoted a program of Hellenization throughout Judaea. The decline of their society is believed to have begun after the earthquake in 31 B.C.

The Essenes were the smallest of four sects of Jews, the others being the Pharisees, Sadducees, and Zealots. Most of what is known about the Essenes comes from the commentaries of the Jewish historians Philo of Alexandria and Flavius Josephus, from the first century A.D., who both estimate their numbers to be 4,000 by the first century A.D. After the destruction of the temple in Jerusalem by the Romans in A.D. 70, the Essene brotherhood apparently disintegrated. There is, however, evidence that the Essenes may have integrated into the early Christian church; with its similarities as an apocalyptic faith, the practice of ritual bathing and initiation rites by immersion in water, and the emphasis on moral purity and nonattachment to material existence.

The Essenes were first and foremost Jews, who believed in the one almighty God, Yahweh, and followed the laws of God as set forth by the patriarch Moses (see "Judaism"). According to Josephus, the Essenes believed "that bodies are corruptible, and that the matter they are made of is not permanent; but that the souls are immortal, and continue forever; and that they come out of the most subtle air, and are united in their bodies as in prisons into which they are drawn by a certain natural enticement; but when they are set free from the bonds of flesh, they then, as released from a long bondage, rejoice and mount upward." They also believed that good (pious) souls would be liberated and rewarded by God, and that bad (ungodly) souls would be doomed to Hades (Hell). Many, but not all, lived in communes, and all of them shared income and property equally among themselves. They had disdain for accumulated material possessions and for lascivious behavior, and esteem for continence and conquest over passions. They were strong advocates of peace and justice, and did not believe in animal sacrifices at the temples (which was the norm at the time). The most distinctive attributes of the Essenes were their belief in the imminent battle between the forces of good and evil, and in the coming of *Messiahs* to deliver and lead their people.

The Essenes were a select group, which accepted members only after testing the candidates over a period of several years. For one year the candidate would live with them so that his character and temperament could be observed and tested. After one year's time, if the candidate passed these rigors, he would then participate in a purification by bathing in water. For two more years the neophyte would be tested before being accepted into the brotherhood. An oath was also required that the brother maintain piety toward God and justice toward men. They must harm no one, and maintain fidelity to their fellow man, honesty, and the secrecy of their doctrines. Those who broke this oath were cast out of the society. The society studied the writings of the ancients, and had knowledge of medicinal roots and stones. They held prayers first thing in the morning and before the afternoon meal (after a ritual bath for purification), as well as before the evening meal. They were strict in observing the sabbath of the seventh day, and would not even cook food on this day. They were also noted for wearing white robes and observing periods of silence.

For more information: ████████████████████████

I am not familiar with any direct lineage of the Essene brotherhood. However, the International Biogenic Society (see under New Age Teachings) has founded their organization on the principles of the Essenes as researched by Edmond Bordeaux Szekely. Other smaller groups that have adopted Essene beliefs, or have "channeled" the teachings, have formed around the world. Independent investigation of these groups through metaphysical organizations is suggested.

Recommended Reading:

The Complete Works of Josephus
Translated by William Whiston
(look in index under Essenes)

The Dead Sea Scrolls
by Geza Vermes

Note: Unfortunately the principal source of documentation of the life and practices of the Essenes, the Dead Sea Scrolls from Qumran, are not made available to the public. So, a great deal more about this group has yet to be learned.

GNOSTICISM

*G*NOSTICISM IS a term that comes from the Greek word for "knowledge," *gnosis*, referring to the inner, hidden knowledge or transcendental understanding of God gained experientially. Gnosticism is a mixed and diverse body of thought. Though the origins seem to have been in pagan and Jewish (perhaps Kabbalistic) sects before the coming of Jesus Christ, the term *Gnostic* generally refers to the teachings of those Christians in the first century A.D. who were not members of the orthodox Christian churches. By the second and third centuries A.D., Gnosticism had grown into numerous scattered groups, which generally fell into two main schools—the Basilideans and the Valentinians, both of which were considered heretics by the orthodox Church authorities.

Until recently, all that was generally known of Gnosticism was recorded by the critics of the time (e.g., Irenaeus, Hippolytus, Tertullian, Origen, and Plotinus). However, in 1945 "Apocryphal Documents," which are believed to contain the scriptural basis for Gnostic beliefs, were discovered at Nag Hammadi in Egypt. These Gnostic gospels include The Apocryphon of James; the Gospel of Truth; the Gospel of Thomas (Jesus' brother); the Gospel of Philip; the Exegesis of the Soul; the Origin of the World; the Dialogues of the Savior; the Apocalypse of Paul; the Acts of Peter and the Twelve Apostles; and the Gospel of Mary (Magdalene), as well as many others. These Coptic texts profess and document the teachings of Adam and of Jesus Christ and the disciples (among others) and explain many of the esoteric or "hidden" teachings of Judaism and Christianity.

Gnosticism generally emphasized one's individual pursuit of spiritual knowledge and personal experience with the Holy Spirit, over the established beliefs, or dogma, propagated by the Church. Gnostics apparently rejected the Church doctrines of blind faith and the belief that accepting Jesus Christ as the Savior was the sole source of salvation. Gnostics appeared to perceive Jesus as an enlightened Spiritual

Master, or God Man, who showed the way to salvation by providing a means of attaining Gnosis, or experiential knowledge, through his Grace. More than just believe, you had to realize God to be saved. Gnostics sought freedom from the illusory material world by way of spiritual insight and development of their inner awareness.

The Nag Hammadi documents present a significantly different interpretation of Christian theology, which accounts for the Gnostics being so heavily persecuted by the churches and almost all the Gnostic writings being destroyed. These esoteric documents give new accounts about Adam and Eve's discovery of knowledge in Eden; the inner light of God (which is something actually experienced, not just a metaphor); meditation techniques; experiences of leaving the physical body and traveling to the heavenly spheres and returning again; and various other esoteric teachings. It suggests the possibility of attaining a realization of God through techniques that Jesus himself taught, through self-inquiry and personal experience.

Modern Gnosticism is practiced either through independent research and contemplation or through traditional services, which are quite similar to a Catholic Mass. Traditional services include the celebration of the Holy Eucharist, but also include unorthodox services such as the "Feast of the Holy Mary Magdalene" and various healing services. Gnostic practices place emphasis on individual "gnosis" rather than on faith or on rules to live by. With English translations of most of the Nag Hammadi library only becoming available in the last decade, not too many people have become familiar with their contents. But as more people are questioning traditional dogmas, Gnostic congregations continue to grow.

For information contact: ████████████████

The Gnostic Association
1316 Glendale Boulevard
Los Angeles, CA 90026
Phone: (213) 664-8241

See also: *Gnosis*, A Journal of the Western
Inner Traditions. Lists Gnostic
organizations.
Phone:(415) 255-0400 for subscriptions

Recommended Reading:

The Nag Hammadi Library in English
edited by James M. Robinson

The Gnostic Religion
by Hans Jonas

The Gnostic Gospels
by Elaine Pagels

Gnostics and Their Remains
by Charles William King

CHRISTIAN MYSTICISM

*C*HRISTIAN MYSTICISM is a rather broad category of belief that generally pertains to personal experiences with Jesus, or God. The literature of this field spans nearly 2,000 years, beginning with the advent of the Christ and continuing to evolve even to the present day. The themes generally involve the individual inner experiences of various saints written in the form of guides, poems, and autobiographies. Most of the literature comes from ascetic monks and nuns within the Church, who describe such things as the necessary discipline of the mind and body to receive mystical experiences, the nature of the experiences, and the effect that these mystical experiences have had on their lives. The following is only a brief summary of some of the better known Christian mystics (see also "Swedenborgianism").

Recommended Reading:

> *Light from Light: An Anthology of
> Christian Mysticism*
> by Louis Dupre & James A. Wiseman,
> eds.

and   *The Cloud of Unknowing and The Book
> of Privy Counseling* (anonymous)

SAINT AUGUSTINE

Aurelius Augustinus (354-430), a North African bishop of Hippo Regius in what is now Algeria, is one of the most influential theologians in Christian history. Augustine's writings established a precedent in acknowledging mystical experience as an important aspect of spiritual practice. His writings show a shift in emphasis from Faith (in God's promise), to Will (God's intention for a person), to perfect

Love (in loving God, God's love is reciprocated and salvation is assured). The emphasis changes from theological to experiential, and from faith to conscious awareness.

Recommended reading:

> *The Confessions of Saint Augustine*
> by Saint Augustine

THE DESERT FATHERS

During the last decades of the third century, several devout Christians, despairing of the worldliness of the Church, left to live in the desert as hermits. They lived ascetic lives, practicing austerities and forming monastic communities. Their practices led many to mystical experiences that have inspired many monks and nuns throughout the history of the Church.

Recommended reading:

> *Conferences*
> by John Cassian

and *Lives of the Desert Fathers*
> Norman Russell, Tr.

and *The Wisdom of the Desert*
> by Thomas Merton, Tr.

SAINT FRANCIS OF ASSISI

Saint Francis (1182-1226) is probably the most popular and best known of the Christian mystics. During a visit to Rome he had a vision of Christ, who told him to rebuild the Church. Francis was known for his renunciation of worldly life, and for his work among the lepers and the poor. His simplicity, charity and, love for nature have set an example for the Christian brotherhood. Francis is the founder of the order of the Friars Minor (OFM), which has since been divided into liberal, moderate, and conservative wings. The Franciscan orders are founded upon principles set forth by St. Francis.

Recommended reading:

> Francis and Clare: The Complete Works
> by St. Francis and St. Clare

and The Little Flowers of St. Francis
by St. Francis. Trans. by Raphael Brown

MEISTER ECKHART

Meister Eckhart (1260-1327) was a Dominican friar from Germany. He is one of the best known of the Christian mystics. His ideas were condemned by the Church. Eckhart emphasized that one must strip the mind of all active thoughts and images in order to obtain mystical experiences. Eckhart taught that through mystical experiences one would know the "Eternal Word of the Soul."

Recommended reading:

> *Meister Eckhart: The Essential
> Sermons, Commentaries, Treatises
> and Defense*
> by Meister Eckhart

HESYCHASM

Hesychasm formed in the Eastern Christian churches during the thirteenth and fourteenth centuries. The practice involves a discipline of special breathing exercises, physical postures, and the continuous repetition of the Jesus Prayer as a means of obtaining an inner quiet that leads to inner visions. It was given theological justification by Gregory Palamas (a fourteenth-century Byzantine saint), and was received as official doctrine of the Greek Orthodox church in 1351.

Recommended reading:

> *Saint Gregory Palamas and Orthodox Spirituality*
> by John Meyendorff

See also: *The Philokalia* (a collection of texts) by St. Nicodemos of the Holy Mountain & St. Makarios of Corinth (3 vols) (discusses how man may develop his inner powers and awaken from illusion and know God from personal experience)

SAINT JOHN OF THE CROSS

Saint John (1542-1591) was a mystic and reformer who was a member of the Carmelite order. His poems are recognized as among the finest in the Spanish language. Saint John is popularly known for his explanations of the "Dark night of the Soul," the struggles one must go through in purifying oneself and receiving God's grace.

Recommended reading:

> *The Collected Works of Saint John of the Cross*, by St. John of the Cross.

SAINT TERESA OF AVILA

Saint Teresa (1515-1582) was a mystic and reformer within the Carmelite order, and was a contemporary of St. John of the Cross. After eighteen years of troubled spiritual life, she underwent a spiritual transformation and began to have visions and mystical experiences. Her works are considered some of the most powerful in Christian mysticism.

Recommended reading:

> *The Collected Works of Saint Teresa of Avila*, by St. Teresa of Avila

and   *The Way of Perfection*
             St. Teresa of Avila

JAKOB BOEHME

Jakob Boehme (1575-1624) was a German lay theologian and mystic who describes visions he had in the book *Aurora*. Through his own symbolic language, he describes a step-by-step method of attaining union with Christ. Though denounced by the Lutheran clergy, he has been an inspiration to many Christians seeking mystical experiences. Jakob Boehme's writings were influential in the Theosophy Movement started by Helena Petrovna Blavatsky and Henry Alcott in 1875 (see also "Theosophy").

Recommended reading:

The Way of Christ
by Jakob Boehme

THOMAS MERTON

Thomas Merton (1915-1968) is perhaps the best known of the modern-day mystics and the most influential theologian among monastics in recent history. Merton's work emphasizes discipline, meditation, and contemplation, and acknowledges spiritual experiences as a test of spiritual development.

Recommended reading:

Spiritual Direction and Meditation and What Is Contemplation?
by Thomas Merton

SWEDENBORGIANISM

SWEDENBORGIANISM, OR the Church of New Jerusalem, is based upon the teachings of Emanuel Swedenborg. Swedenborg was born in Stockholm, Sweden, in 1688. He was a distinguished scientist in the fields of cosmology, mathematics, geology, and anatomy before turning seriously to theology. Swedenborg was uniquely gifted as a scientist, as he was able to communicate with the "other world." He was granted daily visions of heaven and hell, and had frequent conversations with spirits. Through these experiences Swedenborg learned that a new church was to be born, and that his writings were to be part of its teachings.

Swedenborg himself never preached or founded a church, but by about ten years after he died in 1772 his followers had formed a group to disseminate the teachings of this man, whom they considered to be a divinely illuminated seer and revelator. An organized church was established in London in 1789, when a follower named Robert Hindmarsh gathered friends to discuss Swedenborg's teachings. The first Swedenborgian society in America formed in Baltimore in 1792. The Church of New Jerusalem developed from these societies, and today remains a relatively small congregation of several thousand followers, mostly in northeastern Europe and on the East Coast of the United States.

Swedenborg held that "God is Man," and that the origin of all that is truly human is in one God. Christ, as God incarnate, glorified his humanity, and thereby established a new unity between the spiritual and natural dimensions of reality; a unity each person can now participate in. Church doctrine includes: (1) That there is One God, in whom there is a Divine Trinity; and that He is the Lord Jesus Christ. (2) That saving faith is to believe in Him. (3) That every man is born to evils of every kind, and unless through repentance he removes them in part, he remains in them, and he who remains in them cannot be saved. (4) That good actions are to be done, because they are of God and from God. (5) That these are to be done by a man as from himself; but that it ought to be believed that they are done from the Lord with Him and by Him. (from "The Christian Religion," por. #3)

For information contact: █████████████████

The Swedenborgian Church
112 E. 35th Street
New York, NY 10016
Phone:(212) 685-8967

or   The Wayfarers Chapel
5755 Palos Verdes Road South
Rancho Palos Verdes, CA 90274
Phone:(213) 377-1650

Recommended Reading:

Arcana Coelestia
by Emanuel Swedenborg

SUFISM
(TASAWOF OR TASAWWUF; DARVISH)

SUFISM IS the English name given to the religion known as Tasawof in Arabic. The term *Sufism* is derived from the word *sufi*, which, in both Arabic and English, refers to one who follows the Tasawof religion. The word *sufi* may be derived from the Arabic word safa, meaning "honesty" and "purity"; from the Arabic word *suf*, meaning "wool" (referring to the traditional dress of the Sufi); or from the Arabic word *suffe* meaning "platform," referring to the platform on which the prophet Muhammad used to worship and instruct. The East Indian followers of this religion are known as dervishes.

Sufism is generally considered to be the mystical teachings of the religion of Islam. The origins of the Sufi movement are obscure. The root of the religion comes from the teachings of the prophet Muhammad, the founder of Islam, who was born in Mecca, Arabia, about 572 A.D. Muhammad taught his disciples the way to true knowledge of *Allah* (God), and out of these teachings evolved the religion that later became known as Tasawof, or Sufism. As these disciples went off and gathered more disciples, centers of Sufism were formed in different parts of the land, including Baghdad, Khurasan, Shiraz, Kurdestan, and Karaj. Sufism has spread throughout the Arab world and Persia, and as far as India, Indonesia, West Africa, and quite recently to the United States.

The practice of Sufism is explained in the very derivation of the Arabic word for the religion—*Tasawof*. As one of Muhammad's disciples, Imam Ali, explains, the word *Tasawof* is a combination of four words embodying three concepts each. These are as follows: (1) *Ta*, representing tark, to shun everything other than God; *toubeth*, "repentance"; and *tougha*, "purification." (2) *sa*, signifying safa, "purity and honesty"; *sabr*, "patience"; and *sedgh*, "truthfulness." (3) *wo*, delineating *wafa*, "faith"; *werd*, remembrance of God; and *woud*, "love." And (4) *fe*, embodying *faghr*, "poverty"; *fana*," "to become one with God"; and *fard*, "individuality." Thus the aim of the Sufi is to renounce all physical desires and attachments, purify the heart so only thoughts of God remain, develop and maintain complete faith and love for God, and finally give up the self completely in order to pass away or become one with God.

In Sufism, the aspirant, or *salek*, places complete trust in his Sufi Master, a "Murshed" (or "Ghotb," "Agha," "Pir"). Upon being accepted as a salek, the Murshed instructs the salek in the proper use of a spiritual word (similar to a mantra) which is known as a *zekr*. In addition to personal zekrs, there are special ceremonies which take place in the "Khanegheh" (place of worship) called the "circle of zekr," where worshipers sit in a circle on the floor with their knees touching and chant in unison another zekr. These spiritual exercises assist the salek to be purified of all worldly desires, so that he may come to know God. The aim of the salek is to pass through some forty stages of spiritual development, which starts with "willingness" and ends with "gnosis," or the achievement of true self-knowledge and knowledge of God.

Sufis can be of different sects, such as Sunni or Shi'ite, and maintain different beliefs and practices, depending on the school the Sufi had studied in. All Sufism is based on Islam, and therefore the primary scriptural source is the Qur'an (or Koran). Other great Sufi works include *Kashf Al-Mahjub*, by Ali Hujwiri, perhaps the oldest Persian treatise on Sufism, written sometime late in the tenth century. Another Sufi theologian and poet, Mawlana (Jalal ad-Din ar-Rumi), inspired the Sufi order Tariaa, popularly known as Whirling Dervishes (referring to a spiritual dance that puts the salek into an ecstatic state), and wrote such Sufi collections as "Ma`navi" and "Divan-e Shams-i Tabrizi." Other great works include "Ghoshairi's Treatise" by Abol Ghasem Ghoshairi, and *Ihya'`ulum ad-din*, by Abu Hamid al-Ghazali. Many great Sufi Masters have in turn established their own interpretations of Sufi theory, and Sufism as it has been introduced in the West has adopted its own style and form.

For a listing of Sufi organizations contact:

The Sound
248 Laurel Place
San Rafael, CA 94901
($10.00 subscription as of 1990)
Phone:(707) 538-1358

or   Aegis
RD 1 - Box 1030D
New Lebanon, NY 12125
Phone:(518) 794-8095

Also see: *The Sufi Order of the West*
(in the section "Masters and
Movements")

Recommended Reading:

Sufism
by Dr. Ronald Grisell

The Sufis
by Idries Shah

FREEMASONRY

*T*HE SOCIETY of Free & Accepted Masons is a worldwide men's fraternal club that meets primarily for social purposes and stresses the importance of civic, patriotic, and charitable activities among its members. Masons, as they are commonly called, differ from most fraternal bodies in that (1) a belief in God is a necessary qualification for admission, and (2) great emphasis is placed upon members maintaining the highest moral standards and constantly endeavoring to improve themselves spiritually. The Society of Free and Accepted Masons was founded in the seventeenth century in England. The founders were "gentlemen," *not* laborers such as stone cutters or carvers as is commonly believed. These men formed clubs called Lodges, not only for social purposes, but to discuss and advance their knowledge in the liberal arts and in science (which was in its infancy at that time).

The union of the local lodges was made in 1717, when four London lodges formed the first "Grand Lodge." Grand Lodges were subsequently formed in Scotland and Ireland, and Freemasonry quickly spread from the British Isles throughout the world. Freemasonry is now the largest fraternity in the world, with over 4 million members, 3 million in the United States. The Eastern Star, composed of female relatives of Masons, is the world's largest women's fraternity. Many prominent figures in history were Masons, including George Washington, John Hancock, Benjamin Franklin, John Paul Jones, Charles Lindbergh, Henry Ford, Rudyard Kipling, David Crockett, and Norman Vincent Peale. Many English kings and thirteen U.S. Presidents have been Masons, including, recently: Truman, and Ford.

The seventeenth century founders of Freemasonry, having formed their lodges in imitation of actual operative lodges of masons, decided that they would illustrate the teachings of Freemasonry by the use of the working tools of the operative mason. An example: "The Plumb is an instrument made use of by operative Masons to try perpendicular; the Square, to square their work; and the Level, to provide horizontals; but we, as Free and Accepted Masons, are taught to make use of them for more noble and glorious purposes. The Plumb admonishes us to walk uprightly in our several stations before God and man, squaring our actions by the Square of virtue, and ever remembering that we are traveling upon the Level of time to 'that undiscovered country from whose bourn no traveler returns.' "

Masons advance in what are called "degrees" within the fraternity. In the first degree a candidate learns the first principle tenet of Freemasonry, which is Brotherly Love. A candidate for membership is asked to memorize the following: "By the exercise of Brotherly Love we are taught to regard the whole human species as one family, the high and the low, the rich and the poor, who, as created by one Almighty Parent, and inhabitants of the same planet, are to aid, support and protect each other. On this principle Masonry unites men of every country, sect, and opinion; and causes true friendship to exist among those who might otherwise have remained at a perpetual distance."   In the United States, meetings are opened by repeating the Pledge of Allegiance to the Flag (which was written by a Mason), and reciting a nondenominational prayer. Much of the activities conducted by Masons focuses on charitable causes, such as support of youth organizations, public schools, and hospitals.

For more information:

The Most Worshipful Grand Lodge
of Free and Accepted Masons of
California
1111 California Street
San Francisco, CA 94108

Recommended Reading:

> *The Craft and Its Symbols*
> by Allen E. Roberts
>
> *Freemason's Guide and Compendium*
> by Bernard E. Jones

Note: There are numerous books written about Freemasonry that suggest an association with the masons who build the cathedrals of Europe, and even the pyramids of Egypt, and imply that the teachings are occult. While ancient masons may have had occult or esoteric knowledge, the organization of Freemasonry is not associated with those masons or their occult knowledge.

THE ANCIENT MYSTICAL ORDER ROSAE CRUCIS (A.M.O.R.C.)

*T*HE ANCIENT and Mystical Order Rosae Crucis, or AMORC, is a fraternity of men and women who strive to attain knowledge of the higher truths through the study of preserved ancient teachings. The A.M.O.R.C. traditionally traces its lineage to the mystery schools of ancient Egypt. These mystery schools are said to have begun evolving as early as 5000 B.C.; however, the first pharaoh to conduct private classes on the arcane arts and sciences was Ahmose I (1580-1557 B.C.). Thutmose III (1500-1447 B.C.) is accredited with the organization of the first secret brotherhood for the preservation and dissemination of these teachings. This brotherhood has come to be called the **Illuminati**. It was Amenhotep IV (later called Akhnaten, 1378-1350 B.C.) who introduced the rose and the cross as the symbol of that brotherhood. And, it was Akhnaten who is traditionally credited with the construction of a cross-shaped temple at Egypt's al-'Amarna.

During the centuries that followed, this brotherhood (sometimes called the **Great White Brotherhood**) achieved a reputation as a center of knowledge for these arcane teachings of higher truth. Seekers came from throughout the world to become initiates of the brotherhood, study its teachings, and disseminate its wisdom.

Many great teachers are said to have been members of this early Rosicrucian brotherhood: Hermes Trismegistus (1399-1257 B.C.); Solomon (who came to the temple at al-'Amarna around 1000 B.C.); Pythagoras (who entered the Illuminati in 529 B.C.); as well as the Greek philosophers Democritus, Socrates, Plato, and Aristotle. The biblical Moses is said to have been a High Priest of this brotherhood. As these Rosicrucian workers carried their knowledge into other lands, they became known as the **Essenes** in Palestine, and as the **Therapeuti** in Greece. It is said that Jesus the Christ was a Master, and that his disciples were high officers of this Great White Brotherhood.

It was during the pre-Christian era that the Rosicrucian Order entered a period of active (visible) and inactive (invisible) cycles of 108 years. Some of the periods of important revival include the reign of Charlemagne (around A.D. 778), early seventeenth-century Germany (where the invention of the printing press rapidly accelerated the dissemination of Rosicrucian teachings), and, most recently, the 1915 establishment of the A.M.O.R.C. in the United States of America. Currently, the Rosicrucian Order, AMORC, is represented by thousands of members throughout the world, and has its headquarters in San Jose, California.

As the Rosicrucian Order is not a religion, it does not exclude the adherents to any religious belief from its brotherhood. The Order guides the student/seeker into a greater understanding of his or her own being and the recognition of the purpose of earthly existence. Through personal experiences, the student learns of the invisible cosmic influences that can be utilized to shape life through the attainment of higher levels of consciousness. The lessons, or monographs, are received by mail and studied in the privacy of the home. Simple experiments are also provided to allow the student to demonstrate the principles studied.

For more information:

The Department of Member
Services
The Rosicrucian Order, AMORC
Rosicrucian Park
San Jose, CA 95191

Recommended Reading:

*Rosicrucian Questions and Answers
With a Complete History*
by H. Spencer Lewis, Ph.D., F.R.C.

ROSICRUCIAN FELLOWSHIP

*T*HE ROSICRUCIAN Fellowship is an international association of Christian mystics. In the thirteenth century a high spiritual teacher with the symbolic name Christian Rosenkrenz (the Christian charged to explain the mysteries of the Cross) appeared in Europe. As a symbol of this mystery the Rose was added to the cross. Rosenkrenz founded the mysterious Order of Rosicrucians with the object of throwing occult light upon the misunderstood Christian religion and explaining the mystery of Life and Being from the scientific standpoint in harmony with religion. The messenger of the Rosicrucian Order and the founder of the Rosicrucian Fellowship is Max Heindel. Mr. Heindel was born in Denmark on July 23, 1865, and later emigrated to the United States. For several years Mr. Heindel studied metaphysics, searching for spiritual knowledge.

In 1907, one of the Elder Brothers of the Rosicrucian Order made contact with Mr. Heindel on the physical plane; then, in the etheric Temple of the Rose Cross, the Elder Brothers imparted to him the greater part of the teachings contained in the Rosicrucian Cosmo-Conception, which was published in 1909 and is the main text of the Rosicrucian teachings today. The Rosicrucian Fellowship was founded by Max Heindel in 1909, and has grown into an international body, disseminating the Western Wisdom Teachings around the world and preparing the Western people for the New Age of Aquarius.

The Rosicrucian philosophy is Christian, as taught through the medium of occult or esoteric knowledge. The teachings provide accounts of the nature of the visible world and of the invisible worlds, the evolution of man, the nature of soul and of the spirit. The divine essence of the spirit, the past, present and future evolution of man, and the applications of the laws of Nature — Law of Consequence, Law of Rebirth, for example — are the focus of the Western Wisdom Teaching, which is supported by reason and logic, and also by the personal experiences of the aspirant.

The purpose of presenting the Rosicrucian philosophy is to: (1) explain the hidden sides of life—by knowing what forces are at work within himself, man can make the best of his present faculties, (2) teach the purpose of evolution — this enables man to work in harmony with the Plan of God and develop still unrecognized possibilities; (3) show why service to others is the most direct path to spiritual unfoldment. The aim of the Rosicrucian Fellowship is to spread the Western Wisdom Teachings through correspondence courses of philosophy, Bible studies, and astrology, thus enabling people to understand and to accept the Christian religion through the medium of occult or esoteric knowledge. The Rosicrucian Fellowship is also involved in spiritual healing and spiritual astrology. Daily services are also performed, and a Sunday service is held at the Rosicrucian Fellowship headquarters in Oceanside, California.

For additional information contact:

The Rosicrucian Fellowship
P.O. Box 713
2222 Mission Avenue
Oceanside, CA 92054
Phone:(619) 757-6600

Recommended Reading:

The Rosicrucian Cosmo-Conception
by Max Heindel

The Rosicrucian Mysteries
by Max Heindel

The Rosicrucian Philosophy in Questions and Answers, Volumes I and II
by Max Heindel

BUILDERS OF THE ADYTUM
(B.O.T.A.)

*B*UILDERS OF the Adytum (abbreviated B.O.T.A.) is a Western mystery school whose teachings are based on the Holy Kabbalah and the Sacred Tarot. The Holy Kabbalah is the Mystery Wisdom Teachings of ancient Israel. The great prophets of the Bible (including Jesus of Nazareth) were versed in the Kabbalah and received their spiritual training therefrom. The Kabbalah is based on a diagrammatical and symbolic glyph called the Tree of Life. It is a pictorial-symbolic representation of the One God and man's relationship to God and creation. The Tarot is a pictorial textbook on Ageless Wisdom. B.O.T.A. was founded in 1922 by Dr. Paul Foster Case for the study of practical occultism. As a recognized world authority on the Tarot and Kabbalah, Dr. Case was given the task by the Inner School of reinterpreting the Ageless Wisdom into terms understandable to the modern Western mind.

The primary purpose of B.O.T.A. is to teach and practice the doctrine of the Oneness of God, the brotherhood of man, and the kinship of all life patterned after the Ageless Wisdom mystery schools of spiritual training, as particularly exemplified by the Kabbalah. The major objective of B.O.T.A. is to promote the welfare of humanity, which is embodied in their seven-point program: (1) universal peace, (2) universal political freedom, (3) universal religious freedom, (4) universal education, (5) universal health, (6) universal prosperity, (7) universal spiritual unfoldment.

Dedicated work with the Tarot techniques, as embodied in the B.O.T.A. curriculum, transmutes personality. A transformed personality will bring the ability to change the environment to bring it closer to the heart's desire. A fulfilled life becomes a positive radiating center, an effective channel through which the Higher Self can function, and serves as a living example for others. B.O.T.A. offers courses in the Kabbalah and the Sacred Tarot, correspondence courses are also available.

For more information:

Builders of the Adytum, Ltd.
5105 N. Figueroa Street
Los Angeles, CA 90042
Phone: (213) 255-7141

Recommended Reading:

The Tarot: A Key to Wisdom of the Ages
by Dr. Paul Foster Case

The Book of Tokens
by Dr. Paul Foster Case

SHAMANISM
(NATIVE AMERICAN SPIRITUAL
TRADITIONS)

SHAMANISM IS the practice of attuning to, and working with, the spiritual realms; both in the heavens and on earth. The word *shaman* is derived through Russian from the Siberian Tungusic word *saman*. Technically, shamans are indigenous to Siberia and Central Asia, but shamanism as it is known in the West refers to the practices of the "men of knowledge" or "medicine men" within the Native American tribal religions. Shamanistic elements are found around the world, dating back to Paleolithic times. Native American ancestors came to North America from Siberia by way of a land bridge across the Bering Strait during the last glacial period, about eleven thousand years ago.

As different groups spread out across the continent, different cultures and religions developed among the tribes, but a close relationship between man, God, and all creation was maintained. As the European races, primarily the Spanish, French, and English, conquered North America, they destroyed the Native American civilization and imposed their religions (Catholicism and Protestantism) upon the native people. However, shamanistic practices were maintained by enough people to carry the traditions and knowledge into the present. In the last twenty years more westerners have seen the value of the shaman's relationship with the creator and the earth, and have been drawn to study the ancient teachings of these adepts. Today Shamanism is widely practiced, primarily in rural or undeveloped areas, around the world, and is becoming increasingly popular with westerners in North America and Europe.

Beliefs among shamans vary, but a common relationship is often seen, with God represented as the Great Mystery that moves in all things, and the earth representing creation (a living being). All living things (including animals and plants) are the brothers of mankind. The earth does not belong to man, but man belongs to the earth. Shamans respect and revere the earth and all creation. They observe the spirits that lie within all living things, and learn to commune with these spirits through their daily activities and through special rites. Shamans work with spirits, and spirits will in turn work with the shaman; thus the shaman has a special relationship with the world of spirits. Often the shaman will enter into ecstatic states of consciousness in order to make contact with the spirit world, and may even visit with spirits in their heavenly abode. The shaman has developed the ability to participate directly in the spiritual dimensions of reality, and may have other abilities as a healer, diviner, or clairvoyant. Shamans may also play the role of psychopomp, escorting the deceased soul to the domain of the dead.

Shamanistic practices vary, depending on which cultural group the shaman is from. Generally hunting and gathering tribes pay tribute to the spirits of the animals they need to hunt, while the agricultural tribes pay tribute to the elements that foster a good harvest (the sun, the rain, the corn, etc.). Special rites may also be performed when a child reaches puberty, or adulthood. Sometimes the seasons are observed, and special occasions, such as marriages, births, and deaths. Sometimes the shaman will use the mind-altering properties of hallucinogenic plants such as wild tobacco, peyote, and mushrooms in order to enter ecstatic states and to commune with spirits.

On special occasions a "medicine wheel" may be constructed in order to create the power to connect human beings to the infinite. At a medicine wheel gathering, special stones are placed in various configurations within a circle, and special ceremonies are performed. Sometimes dances or plays are acted out to reflect spiritual principles, or a "peace pipe" will be passed around to foster solidarity. Other observances may include ritual chants or singing. Another common Native American practice is purification in a "sweat lodge." This practice begins when "stone people" (spirits of the mineral kingdom located within stones) are scouted out at special times, and than heated up in a ceremonial fire. At the appropriate time, the participants are smudged (covered with smoke from a sacrificial fire), pay respects to their relatives and guiding spirits, and then enter the sweat lodge, which is basically a dome covered with skins or blankets. Once the participants are seated, the heated stone people are brought in and placed in a pit in the middle of the lodge, and the openings are closed to keep the heat in. While the heat increases, the participants take turns letting go of those feelings that have been troubling them, as they sweat from the heat of the stone people. In the sweat lodge, one prays to the spirits and asks for guidance, to purge oneself of negative feelings, and to prepare for changes in one's life. One of the strongest disciplines the shaman performs is to go on a "vision quest." During a vision quest, the participant goes off into the wilderness by himself or herself for several days; typically without eating. During this time the trekker severs his or her worldly attachments, and calls upon God to show a sign for direction and guidance, which takes the form of a vision.

For more information...

... on Native American traditions and/or Shamanism, look up a tribal group or representative in your area. The Bureau of Indian Affairs (listed under Federal Government) may be able to direct you. You may also look under the Native American Church for additional information. The Bear Tribe and the Deer Tribe both offer programs that are available to the public, they can be contacted through the following:

> The Bear Tribe
> P.O. Box 9167
> Spokane, WA 99209
> Phone:(509) 326-6561

> *or*   The Deer Tribe
> P.O. Box 1519
> Temple City, CA 91780
> Phone:(818) 285-9062

Recommended Reading:

> *The Sacred Ways of a Lakota*
> by Wallace Black Elk
>
> *Black Elk Speaks*
> by John G. Neihardt
>
> *The Path of Power*
> by Sun Bear, Wabun, and Barry
> Weinstock
> (or other books from the Bear Tribe)

Other popular books with Shamanistic themes:

> *Medicine Woman*
> by Lynn Andrews
>
> *Return of the Bird Tribes*
> by Ken Carey

*H*UNA

*H*UNA IS a Hawaiian spiritual tradition, which is part of a Polynesian heritage that dates back three to five thousand years (or more). Huna is not a religion, but rather an esoteric philosophy and science that has been passed on through Hawaiian family lineages. The word *huna* means "that which is hidden, or not obvious," and a Kahuna is a Hawaiian shaman, or the "transmitter of the secrets." The Huna teachings were an integral part of Hawaiian culture until the first Christian missionaries came to Hawaii in 1820. These missionaries rapidly began altering the culture and customs of the Hawaiian people and outlawed the practice of Huna in Hawaii. Due to this alienation from their culture and purging by the Christians, the Kahunas became reclusive and did not reveal themselves to any *haoles*, or white people, and the teachings remained a mystery to the West. However, these days Huna can be practiced more openly, and several Kahunas have opened up to share their philosophy with others, and the practice is now gaining in popularity, particularly on the West Coast and in Hawaii.

Huna is not a philosophy that can be accurately understood by reading about it. It is an interactive system between an individual and everything else. In Huna, everything is interrelated. In the Huna teachings God is everything, and everything is of God. Moreover, all things have a higher spiritual nature called *aumakua* or *akuas*, and the personal god or god-self is not limited to mankind but is innate in all creation. The spiritual and material worlds are creations resulting from the interplay between male and female aspects of God. Kane is the principal male god, expressing the masculine (expansive) forces of nature, and Wahine is the primary female god, expressing the feminine (contractive) forces of existence. This dual nature of god-self lies within all creation, and it is the interaction of these energies that creates our existence.

The teachings of the Kahunas have historically been passed on by word of mouth, and the only historical writing of Huna is found in the ancient "creation chant" called the "Kumulipo." The practice of Huna involves looking within all that you perceive; there is a being within a being, and a universe within a universe, and the center of the universe lies within you. This awareness develops as you observe the natural rhythms that are working within you and around you, and which are interconnected to you. Huna is the practice of attuning to the energies around you, and working in concert with those energies. One of the principal energies utilized by the Kahunas is that of "Aloha," or complete unconditional love. The practice of Huna involves expressing the Aloha Spirit in yourself as well as bringing it out in others and in all things.

Kahunas have a reputation for being very psychic. They practice telepathy and mind reading, are clairvoyant, and have the ability to leave the physical body and return at will. Several Kahunas are even said to be able to raise the dead. However, Kahunas typically do not give public demonstrations of their abilities, and concentrate on helping others learn about the nature of themselves, and to live in harmony with their surroundings. Some Kahunas focus on certain areas, such as intuitive navigation or healing, and they are often consulted in Hawaii before launching a ship for the first time, building a house or holy site, or before making a major decision in one's personal life.

For more information on Huna
contact any of the following:

Kahiliopua & Herb Brentlinger
Hawaiian Church of Life
P.O. Box 4878
Hilo, HI 96720
Phone:(808) 959-5877

or   Abraham Kawai'i
c/o Erin
P.O. Box 159001-217
San Diego, CA 92115
Phone:(619) 563-4686

or   Serge King
                Aloha International
                P.O. Box 665
                Kilauea, HI 96754
    Phone:(808) 826-9097

or   c/o Wayne Powell
                Kanaloa Enterprises
                P.O. Box 4509
                Chatsworth, CA 91313
    Phone:(818) 704-0540

Recommended Reading:

Kahuna Healing
by Serge King

Kahuna Magic
by Brad Steiger
(a consolidation of the teachings of
Max Freedom Long's pioneering
work)

Note: Keep in mind that Kahuna teachings have not traditionally been imparted through the written word, and these resources are for information purposes only.

VOODOO

*A*S A RESULT of the slave trade that flourished during the eighteenth and early nineteenth centuries, indigenous tribal religions of the black Africans from, primarily, the western coast of Africa, were introduced to the New World and merged into Western Christian culture as the black slaves integrated into the societies of the Americas. Of the some 15 million slaves who were seized from West Africa, approximately half were taken to South America, forty-two percent were brought to the Caribbean Islands, and the others were sold in North America. As the slaves integrated into the Christian, and primarily Catholic, cultures in Central and South America, tribal ritual and spiritual practices were commingled with Catholicism and modified to suit the new culture.

The most prominent of these religions is Voodoo, or Voudoun, which comes from Haiti, in the West Indies, but which has spread throughout the Caribbean and parts of North America. Other similar religious practices are known as Macoumaba (Macumba) in Brazil and Santeria (or Lucumi) in Cuba. The other Neo-African religions are smaller and tend to remain within their respective communities. Typically these religions are practiced discreetly, due to religious prejudices and racism; however, during the early part of the twentieth century there was a proliferation of various "voodoo" sects, and today the religion is practiced a little more freely (although not entirely).

Voodoo, and the other Neo-African religions, is based on a premise that the material body houses an esprit—a soul or spirit—which is eternal. Moreover, the soul is able to achieve divinity, and can become the "archetypal representative" of some natural or moral principal. The term *Voodoo,* (*Voudoun,* or *Vo-du*) essentially means "introspection into the unknown," and the religion is based upon experiences in the spirit realms. There is a whole pantheon of loa, or gods, that represent different aspects of existence. These loa are known by different names in different tribes, but generally have the same attributes. Voodoo originated in the mystical city of Ife, a replica of which exists in Yoruba in southern Nigeria, from which the revelation or spirit descends through the form of double serpents Danbhalah Wedo and Aida Wedo, representing the male and female aspects of divinity, which are also represented by Legba (male/Sun) and Erzulie (female/lunar).

Voodoo ritual is practiced by the *houn'gan* and *mam'bo*, male and female priests, who can summon the loa, or mysteres, into a special pottery jar called a "govi" or may be incarnated into the physical world by "mounting" or taking possession of another's body. The various loa perform different functions in ritual, such as providing protection, conferring various powers, curing illnesses, and punishing the guilty. Rituals are typically performed in the "Peristyle" or courtyard, or the "Oum'phor" or temple; in the center of the Peristyle lies the "Poteau-mitan," which is a center post that the ceremonies revolve around, the top of which represents the sky or heavens and the bottom the center of hell. Rituals typically involve the use of music—the beating of Rada, Pethro, or Conga drums, chanting and singing, dancing, prayers, possession by loa or mysteres, sacrifices of cattle or other animals, and feasts. Other spiritual services performed by the houn'gan or mam'bo include divination, healing, and exorcisms. Ritual floor paintings, or Veve's, and objects such as ceremonial dishes, pitchers, bottles, flags, and the Asson (calabash rattle, which is a symbol of office), are unique features of Neo-African religions.

For more information:

La Couleuvre Noire
c/o Technicians of the Sacred
1317 No. San Fernando Blvd.,
Suite 310
Burbank, Ca 91504

Recommended Reading:

Secrets of Voodoo
by Milo Rigaud

*Divine Horsemen, the Living Gods
of Haiti*
by Maya Deren

The Voudon Gnostic Workbook
by Michael Bertiaux

RASTAFARIANISM

*R*ASTAFARIANS ARE part of a messianic movement originating in Jamaica. They worship the god "Jah," and believe that Haile Selassie, the emperor of Ethiopia, is the Messiah of the black race. "Ras Tafari," the great-grandson of King Saheka Selassie of Shoa, was crowned Negus of Ethiopia and took on the name of Haile Selassie (Might of the Trinity). Jah is an abbreviation of Jehovah, who is the God of the black races from Egypt and Ethiopia. The Rastafarian movement has its origins with the slave trade and the repression of the black people in Jamaica by the white ruling class. Years of socio-economic struggle and a lack of religious identity of the black majority fostered the rebellious "Back-to-Africa Movement," which was started by a black Jamaican named Marcus Garvey in the early 1900's. This movement spurred sentiments of black supremacy, and called for the abolition of white dominance. This ideology gained a spiritual connotation and fervor with the crowning of Haile Selassie as emperor of Ethiopia in 1930, as it was seen as a revelation of God and fulfillment of the biblical prophecy in Psalm 68: "Princes shall come out of Egypt; and Ethiopia shall soon stretch out her hands unto God."

The redemption of Africa by the Messiah of Africa, Haile Selassie (Ras Tafari), spurred several members of the Back-to-Africa Movement to reconsolidate the members under the name of Rastafarians (Ras-Tafari-ans). Four members in particular: Leonard Howell, Joseph Hibbert, Archibald Dunkley, and Robert Hinds, played the major role in getting the movement going. As heads of rebellious and militant movements, the leaders were at odds with the presiding authorities. By 1953 "Rastas" had begun wearing their hair in long curling locks, now known as "dreadlocks," as a form of group identity, and had formed a commune called "Pinnacle" in the hills twenty miles from Kingston. However, as the Rastafarians had been growing ganga (marijuana, an illegal substance in Jamaica) at Pinnacle for ritual purposes, the police raided and destroyed the commune and arrested many of its members, which put a damper on the movement. Eventually the movement grew less militant, and the followers have become a peaceful, loosely structured, multiracial body, who find fellowship through the music and a cultural identity known as Reggae. This music, with its Rasta themes, has spread throughout both the black and Western nations of the world; and Reggae music has become popular with millions of people of every race.

Rastafarians generally believe that Jamaica is Babylon, or Hell, and that Africa, and Ethiopia in particular, is the Promised Land. Moreover, Haile Selassie is the Messiah, who will deliver the black race from the oppression of the white race in Jamaica to live in Ethiopia (or Africa). The Ethiopians, or black race, are the Israelites, who will one day rule over the world as Jah's chosen people. Jah, or Jehovah, is the one supreme God, who is considered black according to several biblical translations, namely, Jeremiah 8:21, "For the hurt of the daughter of my people am I hurt; *I am black*; astonishment hath taken hold of me"; and Daniel 7:9, describing God with "Hair of his head like pure wool; his throne was like the fiery flame, and his wheels as burning fire" (fire being associated with the black race). Rastafarians generally consider the Bible holy, but believe other faiths have interpreted the Scriptures incorrectly. The vision of the Rastafarians is to create a universal brotherhood and world peace.

Most Rastafarians are vegetarians, and don't believe in killing for any reason. They are identified by wearing the colors red, black, and green, and often wear their hair in natural curls called dreadlocks. The symbol of the Rastas is the lion. Rituals involve prayers, the smoking of ganga, reciting poems and most often playing or singing Reggae music. The controversial use of the ganga plant, which is smoked for religious experiences, is supported by the following biblical passages: Genesis 1:12, "And the earth brought forth grass, and herb yielding seed after his kind, and the tree yielding fruit, whose seed was in itself, after his kind: and God saw that it was good"; and Psalm 104:14, "He causeth the grass to grow for the cattle, and herb for the service of man ..." However, the greatest common denominator of the Rastafarians is in the Reggae music, which expresses their feelings and beliefs. Most notable of the Reggae musicians are Bob Marley, Peter Tosh, Steel Pulse, and the Third World.

For more information contact: █████████████████

The best way to learn more about the Rastafarian movement is to listen to their music and then go to where a Rasta group is playing near you.

Recommended Reading:

The Rastafarians
by Leonard Barrett

Itations of Jamaica and I Rastafari
by Judah Anbesa

Recommended Listening:

Bob Marley
Peter Tosh
Steel Pulse
Third World

SACRED SUBSTANCES

*M*IND-ALTERING substances are those which can temporarily shift the consciousness from a limited reality based on physical perceptions to an expanded view of reality. Evidence of the use of sacred mind-altering substances is noted throughout recorded history. The oldest scripture from the Indian subcontinent, the *Rig Veda* (composed beginning around 1400 B.C.), begins with a hymn (*sukta*) of a ritual in which a holy libation called *soma* is taken to attain superior intelligence or awareness of God (Indra). This *soma* is believed to be made from a leafless vine that grows in the Himalayas and is only picked at astrologically auspicious times, and is picked only with permission of the plant.

Archaeological evidence exists in Central and South America, in Africa, and in parts of Asia and Europe that indicates that various kinds of mushrooms, identified as being hallucinogenic, were either worshiped or considered sacred in rituals. Shamans all over the world are known to utilize plants with mind-altering properties for spiritual development, and such plants are still an integral part of many religious rituals and spiritual practices. In the last few decades, westerners looking for mind-altering experiences have begun experimenting with hallucinogenic substances, all too often without the proper guidance, or purpose, in their use. In modern Western society, the use of mind-altering substances is frowned upon, and in many cases, use of them violates the law.

Some of the most widely used mind-altering substances are found in mushrooms, such as the psilocybin in the red-and-white speckled variety known as Amanita Muscaria (fly-agaric mushroom). Thousands of species of mushrooms with hallucinogenic properties are found and used all over the world. Two other common sacred substances, found primarily in the deserts of North America, are the peyote cactus, which contains the active substance mescaline; and the jimsonweed, a species of Datura plant. The Native

Americans smoked the wild tobacco plant in their peace pipes on auspicious occasions. Smoking this wild variety of tobacco, in conjunction with ritual chanting and the invocation of spirits, provides the smoker a means of communing with the spirit world. The marijuana plant (a member of the genus Cannabis) is commonly used throughout the world. Shivites in India, particularly Tantrics, smoke the leaves of the marijuana or ganji, or a concentrated form of marijuana called hashish, in a pipe called a chillum during ritual practice and worship. Sometimes Tantrics make an intoxicating drink called bhang by mixing marijuana with milk, and drink it before performing sacred sexual acts used to transcend the mind and body. Marijuana is also used for ritual purposes by shamans throughout North, Central, and South America, Asia, and the Middle East.

Opium is a drug that comes from the dried juice of certain species of poppies, and it has been used for ritual purposes throughout Asia for centuries. Both morphine and heroin are made from opium, but I am not familiar with these refined substances being used in any spiritual rituals. Native South American people used to chew coca leaves in their spiritual rituals, or to provide stamina in tasks that require additional strength. Cocaine is made from coca leaves, but I am not familiar with any spiritual groups that make use of this refined drug in their rituals or spiritual practices. The most commonly used mind-altering substance in the world is alcohol. Alcohol has also been used in various spiritual rituals, including those of Christianity, in which wine is imbibed in the Holy Eucharist to commune with the Lord Jesus in a Holy Sacrament. Almost all societies, except Islam, utilize alcohol in one form or another. Alcohol is made from distilled or fermented fruits, grains, and starches, and is consumed in various forms as beverages. Although alcohol is legal in most countries, and not generally considered a drug, it also alters one's perception, and when used with frequency causes deleterious effects on the mind and body, just as any other drug.

Sacred substances are generally taken during some form of ritual, under the guidance of an experienced priest, shaman, or guru. Mushrooms are typically eaten raw, though they can be smoked, snorted as a powder, or made into a tea. The buds of the peyote cactus are generally eaten raw on an empty stomach. Jimsonweed, wild tobacco, and marijuana are typically smoked, but can also be eaten, or chewed raw. Opium is typically smoked or baked in sacramental cakes, as is the custom of the Sikhs. Coca leaves are either chewed raw or boiled in water to make a tea. Alcohol is always made into a beverage, such as wine, beer, or spirits.

Generally, sacred substances are used to get the initiate to break through the veil of this physical existence to experience a separate, or different, reality. While under the influence of these substances, the user will generally perceive emotions, subconscious thoughts, and forms of perception previously unknown. Sacred substances can awaken spiritual energy *(kundalini)* within the user, but prolonged use or excessive amounts can do physical and mental damage. In all cases, the use of sacred substances for spiritual purposes is done under the guidance of one who is familiar with how the substances are to be prepared, and who knows how much to take and under what conditions the substance should be taken. Unsupervised use can be extremely dangerous.

Additional information:

Contact groups that have traditionally used the substance as a part of their spiritual practice. Be discreet, and don't be surprised if you are not invited to partake with them. Please also check the local laws regarding the use of sacred substances.

Recommended Reading:

The Teachings of Don Juan: A Yaqui Way of Knowledge (and other books) by Carlos Castaneda

The Doors of Perception by Aldous Huxley

METAPHYSICAL TEACHINGS

SOMETHING UNPRECEDENTED in world history is now occurring on this planet: mankind is evolving its consciousness into an awareness of itself. Man is becoming aware of his own self, individually and collectively as part of a common consciousness. People are beginning to take a good look at themselves, and are searching for meaning and purpose in their lives. Individuals are beginning to recognize their divine nature, and are looking within to find answers and to commune with God. Metaphysics is the branch of philosophy that deals with the nature of existence and of truth and knowledge. As a result of this resurgence in self-awareness, many new teachings have evolved to facilitate a greater understanding of truth, self, and God.

The term "New Age" has been coined to convey the mass change of consciousness occurring on the planet. It means different things to different people, depending on which vehicle or organization they have been exposed to. Frequently the New Age refers to the Acquarian Age, in which mankind is expected commune with God and live in peace. No one organization is conducting the movement, or transition, but rather various individuals and groups are mobilizing to address the needs of individual seekers. Some of these groups are drawing upon arcane teachings from Eastern or Western cultures, while others are evolving traditional theology to suit the new way of thinking about things. The commonality among all "metaphysical" teachings is that they are addressing the human being's ability to discover, or experience, the Truth for himself or herself. The New Age is

147

directing the responsibility for self-awareness back on the individual; the power of realization is being acknowledged within mankind. The various forms by which these vehicles express themselves are as wide and divergent as the societies that create them.

As you read through the various schools of thought, think about what must have occurred to manifest such teachings and create such a response within our society. Many of these teachings may seem far-fetched, and they may be far-fetched, but the changes that have occurred in society because of these teachings can be easily seen. Not only has the New Age prompted questioning and personal investigation of the Truth, but many individuals are living fuller, happier lives due to their greater understanding of themselves. Moreover, many people who had either developed apathy or disillusionment in their spiritual life are now enthusiastically exploring their spirituality again. More than anything else, the New Age has been a catalyst for change.

The following is a summary of the largest and/or better-known metaphysical organizations. As much of the New Age teaching is based on individual investigation, a resource list for independent study appears at the end of this section. The following list of periodicals may also prove to be useful.

Recommended Periodicals:

New Age Journal
Exploring the Frontiers of
Human Potential
P.O. Box 51162
Boulder, CO 80321-1162
Phone:(617) 787-2005

Body Mind Spirit Magazine
Your New Age Information Resource
P.O. Box 3035
Southeastern, PA 19398-9978
Phone:(401) 351-4320

Halo
(Spiritually Related Subjects)
217 Kenmore
Elmhurst, IL 60126
Phone:(312) 834-5683

National New Age Yellow Pages
A Guide to Consciousness-Raising
Services, Products and Organizations
P.O. Box 5491
Fullerton, CA 92635
Phone:(714) 871-2489

THEOSOPHY

*T*HEOSOPHY (GREEK: *theos*, "God"; *sophia*, "wisdom"), is generally considered to be a strain of Western mystical philosophy. Though theosophical thought is traced back to the Greek philosopher and mystic Pythagoras, it was more recently expounded by Helena Petrovna Blavatsky, who was cofounder with Henry Olcott of the Theosophical Society.

Helena P. Blavatsky was born in Ekaterinoslav, Russia, in 1831, the daughter of a Russian colonel and a princess. In 1851 she went to London and met the legendary Master Morya, who began guiding her inner development and work for mankind. She made several trips through Asia and into Tibet to complete her training in occult powers. In 1875 she cofounded (with Colonel H. S. Olcott and W. Q. Judge) the Theosophical Society in New York, to "collect and diffuse a knowledge of the laws which govern the Universe." H. P. Blavatsky has written several books, which form the basis for contemporary theosophy, including *Isis Unveiled* (1877) and *The Secret Doctrine* (1888). In 1878 the founder moved the international headquarters of the Theosophical Society from New York to Adyar, India, where it is today. Theosophy is now studied throughout the world, with centers in many countries.

Theosophy is the study of the science of God, or "Divine Wisdom." It attempts to "gather the oldest of the tenets together and to make of them one harmonious and unbroken whole." The teachings are not those of any Eastern or Western religion, but rather the essence of all the world's spiritual teachings. The "Secret Doctrine" of theosophy is stated as being the synthesis of science, religion, and philosophy, and proposes to explain the fundamental unity in all religions and unite these findings with science.

The objectives of the Theosophical Society are as follows:

> *To form a nucleus of the Universal Brotherhood of Humanity, without distinction of race, creed, sex, caste, or color.*

*To encourage the study of Comparative
Religion, Philosophy and Science.*

*To investigate unexplained laws of
nature, and the powers latent in man.*

For more information:

The Theosophical Society
P.O. Box 270
Wheaton, IL 60189-0270
Phone:(708) 668-1571

or

Theosophical University Press
P.O. Bin C
Pasadena, CA 91109
Phone:(818) 798-3378

Recommended Reading:

An Abridgement of the Secret Doctrine
by H. P. Blavatsky

The Secret Doctrine
by H. P. Blavatsky

*Isis Unveiled "a Master Key to the
Mysteries of Ancient and Modern
Science and Theology"*
by H. P. Blavatsky

Letters That Have Helped Me
by William Q. Judge

Fountain-Source of Occultism
by G. de Purucker

RELIGIOUS SCIENCE
(SCIENCE OF THE MIND, UNITED CHURCH OF RELIGIOUS SCIENCE)

*R*ELIGIOUS SCIENCE is a spiritual teaching that corre-
lates "the laws of science, the opinions of philosophy, and the
revelations of religion applied to the needs and the aspirations of man." This teaching was founded by Ernest Holmes
(1887-1960), who synthesized his personal spiritual studies
into the basic text for Religious Science, *The Science of Mind*
first published in 1926. Holmes started lecturing on his
insights in 1916 in Los Angeles. By 1927 he had formed the
Institute of Religious Science and School of Philosophy, Inc.,
which became known as the Church of Religious Science in
1954 and became known by its official name of the United
Church of Religious Science in 1967. This organization is
now represented internationally, and its *Science of Mind*
magazine is read by hundreds of thousands. Its Founders
Church of Religious Science in Los Angeles is said to have the
largest metaphysical congregation in the world.

The teachings of Religious Science are best expressed by
Ernest Holmes himself in an article called "What We Believe," published in the first issue of *Science of Mind* Magazine, October 1927. To quote:

WHAT WE BELIEVE

*We believe in God, the Living Spirit Almighty; one,
indestructible, absolute, and self-existent Cause.
This One manifests itself in and through all creation but is not absorbed by Its creation. The manifest universe is the body of God; it is the logical and
necessary outcome of the infinite self-knowingness
of God ... We believe in the incarnation of the Spirit
in man and that all men are incarnations of the One
Spirit ... We believe in the eternality, the immortality, and the continuity of the individual soul, forever*

and ever expanding...We believe that the Kingdom of Heaven is within man and that we experience this Kingdom to the degree that we become conscious of it...We believe the ultimate goal of life to be a complete emancipation from all discord of every nature, and that this goal is sure to be attained by all...We believe in the unity of all life, and that the highest God and the innermost God is one God...We believe that God is personal to all who feel this indwelling Presence...We believe in the direct revelation of Truth through the intuitive and spiritual nature of man, and that any man may become a revealer of Truth who lives in close contact with the Indwelling God...We believe that the Universal Spirit, which is God, operates through a Universal Mind, which is the Law of God; and that we are surrounded by this Creative Mind which receives the direct impress of our thought and acts upon it...We believe in the healing of the sick through the power of this Mind...We believe in the control of conditions through the power of this Mind...We believe in the eternal Goodness, the eternal Lovingkindness, and the eternal Givingness of Life to all...We believe in our own soul, our own spirit, and our own destiny; for we understand that the life of man is God.

For additional information...

...look up the local member church in your telephone directory, or contact:

United Church of Religious
Science
3251 West 6th Street
P.O. Box 75127
Los Angeles, California 90075
Phone:(213) 388-2181

Recommended Reading:

The Science of Mind (the text)
by Ernest Holmes

Science of Mind Magazine
by Science of Mind Communications

SCIENTOLOGY
(CHURCH OF SCIENTOLOGY, DIANETICS)

SCIENTOLOGY IS "an applied religious philosophy dealing with the study of knowledge, which through the application of its technology, can bring about desirable changes in
the conditions of life." Scientology was founded by the
prolific writer and philosopher L. Ron Hubbard. Mr. Hubbard
was born in Tilden, Nebraska, on March 13, 1911, and most
of his life was spent exploring all over the globe observing
man, the mind, and humanity, and writing. From the culmi-
nation of his observations, he developed a philosophy and
science he called "Dianetics," which means "through thought
of mind." Mr. Hubbard published this new concept of the
nature of life and the human mind in 1950 in his book
Dianetics: The Modern Science of Mental Health, which
quickly became a best-seller. In 1951 he released his findings
on the spirit of man in his book *Science of Survival*, which
contained the foundation of the religion of Scientology.

Over the past fifty years, L. Ron Hubbard has published
over 589 works, delivered over 4,000 lectures and, through
the Churches of Scientology, spread the science of Dianetics
to every continent through over 600 churches, missions, and
groups.

Scientology evolved from Dianetics. Its aim is for humanity to evolve, individually and collectively as a society, to
a higher state of being. Quoting L. Ron Hubbard, "A civilization without insanity, without criminals and without war,
where the able can prosper and honest beings can have
rights, and where Man is free to rise to greater heights, are
the aims of Scientology." The faith is in man, and the
teaching is concerned with how to show man how he can set
himself free. The belief is that the route to freedom lies in
knowledge. *Scientology* means "knowing how to know."

Scientology is practiced in classes that allow the student
to realize a greater self. Much of the work involves "clearing"
the "preclear" (a person who through Scientology processing,

is finding out more about himself and life) of unwanted behavior patterns and discomforts, in order to become a "clear," an individual who, as a result of Dianetics therapy, has neither active nor potential psychosomatic illness or aberration. Such clearing allows the student (preclear) to come to know his true self, or Thetan. The greater realization in Scientology is to know yourself as "that which is aware of being aware; the identity which is the individual," or spirit.

For information contact: ▮

Scientology Information Center
4833 Fountain Avenue
Los Angeles, California 90029
Phone: 1 (800) FOR-TRUTH

or look in the phone directory under Church of Scientology.

Recommended Reading:

Dianetics: The Modern Science of Mental Health
by L. Ron Hubbard

Science of Survival
by L. Ron Hubbard

Scientology, the Fundamentals of Thought
by L. Ron Hubbard

MENTALPHYSICS

*T*HE SCIENCE of Mentalphysics, or Brahma Vidya as it is known in the East, is a methodology for self-realization that has been passed on throughout time to a select few, and was brought from Tibet to the West by Edwin John Dingle in the early part of the twentieth century. Edwin John Dingle was born in England on April 6, 1881. His mother and father both died while he was young, and he was raised by his paternal grandmother in Cornwall. Edwin was a solitary boy, who used to take imaginary trips to Tibet and yearned to travel there. After completing school, Edwin was apprenticed in the printing trade and later became editor of the *Strait Times of Singapore*. In Singapore, Edwin met a Sage who instructed him in certain methods and practices for spiritual development, and then told him to make a pilgrimage to the Tibet. When Edwin arrived in western China and Tibet, he was surprised to find his spiritual masters and brothers waiting for him, and began an arduous training in the mysteries of the East.

Mr. Dingle spent twenty-one years in the Orient, where he built a large publishing company with offices in Shanghai and Hong Kong, and developed a reputation as a geographic authority on China. During the Boxer Rebellion he served as a war correspondent. He was later given the Chinese name of Ding Le Mei, and went on to teach aspirants from the West the mysteries of the ancient science of Brahma Vidya, or what he refers to in the West as the Science of Mentalphysics. In 1927 Ding Le Mei founded the Institute of Mentalphysics in New York, which pioneered the evolving Western interest in Eastern esoteric teachings. To date, the Institute has inspired over 200,000 students from all over the world. Edwin Dingle passed away in 1972, and the Institute is now guided by Chancellor Donald L. Waldrop at their headquarters in Yucca Valley, California.

Mentalphysics is based on the "Eternal Truth of Life," and serves to spread the Light of Divine Wisdom, working through Natural Law in the Holy Trinity of Body, Mind, and Spirit of Man. The underlying belief is that there is a spark of the divine in every human being, and through the practice of Mentalphysics that divinity can be realized more clearly. Through this practice one will see "the universality and oneness in life, embodied in all substance, energy and thought." Moreover, "Man is the Temple of the Living God, and the knowledge of God's Universal Law as taught by us enables him to demonstrate 'perfect mind in a perfect body.'" Mentalphysics is a practice, not a creed. The truth cannot be fully understood by our intellect, but must be "felt" within the depth of the soul, and made "a MAINSPRING of every thought and action from within us." Students take universal truths as are offered in the teachings into the laboratory of their own lives—to prove for themselves. Thus the teachings are called THE SCIENCE OF MENTALPHYSICS.

Central to the practice of Mentalphysics is the use of the breath, or *pranayama* as it is referred to in the East. Within the air we breath is the vital life force, which provides the energy to sustain the body, and by cultivating this energy we increase our vitality and increase our capacity for higher awareness. Various breathing techniques are used to develop and direct the *Prana* for specific applications such as health, clarity of mind, and inspiration. Sometimes affirmations and visualizations are included as part of the meditation process, and a particular diet and exercise is prescribed to enhance the body's capacity for utilizing the spiritual energy.

For more information... ▐

...on Mentalphysics, contact their headquarters at:

Institute of Mentalphysics
P.O. Box 1000
Joshua Tree, CA 92252
Phone:(619) 365-8371

Recommended Reading:

Breaths That Renew Your Life
by Edwin John Dingle

My Life in Tibet
by Edwin John Dingle

THE TEACHINGS OF THE ASCENDED MASTERS

*T*HE TEACHINGS of the Ascended Masters are the Universal Truths taught by the "Great White Brotherhood," as dictated by the Masters to Mark L. Prophet and Elizabeth Clare Prophet. The Great White Brotherhood is a spiritual order of Western Saints and Eastern Adepts known as the "Ascended Masters," who work with earnest seekers and public servants of every race, religion, and walk of life to assist humanity in their forward evolution and to save the planet. Among the Ascended Masters are Jesus Christ, Gautama Buddha, Saint Michael the Archangel, Maitreya, Kuthumi, El Morya, Saint Germain, and the Mother Mary. Mark and Elizabeth Prophet were anointed as messengers for the Ascended Masters to deliver God's prophecy and to convey the truths for this necessary change in consciousness.

Mark L. Prophet was born on December 24, 1918, in Chippewa Falls, Wisconsin. Mark was a very religious child; he was raised in the Pentecostal church and received all nine gifts of the Holy Spirit before finishing high school. Later he studied the teachings of Paramahansa Yogananda in the Self-Realization Fellowship, was associated with the Rosicrucian Order, and was apparently inspired by Theosophy and the "I AM" movement of Guy Ballard. Mark lectured on Christian and Eastern mysticism from 1945 to 1952, then began publishing a series of letters to his students called *Ashram Notes* that were dictated by the Ascended Master El Morya. Mark founded The Summit Lighthouse in 1958 to publish the Teachings of the Ascended Masters and launch a worldwide movement.

In February 1973, Mark L. Prophet passed on and the ministry was carried on by his wife and partner, Elizabeth Clare (Wulf) Prophet. Elizabeth was born in Red Bank, New Jersey, in 1939. As a young girl she was very interested in finding Truth and could hear Jesus speaking to her in her heart as she pursued her quest. From the ages of nine to eighteen she studied the works of Mary Baker Eddy and attended the Christian Science Church. In 1961 she attended a meeting of The Summit Lighthouse in Boston and met Mark L. Prophet. While Elizabeth was studying for her bachelor's degree in political science at Boston University, the Ascended Master El Morya appeared to her and told her to go to Washington, D.C., to study with Mark Prophet, who would train her to become a messenger. With Mark, she underwent intense spiritual training, and three years later she received Saint Germain's anointing to be the messenger of the Great White Brotherhood. Mark and Elizabeth were married on March 16, 1963, and have raised a son and three daughters. Today the Teachings of the Ascended Masters are disseminated throughout the world. Elizabeth has lectured in over thirty countries and written over fifty books, which have sold over a million copies. Her cable television shows have a viewing audience of 36 million.

A long time ago, cosmic councils had determined that no further opportunity should be given to humanity, so great was their departure from cosmic law and their desecration of life. It was at this time that Sanat Kumara, one of the Seven Holy Kumaras who focused the light of the seven rays, offered his heart to serve the people of earth until the few, and eventually the many, would once again keep the flame of Life and come to know their True Self as God. The solar lords granted Sanat Kumara this dispensation, and he proceeded with his spiritual sons and daughters to Earth and established the retreat of Shamballa in what is now the Gobi Desert. This retreat, once physical, was withdrawn to the etheric octave, or heaven-world, in subsequent dark ages. It is one of many retreats on the etheric plane from which the Ascended Masters minister to those on earth and work together to uplift the consciousness of the world. The Masters teach that each soul has the potential to externalize its own divine nature, and that we have the ability to realize the Light of God, as the Inner Christ or the Inner Buddha, within. Moreover, each individual has the ability to walk the path of personal Christhood and to Ascend, as Jesus did. The ascension is a spiritual acceleration of consciousness that takes place at the natural conclusion of one's final lifetime on earth.

The practice focuses on the science of the spoken Word through "dynamic decrees," which combine prayer, meditation, and visualization, with a special emphasis on affirmations using the name of God: "I AM THAT I AM." Emphasis is also placed on reading and contemplating the Teachings of the Ascended Masters. Students of the Ascended Masters use decrees to direct God's light for the solving of personal and planetary problems. Some students practice independent study, while others may subscribe to the weekly *Pearls of Wisdom* discourses, dictated by the Ascended Masters. There is also a Keepers of the Flame fraternity, which is a secular organization "dedicated to keeping the flame of Life in earth's evolutions and to planetary enlightenment." The movement is based at the 33,000-acre Royal Teton Ranch in Park County, Montana, which is home to a self-sufficient spiritual community-in-the-making and is the international headquarters for Church Universal and Triumphant, The Summit Lighthouse, Summit University (which sponsors twelve-week retreats and summer courses), Montessori International School, and Summit University Press.

For more information: ████████████████████████

> Summit University Press
> Box A
> Livingston, MT 59047-1390
> Phone:(406) 222-8300

Recommended Reading:

The Chela and the Path
by the Ascended Master El Morya
(a brief introductory book)

Saint Germain On Alchemy
by the Ascended Master Saint
Germain

The Lost Teachings of Jesus
(Vols 1 & 2)
by Mark L. Prophet & Elizabeth Clare
Prophet

The Lost Years of Jesus
by Elizabeth Clare Prophet

INTERNATIONAL BIOGENIC SOCIETY

*T*HE INTERNATIONAL Biogenic Society "is a nonsectarian, nonpolitical, scientific, educational association of Individual Associate Members and Associate Teachers, for the teaching of the various aspects of Biogenic Living, as well as the many all-sided practical applications of the ancient Essene Teachings in our daily lives in the twentieth century." The Society was founded in Paris in 1928 by the Nobel prize-winning author Romain Rolland and the philosopher Edmond Bordeaux Szekely, Ph.D. The IBS evolved out of Dr. Szekely's research on ancient civilizations and religions, and in particular on the Essene brotherhood of first century A.D. Judaea. Early in his education, Dr. Szekely earned the privilege of studying ancient manuscripts at the Archives of the Vatican, under the direction of Msgr. Mercati. His research began with the study of the venerable Saint Francis, which led him to the writings of Saint Benedict and the manuscripts that he had preserved that dated back to the fourth century A.D. These manuscripts were Saint Jerome's translations of first-century biblical codices, which included Hebrew writings of the Essene Brotherhood.

During the middle of the fourth century A.D., Saint Jerome spent twenty years traveling in the Holy Land deciphering fragments of ancient first-century A.D. manuscripts. During this time he gathered letters from an ancient brotherhood of the desert known as the Essenes, and began translating these fragments from Hebrew into Latin. Having gained a reputation as a scholar of first-century Hebrew manuscripts, he was commissioned by Pope Damasus I (St. Damasus), who founded the Papal Library, to revise the New Testament, using the newly translated first-century letters. These new translations included a number of "Apocryphal Documents" which were preserved at the Vatican, and were recently rediscovered and translated by Dr. Sezekely. These writing explained a formula for living that the Essenes practiced, which Dr. Sezekely calls "Biogenic Living." In

1928 Dr. Sezekely translated "The Essene Gospel of Peace" into modern languages, and today over ten million readers have absorbed its message. Moreover, the International Biogenic Society is now represented around the world, instructing people in "The Essene Way of Biogenic Living."

The philosophy of the International Biogenic Society is summarized by its credo, which is as follows:

We believe that our most precious possession is Life.

We believe we shall mobilize all the forces of Life against the forces of death.

We believe that mutual understanding leads toward mutual cooperation; that mutual cooperation leads toward Peace; and that Peace is the only way of survival for mankind.

We believe that we shall preserve instead of waste our natural resources, which are the heritage of our children.

We believe that we shall avoid the pollution of our air, water, and soil, the basic preconditions of Life.

We believe we shall preserve the vegetation of our planet: the humble grass which came fifty million years ago, and the majestic trees which came twenty million years ago, to prepare our planet for mankind.

We believe we shall eat only fresh, natural, pure, whole foods, without chemicals and artificial processing.

We believe we shall live a simple, natural, creative life, absorbing all the sources of energy, harmony and knowledge, in and around us.

We believe that the improvement of life and mankind on our planet must start with individual efforts, as the whole depends on the atoms composing it.

*We believe in the Fatherhood of God, the Mother-
hood of Nature, and the Brotherhood of Man.*

Biogenic means "life-generating," and Biogenic Living
involves presenting life rather than destroying it—learning
to cultivate and assimilate natural foods ecologically, and
learning how to interact with our environment without
damaging it. The spiritual practice involves "dynamic communion," which is a way of "tapping a source of knowledge
which does not depend on superficial dogmatic convictions,
but is eternal and timelessly valid from which our own
human existence was formed, and with which we are forever
connected." Biogenic Living also involves self-analysis, and
reflection on life's purpose, not based on abstract theories,
but arrived at through empirical life experiences. Biogenic
Living is the most natural, healthy, and happy way of living.

For more information...

... on the International Biogenic Society and
the Essene Way of Biogenic Living, contact:

I.B.S. International
Box 205, Matsqui, B.C.
Canada VOX 1SO

Recommended Reading:

The Essene Gospel of Peace
by Edmond Bordeaux Szekely

The Essene Way—Biogenic Living
by Edmond Bordeaux Szekely

THE BAHA'I FAITH

*B*AHA'I IS a faith founded by Baha'u'llah, and is based on the tenets of the unity of all religions and of mankind. Baha'i is the outgrowth of a movement within Islam known as Babism. In 1844 a young man named Siyyid 'Ali Muhammad from Shiraz, Iran, who was a direct descendent of the prophet Muhammad, proclaimed himself to be the Bab (the "gate" or "door"). Within the Shi'ite sect of Islam, it is believed that the Imam Mahdi, or "rightly guided imam," will come forth and bring in an era of justice and peace. By proclaiming himself the Bab, Siyyid 'Ali Muhammad was declaring himself as the expected imam and forerunner to "He whom God shall make manifest" who Baha'is believe was Baha'u'llah.

The Bab was rapidly gathering disciples, which threatened the established clergy in Iran, so they quickly put him to death by firing squad in 1850, and many of his followers, or Babis, were massacred or exiled. One such exiled follower, Mirza Husayn-'Ali, who was known as Baha'u'llah (born in Teheran, Iran, in 1817, the son of a nobleman and minister), declared himself "He who God shall make Manifest" to a small group of followers while in Baghdad in 1863. Shortly thereafter he was banished to Istanbul and then to Adrianople, Turkey, where he publicly proclaimed his mission. While in exile he wrote many letters to world rulers and developed the unifying concepts that characterize the Baha'i faith. In 1868 Baha'u'llah was exiled to Akka, Palestine, where he suffered harsh imprisonment for two years, followed by a house arrest that lasted until his death in 1892. Leadership passed to one of Baha'u'llah's sons, who was known as "Abdul-Baha" or "The Servant of Baha." Abdul-Baha was released from prison in 1908 and promptly set out on missionary journeys to Egypt, Europe and America. After the death of Abdul-Baha in 1921, his grandson, Shoghi Effendi Rabbani, was appointed the Guardian, or next leader of the Baha'i religion. After Shoghi Effendi's death in 1957, the administrative duties were delegated to the Universal House of Justice in

Haifa. Baha'i is currently represented throughout the world, with over 5 million Baha'is, with large followings in Iran, India, Europe, and the United States.

The main tenet of the Baha'i Faith is the unification of all religions and teachings and the promotion of the unification of humanity. Baha'is perceive God as an essence that manifests in numerous ways. Baha'i theology recognizes the great prophets and saviors of all major religions, but emphasizes the most recent revelations given by Baha'i prophets such as the Bab, Baha, and Ullah, as their teachings are designed for the scientific age. The teachings and laws of the Baha'is are set forth in such books as the *Kitab al-Aqdas* or *The Most Holy Book*, the *Bayan*, or *Statement of Explanation* by the Bab.

The Baha'i Faith is a religion without a clergy. Each individual in the faith is encouraged to look into religious teachings with an unbiased mind and be responsible for his or her own individual beliefs and actions. Spiritual assemblies are elected to carry on various activities such as marriages and funerals. Baha'is often meet for small group discussions called "firesides" and observe various Holy Days such as the birth and death of the Bab and Baha'u'llah. Fasting is observed, from March 2 through March 20, when Baha'is abstain from all food and drink from sunrise to sunset. The Baha'i Faith also has the institution of obligatory prayer; Baha'is are obligated to say one of three obligatory prayers each day. Baha'i teachings have as their goal the improvement of the conditions of human life.

For more information... ▮▮▮▮▮▮▮▮▮▮▮▮▮▮▮▮

... look up Baha'i in the phone book for a community nearest you, or contact:

Baha'i National Center
Wilmette, IL 60091
Phone: (708) 869-9039

Recommended Reading:

The Baha'i Faith, an Introduction
by Gloria Faizi

Baha'u'llah and the New Era
by John Esslemont

EMISSARIES OF DIVINE LIGHT

*T*HE EMISSARIES of Divine Light was founded by Lloyd Arthur Meeker, who was born in Iowa in 1907 and moved to Colorado at the age of two. He was the son of a poor farmer and minister, whose strict interpretation of religious dogma prompted Lloyd to question the spiritual values he was raised with and contemplate the deeper meaning of life. In September 1932, Lloyd had an experience of enlightenment that opened his eyes to the purpose of existence and man's relationship with God. Lloyd quickly began to find others who shared his spiritual values and who found great benefits from his insights on God and man. His following grew, and in 1940 he incorporated his program into a church under the name of Emissaries of Divine Light.

In 1939 Meeker was introduced to a cattle rancher of the English aristocracy from British Columbia named Martin Cecil. Martin was instrumental in developing and spreading the work of the Emissaries. In 1945 the Emissaries established its international headquarters at Sunrise Ranch near Loveland, Colorado. In 1948 another spiritual community was formed at Cecil's 100 Mile House Lodge in British Columbia. The work of the Emissaries inspired many, and other communities formed around the world. In 1954 Lloyd Meeker died in a plane crash, and Martin Cecil assumed the leadership of the Emissaries. Under Martin's leadership the Emissaries continued to grow. In 1981 Martin succeeded to the title of 7th Marquess of Exeter with the passing of his brother, David, and took his seat in England's House of Lords in March 1982. In 1987, the Emissaries held their "The Signs of the Times" public event, which was broadcast to 70 locations in 23 countries, reaching an estimated 4,600 people. In 1988, Martin Cecil died, and now his son Michael Cecil provides leadership for the Emissaries. Michael succeeded his father as the 8th Marquess of Exeter and has taken his seat in the House of Lords.

The purpose of the Emissaries is "to assist in carrying forward a work of Spiritual regeneration of the human race, under the inspiration of the Spirit of God." The Emissaries provide a forum to align the individual with the true character of spirit. No specific teachings are adhered to, but rather individuals are assisted to release the spiritual nature within themselves. Lloyd Meeker affirmed that "Incarnate within all people dwells an aspect of the spirit of God, eternal and perfect, having no need to evolve or to grow. Where there is a willingness to align with that, so that mind and emotions become clear channels through which the essence of that incarnate spirit may find release, all problems immediately begin to dissolve."

The Emissaries have established spiritual communities which provide a setting where people have the opportunity to awaken the spirit within themselves. Classes and seminars are offered regularly. As Martin Cecil stated, "Such awakening is easier, in many ways, when one shares the process with others; as when a team climbs a mountain, there is the advantage of comradeship, mutual encouragement, and shared purpose." Each individual in the community is encouraged to exemplify the Truth, to become a walking example of the very nature of spirit. However, many Emissaries do not live in these communities, which have developed as regional headquarters, but merely visit as time permits. Transcripts of Michael Exeter's recent addresses are sent to those interested twice monthly, and a correspondence course is available at no charge, featuring introductory material. The Emissaries now have centers throughout North America and in South America, South and West Africa, Australia, and Europe. Visitors are welcome to visit their communities or attend their Sunday services.

For more information:

The Emissaries of Divine Light
5569 North County Road 29
Loveland, Colorado 80538

Recommended Reading:

       Introductory pamphlets
       Martin Cecil's biography
       Martin Cecil's books

ECKANKAR

*E*CKANAR IS the ancient path to God-Realization through the inner light and sound and the Living Eck Master, or Mahanta. Eckankar has always existed, it predates history as we know it, and is practiced not only throughout the physical universe but also throughout all higher levels of consciousness, or Heaven. Eck Masters have always been available on earth to assist aspirants (seekers) to reach God-Realization. However, since very few people were ready for such a direct path to God, the teachings were not made available to the masses. As many evolved souls are now incarnating during the coming Aquarian Age, the Eck teachings are becoming more readily available.

Paul Twitchell brought Eckankar to Western civilization in the early 1960s and made it accessible to the masses. Eckankar is now practiced around the world by many thousands, and is growing rapidly as more people make contact with the inner light and sound. The current Living Eck Master is Harold Klemp, who works with seekers outwardly through his writings, correspondence, and speaking engagements, and on seekers inwardly (personally) through dreams and soul travel (such as out-of-body experiences).

Eckankar teaches on the basis of direct personal experiences. Spiritual exercises are given to Eckists as a vehicle for learning, along with written discourses, which can be studied in private or in classes. These spiritual exercises connect the aspirant (or Chela) with an inner light and sound, which are seen and heard from within. This light and sound connect the seeker, via the Eck (holy spirit), to the Sugmad (the all that is, or God). To overcome the limits of physical awareness, the Mahanta (Living Eck Master) assists the Eckists to ascend, as soul, into the higher levels of consciousness (heaven) where greater truths can be realized through direct experiences.

Eckankar, the religion of the light and sound of God, is geared to the spiritual needs and goals of the individual.

Spiritual concepts are provided for contemplation, but the beliefs are based on the direct personal experiences of the individual. Through the purification of the soul, via these spiritual exercises, the Eckists aim to reach higher states of consciousness and to become coworkers with Sugmad, or God.

For additional information...

... look up Eckankar in the phone book or contact the headquarters at the following address:

Eckankar
Attn: Information
P.O. Box 27300
Minneapolis, MN 55427
Phone: (612) 544-3001

Recommended Reading:

Child in the Wilderness
by Harold Klemp

The Living Word
by Harold Klemp

Eckankar the Key to the Secret Worlds
by Paul Twitchell

The Spiritual Notebook
by Paul Twitchell

THE MONROE INSTITUTE

*T*HE MONROE Institute is a school that provides research and education in the field of human consciousness. The Monroe Institute was founded by Robert Monroe in 1971. Mr. Monroe is a former broadcasting executive who began to have spontaneous out-of-body experiences (OOBE) in 1958. These OOBE's led him into an investigation into the nature and causes of such experiences that has lasted over thirty years. To date Mr. Monroe has written two best-selling books on his experiences: *Journeys Out of the Body* and *Far Journeys*. He has lectured extensively throughout the country, has trained thousands how to access other states of awareness, and is considered one of the world's foremost scientists in the field of human consciousness.

Moreover, the Monroe Institute has developed audio tapes with sound patterns that create electrical patterns in the brain that assist in focusing the consciousness toward desired results, such as health, learning, and expanding consciousness. These "Hemi-Sync" tapes act by synchronizing the energy frequencies of the left and right hemispheres of the brain, which creates a stimulus that activates higher levels of awareness. It is estimated that over 200,000 people have experienced the Hemi-Sync tapes to date.

Mr. Monroe does not purport to have the Truth, and the Monroe Institute does not pretend to have all the answers to the nature of human consciousness; however, the Institute does provide a facility for individuals to have personal, direct experiences that will assist them in determining the Truth for themselves. The underlying premise that is to be tested through his methods for having OOBE's is that there is something more to our existence than our physical world. Monroe reasons that "our physical reality is only one band or frequency in a vast spectrum of realities in the 'universal energy system.'"

Monroe goes into considerable detail as to how he manages to enter into these higher (and lower) states, and explains to the best of his ability (relating to nonphysical experiences) what these other realities are like. His methodology is very scientific and his approach is very objective and clinical. Most interestingly he is able to document and repeat his experiences, and has been able to teach his techniques to many others with positive results. Moreover, there are higher forms of consciousness that work with Monroe as well as the others who practice his techniques. These OOBE's include: Seeing your physical body from outside yourself (which he estimates is an experience over 20 percent of the population has had); visiting entities that have either physically died, or are from other universes or energy systems; going forward or backward in time, and even beyond time; and transcending the limits of his physical consciousness.

Various techniques are employed to initiate OOBE's, including the following: First, emptying all your thoughts and worries into an imagined "Energy Conversion Box," and then practicing "Resonant Tuning," which is a form of chanting combined with rhythmic breathing. The final step is to recite a prescribed affirmation, which states that you are more than your physical body, that you desire to experience other energy systems, and that you desire assistance from beings "whose wisdom is equal to or greater than" your own. This technique is best practiced just as you fall off into sleep. It is also recommended that you practice remembering your dreams, and that you keep track of the dreams and experiences that you have. To assist in developing the ability to have control over expanded states of consciousness, the Monroe Institute has developed a series of Hemi-Sync cassette tapes, which are played in a sequence to enhance your experience.

For more information...

... on the Monroe Institute, and the Hemi-Sync programs for learning, write or phone:

The Monroe Institute
Route 1, Box 175
Faber, Virginia 22938
Phone:(804) 361-1252

Recommended Reading:

> *Journeys Out of the Body*
> by Robert A. Monroe
>
> *Far Journeys*
> by Robert A. Monroe

PSYCHOTECHNOLOGIES

*P*SYCHOTECHNOLOGIES IS a broad term used to encompass the gambit of scientific approaches, and technological means, of altering an individual's state of consciousness. Inducing an altered state of conscious is a means by which individuals can relax, utilize a greater potential of the brain, and/or attain inner spiritual experiences such as out-of-body states, visions, and an expansion of consciousness. A brief explanation of some of the methods and devices available is as follows:

Flotation tank. A flotation tank is basically a tub that is covered in order to keep any sound or light from entering the vessel. The tub is then filled to a shallow depth and heated to body temperature. Several hundred pounds of epsom salt is dissolved into the water, so that when people lie on their back they can float effortlessly. With a lack of external sensory perception—sound, light, touch, etc.—the floater can relax and become more aware of their inner perceptions, and often an altered state of consciousness can occur.

Synchro-Energizer. The Synchro-Energizer is basically a set of goggles with strobing lights and earphones with strobing sounds or music, which pulse in such a way that your brain waves attune to the frequency settings. As the participant reclines and tunes into the frequency selected— Beta, Alpha, Theta, or Delta—the Synchro-Energizer brings the analytical left brain into hemispheric synchronization with the creative right brain, and an altered state of consciousness can be achieved.

Graham Potentializer. The Graham Potentializer is basically a massage table with an electrical current running through it, which rotates up and down slowly in small circular motions like a Ferris wheel. As you are being gently rocked to a rhythmic motion, an electromagnetic current runs through your entire body. The movement of the table stimulates cilia on hair cells in fluid filled sacs of the inner ear and those hair cells send impulses to the cerebellum which results in altering brain wave frequencies. These lower brain-wave frequencies (measured in cycles per second) can induce a deep meditative state, which can alter your consciousness. The Graham Potentializer is also used in conjunction with hypnotic self-improvement tapes, which provide messages played while you are in an altered state.

Mind Mirror. The mind mirror is essentially a biofeedback machine; that is, it measures brain-wave activity through electrodes placed along a band around the head, and brain-wave patterns are then displayed on a screen. As you observe the screen and practice changing your state of mind through visualization, controlled breathing, meditation, or contemplation, the results are displayed in order to gauge the various responses. As the desired response is achieved, the participant can focus the attention in the area which creates the desired response, such as a deep meditation state in the delta-wave frequencies.

Sensory Enhancement Environment. The Sensory Enhancement Environment is a small box of mirrors that reflects over 800 images of yourself. As you gaze into the reflections, various levels of self-awareness are achieved. The box, which is designed to accommodate you sitting cross-legged, can be either dimly or brightly lit. You can sit in the box in total silence for contemplation, or enhance the experience by using Hemi-Sync audio cassette tapes. These Hemi-Sync tapes play sounds at various frequencies, which work in a manner similar to the synchro-energizer in that they help manipulate the mind's brain-wave frequencies and create an altered state of consciousness.

For more information contact: ▐█████████████████▌

Mega Brain
P.O. Box 2205
Sausalito, CA 94965-9998
Phone:(415) 332-8323

or   Altered States
8704 Santa Monica Blvd
West Hollywood, CA 90069
Phone: (213) 854-4497

179

Westside Relaxation Center
500 West End Avenue #9C
New York, NY 10024
Phone:(212) 874-3120

or   John-David's Brain/MindSalons
in:
San Diego, CA (619) 931-0456
Denver/Boulder,CO
(303)449-6266

Recommended Reading:

Mega Brain
by Michael Hutchison

The Awakened Mind
by Anna Wise

ALCOHOLICS ANONYMOUS

ALCOHOLICS ANONYMOUS is a society of alcoholics that help each other to keep sober and to enjoy life more fully. This fellowship started when an alcoholic stockbroker from New York met up with a physician from Akron, Ohio, in 1935. Six months prior to their meeting, the stockbroker, Bill W., had had a spiritual experience that had relieved him of his obsession with drinking. Bill had learned of the "grave nature of alcoholism" from the late Dr. William D. Silkworth, a specialist in alcoholism, and became convinced of the "need for moral inventory, confession of personality defects, restitution to those harmed, helpfulness to others, and the necessity of belief in and dependence upon God." Bill had been working with other alcoholics in New York, on the premise that only another alcoholic could help an alcoholic, but had not been successful. During a business trip to Akron, Bill met Dr. Bob S., who had been struggling with alcoholism and tried other spiritual means to overcome his dependency, but had failed. Bill's words and support were effective in mustering Bob's certitude, and Bob remained sober until his death in 1950.

With inspiration and mutual support, Bill and Bob set off to the Akron City Hospital to offer assistance to other alcoholics in overcoming their disease. They had many failures at first, but several successes; and started the first AA group in the fall of 1935. Shortly thereafter, a second group started in New York, and others picked up the basic idea in other cities. In 1939, the first edition of *Alcoholics Anonymous* was published as a cooperative effort of the group which began to refer to itself as "Alcoholics Anonymous," or "AA." From the writing of this book, the message quickly spread to many thousands. Over 300,000 copies were sold in the first printing, and the second edition, published in 1955, sold over 1,150,000 copies. By September 1983 the combined total of the three editions distributed totalled over 4,000,000. In 1987, AA was composed of approximately 67,000 groups.

Alcoholics Anonymous is represented in almost every country in the world, with countless millions who actively participate in the fellowship of this society and who have been able to remain sober and enjoy life more fully.

The basic underlying premise of AA is that fellow alcoholics can assist each other through the process of becoming and remaining sober, and that there is a power greater than themselves (God, however you perceive him) that we can use in order to overcome the disease that has taken over their life. AA functions in accordance with what is termed the "Twelve Traditions." A summary of these traditions is as follows: (1) Our common welfare should come first; personal recovery depends upon AA unity. (2) For our group purpose there is but one ultimate authority—a loving God as He may express Himself in our group conscience. Our leaders are but trusted servants; they do not govern. (3) The only requirement for AA membership is a desire to stop drinking. (4) Each group should be autonomous except in matters affecting other groups or AA as a whole. (5) Each group has but one primary purpose—to carry its message to the alcoholic who still suffers. (6) An AA group ought never endorse, finance, or lend the AA name to any related facility or outside enterprise, lest problems of money, property, and prestige divert us from our primary purpose. (7) Every AA group ought to be fully self-supporting, declining outside contributions. (8) Alcoholics Anonymous should remain forever nonprofessional, but our service centers may employ special workers. (9) AA, as such, ought never to be organized; but we may create service boards or committees directly responsible to those they serve. (10) Alcoholics Anonymous has no opinion on outside issues; hence the AA name ought never to be drawn into public controversy. (11) Our public relations policy is based on attraction rather than promotion; we need always maintain personal anonymity at the level of press, radio, and films. (12) Anonymity is the spiritual foundation of all our Traditions, ever reminding us to place principles before personalities.

The process of overcoming alcoholism through AA is one of recognizing and acting upon conditions in your life. Through the help of others in similar situations, and with a power greater than himself, an alcoholic becomes sober and can live a happier life. The stages through which one must pass are known in AA as the "Twelve Steps," and they are as follows: (1) We admitted we were powerless over alcohol—that our lives had become unmanageable. (2) We came to believe that a Power greater than ourselves could restore us to sanity. (3) We made a decision to turn our will and our lives over to the care of God as we understood Him. (4) We made a searching and fearless moral inventory of ourselves. (5) We admitted to God, to ourselves, and to another human being the exact nature of our wrongs. (6) We were entirely ready to have God remove all these defects of character. (7) We humbly asked Him to remove our shortcomings. (8) We made a list of all persons we had harmed, and became willing to make amends to them all. (9) We made direct amends to such people wherever possible, except when to do so would injure them or others. (10) We continue to take personal inventory and when we are wrong, promptly admit it. (11) We sought through prayer and meditation to improve our conscious contact with God as we understood Him, praying only for knowledge of His will for us and the power to carry that out. (12) Having had a spiritual awakening as the result of these steps, we tried to carry this message to alcoholics, and to practice these principles in all our affairs.

For more information... ████████

...on AA, look up Alcoholics Anonymous in the phone directory, or contact:

> The General Service Office
> Alcoholics Anonymous
> Box 459
> Grand Central Station, NY 10163

Recommended Reading:

> *Alcoholics Anonymous*, 3rd ed.
> by the A.A. World Services, Inc.
> (principal text for the society)
>
> *Twelve Steps and Twelve Traditions*
> by a cofounder

There is also a support group for the friends and relatives of alcoholics called Al-Anon. To find an Al-Anon group, look in your phone book for the nearest group, or contact them at:

> Al-Anon Family Groups, Inc.
> Box 182
> Madison Square Station, NY 10159

Note: Similar groups have formed for those with other abuses, such as drugs or overeating. You can get additional information through AA groups in your area.

CRYSTALS

CRYSTALS ACT as a catalyst for channeling energies that are used in healing and spiritual development. Crystals are usually found buried in the earth, but may be found in stream beds or washed-out areas. The most common kind of crystals used are natural quartz crystals, which are formed in the earth from the elements silicon and oxygen by a lengthy process involving heat and pressure. Most of the fine quartz crystals are mined in Arkansas, New York, Mexico, and Brazil. Other favorite gems and minerals used for spiritual development and healing include agate, aquamarine, bloodstone, copper, coral, diamond, fluorite, gold, jasper, lapis, magnesium, malachite, moonstone, opal, pyrite, silver, and tourmaline. They have been used by shamans, healers, and royalty throughout recorded history all over the world, and today crystals and gems have become very widely used and are commonly sold in metaphysical bookstores and gem shops.

Crystals are often worn as jewelry to enhance or protect a person from various positive or negative energies, or are placed in rooms to create a particular energy or to protect from negative influences. They come in "hand size" for healing work or meditation, or very large (several pounds) as a single crystal or cluster of crystals called "generators," which are used for spreading energies throughout a room or household. Crystals come in various colors, each of which has a different vibration that can be used for different effects such as healing, grounding, raising consciousness, etc. Crystals typically have six sides and are pointed at one or two ends (single or double terminated). They can also be formed into balls, or made into wands or dorjes (wands with a single terminated crystals of equal size on each end).

As crystals channel energy, they are often used for locating and directing negative energies that are adversely affecting the health of a person, and thereby assist people in their mental or physical healing. Crystals are also applied to the opening of certain spiritual energy centers known as chakras. Typically either light or sound is conducted through the crystal in various ways so as to open these centers, which are located at the heart, the throat, between the eyebrows, or on top of the head. By directing the energy to these spiritual centers, they may be opened to awaken a greater awareness within an individual.

In order to become sensitized to a crystal, vigorously rub the palms of your hand together for thirty seconds. Then gently blow on your palms so that you can feel a tingling sensation. Next, pick up a crystal with one hand so that the point is sticking out, and gently pass the point of the crystal back and forth or in a circular motion about a half an inch over the palm of your other hand. The energy from the hand holding the crystal is easily felt by the other hand without physical contact. Each crystal has its own energy and purpose, and to become familiar with its unique character and use you should handle the crystal and trust your intuition.

Many other spiritual and healing exercises are taught by crystal workers. To find a crystal worker, look for information in metaphysical bookstores, health-food stores, gem/crystal stores, or holistic medical clinics.

Recommended Reading:

The Crystal Book
by Dael

The Complete Crystal Guidebook
by Uma Silbey

The Crystal Sourcebook
by John Vincent Milewski and
Virginia L. Harford

Gem Elixirs and Vibrational Healing
by Gurudas

CHANNELING

*C*HANNELING IS a spiritual vehicle whereby individuals act as conduits, mediums, or channels for the expression of thought from another level of consciousness. The channel generally allows his physical body to be used by an element, or entity of "higher" consciousness, to communicate concepts to the physical world. The messages are generally presented to humanity to raise or increase its spiritual awareness.

Channeling can generally be divided into two kinds. Subjective channeling is where the channel makes conscious contact with a higher level of consciousness or God, and recalls the experience. Many of the world's great spiritual texts, such as the Holy Bible, the Koran, and the Vedas are "God's" word given to man to commit, ultimately, into writing. Subjective channeling is generally not what we consider channeling in the contemporary use of the term.

Objective channeling is where the channel makes contact with another entity, which uses the channel's physical faculties to communicate with other people. The channel may or may not be conscious of what the entity is saying through him or her. During the channeling, the channel is generally in an altered state of consciousness such as sleep, trance, deep meditation, or out-of-body. Most of what is currently referred to as channeling is objective channeling.

Accounts of channeling have been recorded throughout history from many cultures. The source of the information being imparted has been attributed to various entities, including: God, various deities, prophets, saints, saviors and enlightened beings, as well as universal mind, collective consciousness, and unnamed thought-form personalities. Channels have also been known by many names; for example, prophets, apostles, saviors, masters, and holy ones. They have also been referred to as oracles, seers, psychics, savants, soothsayers, fortune tellers, shamans, healers, medicine men, witches, and witch doctors, and in esoteric schools as light markers, teachers, and initiates. However, most of the contemporary objective channels appear as ordinary people with little or no previous spiritual inclination.

The following sections will briefly cover a few of the more well-known entities and teachings being channeled. Currently there is a plethora of channels expressing a wide variety of spiritual teachings. Many of these are only discovered by word of mouth, or may have relatively small followings. I have limited the following section to those channels who are widely known and have made their teaching readily available to the public.

Edgar Cayce

Edgar Cayce is probably the most widely known America channel. He was born in Hopkinsville, Kentucky, in 1877, and worked as a photographer. After he mysteriously lost his voice, a doctor suggested that he learn to hypnotize himself to deal with the symptom. While attempting the hypnosis, Cayce went into a trance state and was able to "tune in to" another awareness. Cayce never apparently had another entity enter into his body or consciousness, but rather would be connected with another aspect of his own being. Even when he was communicating with the minds of those people either living or dead, Cayce's flow of information came through his own voice and consciousness. Cayce was a mild-mannered Christian gentleman who shied away from acclaim and offered himself to be tested by many skeptics.

Cayce was able to see things that had occurred in the past, and knew about the life and times of famous people, such as Jesus Christ, and could also see into the future and predict events to come. Cayce's unique gift among channels is that he was able to provide accurate clairvoyant medical diagnosis for people who he never even met. Before his death in 1945, he had accurately diagnosed over 30,000 cases; these are made available to the public at the Association for Research and Enlightenment (A.R.E.) in Virginia Beach, Virginia.

For more information contact:

> Association for Research and
> Enlightenment
> P.O. Box 595
> Virginia Beach, VA 23451
> Phone:(804) 428-3588

Recommended Reading:

> *The Story of Edgar Cayce*
> by Thomas Sugrue
>
> *The Sleeping Prophet*
> by Jess Stern

SETH CHANNELED BY JANE ROBERTS

Seth is an "energy personality essence" that is no longer incarnated in the physical world. Jane Roberts, now deceased, was an aspiring poet and novelist who was contacted by Seth in September of 1963. While composing poetry Jane had an out-of-body experience, whereupon she was introduced to concepts radically different from anything she had ever thought of before. Later that year, while she was experimenting with a Ouija board, the entity who had contacted her identified himself as Seth. From then on, Jane began going into trances regularly in order for Seth to communicate through her, while her husband Rob took down notes of what Seth had to say. Jane was generally not conscious of what Seth was saying while in the trance state, but was instrumental in editing the material after it was taken down. Over six thousand pages of Seth's material was written during the twenty years Jane had been channeling, and Seth is now one of the best known and widely published entities of this century.

Seth's central theme is that we each create our own reality by the beliefs and desires that we hold. Moreover, Seth maintains that man is a manifestation of a soul that is incarnated in this physical world, as well as in other "realities," in order to experience each respective reality or being to its fullest extent to fulfill his totality of being. Man is constantly learning that he must awaken to discover (or rediscover) his true nature as a God-like being. Seth instructs the reader in methods toward realizing this inner being. Other topics include the nature of time, space, energy and matter, the God concept, reincarnations, health, and comments on the historical Christ.

Recommended Reading:

> *Seth Speaks:*
> *The Eternal Validity*
> *of the Soul* (or other books)
> by Jane Roberts.

A COURSE IN MIRACLES

"A Course in Miracles" is a channeled writing designed to teach us to make the choices that will heal our inherent inner conflict and bring us inner peace. The course is authored, through inner dictation, by Jesus Christ. The course was channeled through Helen Schucman, who previously worked in the Psychiatry Department at Columbia University College of Physicians and Surgeons. As a consequence of Helen's determination to find "a better way," she began to hear an inner voice. This inner voice kept repeating, "This is a course in miracles." With the encouragement of her associate Bill Thetford, she started taking down the notes from the inner voice over a seven-year period. Her notes developed into what is now known as "A Course in Miracles."

The Course comprises 1,200 pages in three volumes, consisting of a text setting forth the theoretical system; a workbook for students, containing 365 daily lessons; and a manual for teachers, based on the premise that "to teach is to demonstrate." The course is a self-study method, and it has sold hundreds of thousands of copies. National and international study groups, spiritual counseling, classes and workshops are also available.

The premise of the course is summed up in the introduction, which states: "This is a course in miracles. It is a required course. Only the time you take it is voluntary. Free will does not mean that you can establish the curriculum. It means only that you can elect what you want to take at a given time. The course does not aim at teaching the meaning of love, for that is beyond what can be taught. It does aim, however, at removing the blocks to the awareness of love's presence, which is your natural inheritance. The opposite of love is fear, but what is all-encompassing can have no opposite. This course can therefore be summed up very simply in this way: 'Nothing real can be threatened. Nothing unreal exists.' Herein lies the peace of God." Emphasis of the course is on inner awareness, letting go of fear and guilt and identifying with the oneness, peace, joy and love which is heaven.

For additional information contact:

> Miracle Distribution Center
> 1141 E. Ash Avenue
> Fullerton, CA 92631
> Phone:(714) 738-8380

or

> Foundation for "A Course in Miracles"
> RD2, Box 71
> Roscoe, NY 12776
> Phone:(607) 498-4116 or

> Foundation for Life Action
> 902 S. Burnside Avenue
> Los Angeles, CA 90036
> Phone: (213) 933-5591

Recommended Reading:

> *A Course in Miracles*
> published by the Foundation of Inner Peace; P.O. Box 1104,
> Glen Ellen, CA 95442

RAMTHA CHANNELED BY J. Z. KNIGHT

Ramtha is a "Sovereign Entity" who lived on earth over 35,000 years ago, and has ascended to a higher level of consciousness to teach mankind how to rediscover the "God who lives within you." J. Z. Knight is a woman who had been Ramtha's foster daughter in a previous lifetime, and now channels Ramtha's messages. Knight was first contacted by Ramtha during a fit of laughter prompted by putting a cardboard pyramid on her head while playing with her husband. Since then Knight has become one of the best known channels, especially after being mentioned in Shirley MacLaine's book *Dancing in the Light*. The Knight/Ramtha channeling sessions are lively and often humorous, and can be seen live at seminars or on videocassettes and heard on tapes.

Ramtha's message is that we human beings are divine and immortal entities that have forgotten our true nature as we became a part of the existence that we created. God is the essence that loves us so much as to provide complete freedom for us to experience beingness without judgment or limitation. Moreover, God lies within us, and there is no other redemption than for mankind to realize their Godhood. Ramtha explains in great detail the science of knowing, and the actual process of achieving, superconsciousness. Spiritual exercises are explained and practical guidelines provided in the literature and tapes. Other topics include: death and ascension, creation and evolution, reincarnation, and the purpose of existence.

For additional information:

Ramtha Dialogues
P.O. Box 1210
Yelin, WA 98597
Phone:(206) 458-5201

SIDDHARTHA GAUTAMA
"THE BUDDHA"

I

SWAMI VISHNU-DEVANANDA
SIVANANDA YOGA CENTER

SRI SWAMI SATCHIDANANDA
INTEGRAL YOGA

GURUDEV AMRIT DESAI
KRIPALU YOGA

SWAMI RAMA OF THE HIMALAYAS
HIMALAYAN INSTITUTE

B. K. S. IYENGAR

MAHARISHI MAHESH YOGI
TRANSCENDENTAL MEDITATION

SRI RAMAKRISHNA
THE RAMAKRISHNA ORDER

YOGIRAJ VETHATHIRI MAHARISHI
SIMPLIFIED KUNDALINI YOGA

IV

SRI SRI SRI SHIVABALAYOGI MAHARAJ

SRI RAMANA MAHARISHI

SRI AUROBINDO

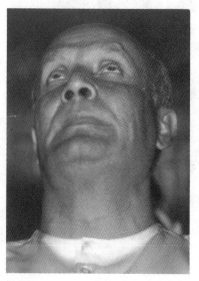

SRI CHINMOY

SWAMI HARIHARANANDA GIRI
KRIYA YOGA

PARAMAHANSA YOGANANDA, FOUNDER
SELF-REALIZATION FELLOWSHIP

SRI DAYA MATA, PRESIDENT
SELF-REALIZATION FELLOWSHIP

BHAGAVAN NITYANANDA

SWAMI RUDRANANDA
NITYANANDA INSTITUTE

SWAMI CHETANANDA
NITYANANDA INSTITUTE

DA AVAVHASA ("THE BRIGHT")
AKA DA FREE JOHN

OSHO RAJNEESH,
THE ENLIGHTENED MYSTIC
(COPYRIGHT NEO-SANNYAS INT'L)

BABA HARI DASS

SATHYA SAI BABA

MEHER BABA

MATA AMRITANANDAMAYI

GURUDEVA SIVAYA
SUBRAMUNIYASWAMI
SAIVA SIDDHANTA

PIR VILAYAT INAYAT KHAN
THE INTERNATIONAL SUFI ORDER

X

DALAI LAMA

SWAMI PRABHUPADA, FOUNDER
HARE KRISHNA MOVEMENT

XI

REV. & MRS. SUN MYUNG MOON
UNIFICATION CHURCH

ELIZABETH CLARE PROPHET
TEACHINGS OF THE ASCENDED MASTERS
(PHOTO BY HARRY LANGDON)

SRI HAROLD KLEMP
LIVING ECK MASTER

XII

JESUS CHRIST

XIII

POPE JOHN PAUL II

MARTIN LUTHER

JOHN CALVIN

JOHN WYCLIFFE
PROTESTANT REFORMER

GEORGE FOX, FOUNDER
QUAKERS

WILLIAM SMITH, FOUNDER
MORMON CHURCH

JOHN WESLEY, FOUNDER
METHODIST CHURCH

MARY BAKER EDDY, FOUNDER
CHRISTIAN SCIENTISTS

MARTIN LUTHER KING, JR.

REVEREND BILLY GRAHAM
EVANGELIST

ERNEST HOLMES, FOUNDER
CHURCH OF RELIGIOUS SCIENCE

REVEREND ROBERT H. SCHULLER,
FOUNDER, CRYSTAL CATHEDRAL

EDGAR CAYCE
AMERICAN CHANNEL

SUN BEAR, FOUNDER
BEAR TRIBE MEDICINE SOCIETY

XVII

EDMOND SZEKELY, FOUNDER
INTERNATIONAL BIOGENIC SOCIETY

L. RON HUBBARD, FOUNDER
SCIENTOLOGY

ROBERT A. MONROE, FOUNDER
MONROE INSTITUTE

Recommended Reading:

> *Ramtha*
> Channeled by J. Z. Knight.
> *Love Yourself Into Life*
> Edited by Dr. Stephen Lee Weinberg
>
> *A State of Mind*
> by J. Z. Knight

LAZARIS CHANNELED BY JACH PURSEL

Lazaris is a consciousness without form, an energy that has never chosen to take human form. This nonphysical entity is often referred to as "the one who waits for us at the edge of our reality." Jach Pursel was an insurance supervisor in Florida, who tried meditating at the suggestion of his wife, Penny, in October of 1974. During meditation Jach went into a deep trance, and an entity Jach later named "Lazaris" started speaking with Penny. This process continued, and soon Penny and Jach were taping the channeling and making the information available to the public.

When Jach is channeling, he is unaware of what Lazaris is saying and his eyes remain shut. Lazaris speaks with almost a Chaucerian Middle-English accent. His sessions are quite lively, humorous, and informative. Contemplative exercises or meditations are given at his seminars, lectures, and workshops held around the country. Lazaris has developed quite a large selection of audio and videocassettes which are also available to the public, and his patronage is growing rapidly.

Lazaris' premise is that we (humans) are essentially evolving, spiritual, immortal beings within and at one with a universe that he refers to as the "God-Goddess-All That Is." And in order to realize our true nature as immortal souls, we must work to overcome our negative programming, our debilitating self-image, and our limited worldview. Some of the topics covered in the Lazaris material include: the New Age, loving yourself, forgiveness, dealing with the ego, creating reality, the higher self, the nature of existence, and the journey home. Lazaris offers to guide you on your journey home to a higher consciousness.

For more information contact:
          Concept Synergy
          302 So. Country Rd., Suite 109
          Palm Beach, FL. 33480
          (407) 588-9599

Recommended Reading:

          The Sacred Journey:
          You and Your Higher Self
          by Lazaris

OTHER CHANNELS

In the last decade, a plethora of new channels have come forth. There are literally hundreds, if not thousands, of new channels in the metaphysical marketplace now. For more information on channeling, check advertising in New Age periodicals and metaphysical bookstores.

Additional Resources:

          Channeling, A Resource Guide
          (audio)
          Audio Renaissance Tapes, Inc.
    Call   St. Martin's Press
          (800) 325-5525

          Spirit Speaks
          P.O. Box 84304
          Los Angeles, CA 90073
  Phone:(213) 826-9197
          (A bimonthly publication on
          channeling)

INDEPENDENT STUDY

Much of the information being conveyed through the New Age movement is in books, and there may not be any organization to join or individual to personally study with. The following are just a few of the more popular books that have had an effect upon the New Age. These books are listed from the older classics to contemporary:

Recommended Reading:

Walden
by Henry David Thoreau

Essays
by Ralph Waldo Emerson

The Prophet
by Kahlil Gibran

Modern Man in Search of a Soul
by C. G. Jung

Discipleship in the New Age
by Alice A. Bailey

The Razor's Edge
by W. Somerset Maugham

Knowledge of the Higher Worlds
by Rudolf Steiner

The Perennial Philosophy
by Aldous Huxley

The Murder of Christ
by Wilhelm Reich

The Journey to the East
by Hermann Hesse

Psycho-Cybernetics
by Maxwell Maltz

Initiation
by Elizabeth Haich

The Road Less Traveled
by M. Scott Peck

Illusions
by Richard Bach

The Aquarian Conspiracy
by Marilyn Ferguson

The Quiet Mind
by White Eagle

Out on a Limb
by Shirley MacLaine

The Way of the Peaceful Warrior
by Dan Millman

Your Erroneous Zone
by Dr. Wayne Dyer

*The Inner Path, from Where
You Are to Where You Want to Be*
by Terry Cole-Whittaker

Healing Yourself
by Louise Hayz

Avalanche
by W. Brugh Joy, M.D.

Unknown Man
by Yatri

MASTERS AND MOVEMENTS

*I*N THIS section, I describe the more well-known and accessible teachings of enlightened, or self-realized, Spiritual Masters of the twentieth century, and the organizations that developed from their teachings. There have been innumerable spiritually evolved beings working to raise the consciousness of mankind, but not all of them collect a large following or have their teachings disseminated to the masses. In fact, many spiritual masters will work only with a select few who have demonstrated their sincerity and perseverance, and do not make themselves accessible to the curious or unprepared. Still other Masters work on the "subtle planes," appearing to spiritual aspirants during meditation or dreams. The various Masters and Movements described here are those that make themselves readily available to the public.

There is an ancient saying that "when the student is ready, the teacher will appear." From my own personal experience, and from listening to the accounts of students from many different Masters, this adage appears to hold true. Each teacher is unique, with his or her own message, personality, and method of teaching. When you look at all the different kinds of people in this world, it is not surprising that so many different kinds of spiritual paths and movements have evolved. There are different teachers and methods of teaching to accommodate all the different personalities and proficiencies of the aspirants. We are all here to learn different lessons in life, and each Master has his own special talents and abilities to assist us on the path of self-awareness. Just as in a school curriculum, studying many different subjects can round out your education; but also just like in academics, at some point you must concentrate in one area to really master the subject.

Studying with a Spiritual Master transcends intellectual speculation and conventional understanding. It stretches your awareness beyond the limited grasp of your mind and physical senses. Most of what occurs within the students lies beyond that which they can relate to by other standards of experience. These student-teacher relationships go to the very depths of the soul. The Master can see a side of you that you don't even know yourself, and can bring it out in you. Ultimately, the Master's role is to help you discover and evolve something within you—the very essence of what you are. Each individual must discover the Truth for himself; but the path is a tricky one, so to seek the guidance of one who knows the way is imperative in the journey. A Spiritual Master is the shower of the way on your own path to Truth and self-discovery. The descriptions I've written are from a limited perspective—my own. Each individual gets something different from each teaching, and from each Master. Your understanding should be based on your own personal experience with the Master and his or her teachings.

As you read through this section, you will find numerous names and titles given to the various teachers. These names can get confusing to a Western reader unfamiliar with the Hindu vernacular, so the following brief explanations are in order: **Baba** refers to a holy man, or "father," and is used as a term of endearment. **Swami** literally means "one who possesses," or "lord," referring to someone in a high position, but is used more loosely to describe any spiritually dedicated man. Many renunciates, monks, and spiritual aspirants are referred to as Swami, and it does not necessarily refer to a Spiritual Master, but acknowledges the spirituality of the individual. **Ji** is a sign of respect added to other names to show additional reverence, such as in **Babaji** or **Swamiji**; one who is referred to by such a name is being held in high esteem as a spiritual teacher.

A **guru** is a teacher, generally a spiritual teacher; and in the strictest sense, one who is awakened, or realized, and therefore capable of teaching others the Truth. A term of endearment is **dev**, so one who loves their teacher may refer to the teacher as **Gurudev**, or "beloved teacher." A **yogi** is one who practices or teaches yoga (the science of the self), and when used as a title refers to one who has attained the goal of yoga, self-realization (God realization). A **rishi** is a seer, one who sees through illusion, or maya, and a **raj** is a king. **Maha** means great, thus a **maharishi** is a great seer, and a **maharaj** is a great king. A **yogiraj** is the highest yogi, and a **yogini** is a female yogi. **Ma** and **Mata** refer to the Holy Mother, and a female spiritual aspirant may be referred to as Ma, or Mataji, as **Sri**, **Shri**, or **Shree**, is also used as a a sign of respect, similar to the English "Sir."

Bhagawan, or **Bhagavan**, refers to a God-man, or a venerable saint, as does the word **Sant**. An **avadhuta** is a saint who has transcended body-consciousness, and whose behavior is not bound by social conventions. A **sadhu** is a dedicated spiritual aspirant, usually an ascetic. A **brahmacharya** is generally a spiritual aspirant who has taken a vow of celibacy, and a **sannyasan** is one who has completely renounced all worldly obligations to pursue self-realization. (Nowadays these terms may refer to any spiritual aspirant, although this is not technically correct.)

Ram, **Hari**, **Vishnu**, **Krishna**, and **Shiva** are all names of God, and are frequently used in spiritual names and titles. **Das** or **Dass** refers to a devotee of God, thus **Ram Dass** or **Krishna Das** refers to a devotee of Ram or Krishna. **Mukti** is liberation, **sat** is beingness or truth, **chit**, or **chid**, is absolute consciousness, and **ananda** means bliss; so **Muktananda** refers to one who has attained bliss through liberation, and **Satchidananda** is one who has realized beingness-consciousness-bliss. Both terms refer to one who has attained self-realization. **Master** generally refers to one who has mastered the discipline of yoga, or is the head of a spiritual lineage. The following is arranged by general groupings, and is not intended to favor one group over another.

SIVANANDA
(SWAMI VISHNU-DEVANANDA)

SWAMI SIVANANDA was born Kuppuswami Iyer of a pious family in Pattamadai, South India, in 1887. At a young age, he was inspired to serve humanity. As a medical student, Kuppuswami published a popular medical journal called *Ambrosia* from 1909 to 1913, for which he served as editor, manager, dispatcher, and journalist. In 1913, Dr. Kuppuswami left for Malaysia in response to an appeal for medical care for thousands of Indian workers on the rubber plantations. By 1923, this ceaseless compassionate service had generated such a dispassion for material life that Dr. Kuppuswami renounced the world to follow *parivrajaka*, a traditional practice of wandering as an ascetic. In 1924 his wanderings brought him to the Himalayan village of Rishikesh, an enclave for yogis striving for God-realization. It was here on the banks of the Ganges that he was initiated into the Sringeri line of Sri Sankaracharya by his guru, Swami Viswananda Saraswati, and plunged himself into *sadhana* (the practice of yoga), which included intense meditation along with *asanas, pranayama*, study, and service. He used his medical skills to serve sick and needy ascetics in the area. Inspired by these practices Sivananda, as he was then called, began writing down his thoughts and to date has written over 300 books on Yoga theory and practice.

In 1938 Sivananda began his monthly review, *The Divine Life*. He soon built the Sivananda Ashram in Rishikesh, which provided a myriad of services: a printing press, a hospital, a post office, and a Yoga training center. Though Sivananda passed on in 1963, his many books and disciples continue to travel the world over serving as personal representatives of his teachings. Some of the better-known in the West are Swami Chidananda, Swami Satchidananda, Swami Venkatesananda, and Swami Vishnu-devananda. The yoga teacher Lilias Folan (PBS-TV "Lilias, Yoga & You") was also trained by Swami Sivananda.

One of Sivananda's main disciples, who became the founder and president of the International Sivananda Yoga Vedanta Centres, is Swami Vishu-devananda. In 1957, Swami Vishnu-devananda was sent to the West by Sivananda with the words, "people are waiting." After traveling coast to coast by car, and a brief residence in New York, Swami Vishu-devananda founded the first Sivananda Ashram Yoga Camp in Val Morin, Quebec (Canada), a 350-acre facility offering retreats and courses in Hatha Yoga, meditation, and Vedantic Philosophy. By 1977 other camps had opened in India, New York, California, and the Bahamas. Swami Vishu-devananda's Yoga instruction has reached millions through his Yoga Centers, which are now found in five continents, and to date over 5,300 Yoga teachers have been trained.

Swami Vishnu-devananda presented Yoga as a popular discipline in the West with a series of five principles, namely: (1) Proper exercise—Yoga postures for overall health and well-being. (2) Proper breathing—to recharge the body and control the mental state by regulating the flow of prana, or life-force energy. (3) Proper relaxation—releasing tension from the body and carrying that awareness to all daily activities to conserve energy and let go of fears and worries. (4) Proper diet—a natural vegetarian diet to keep the body both light and supple, and the mind calm. (5) Positive thinking (Vedanta philosophy), meditation (Dhyana Yoga) to put one in control, purify the intellect, and bring one peace with one's Self by transcending the mind itself.

For more information:

Sivananda Ashram Yoga Camp
Swami Vishnu-devananda
673 8th Avenue
Val Morin, Quebec,
Canada JOT 2RO
Phone: (819) 322-3226
(800) 783-YOGA

Recommended Reading:

The Sivananda Companion to Yoga
by the Sivananda Yoga Vedanta
Centres

Concentration and Meditation
by Swami Sivananda

Meditation and Mantras
by Swami Vishnu-devananda

SRI SWAMI SATCHIDANANDA
(INTEGRAL YOGA)

SRI SWAMI Satchidananda was born as C. K. Ramaswamy Grounder in Chettipalayam, South India, on December 22, 1914. He came from a family of landowners who were devout and often took in *sadhus* and holy men who would instruct the young Ramu, as he was called. After graduating from agricultural college, he took a position with his uncle's firm, which imported motorcycles. At the age of twenty-three he married and has fathered two sons. Five years after his marriage his wife suddenly died, and he turned all his attention to spiritual development. In 1945, at age thirty-one, Ramu went to Palani to study with several *siddhas*, including Sri Sadhu Swamigal, Sri Swami Badagara Sivananda, and Sri Swami Ranga Nath. The next year he entered the Ramakrishna Mission at Tirupurraiturai and received *brahmacharya diksha* (monastic vows), and was given the name Sambasiva Chaitanya. During the next two years he went to Kalahasti to study with Sri Swami Rajeshwarananda, then to Tiruvannamalai to study with Sri Ramana Maharishi, and visited Pondicherry to have the *darshan* of Sri Aurobindo. In May of 1949 Swamiji went to Rishikesh to meet his Gurudev, H. H. Sri Swami Sivanandaji Maharaj. Two months later he was initiated into the Holy Order of Sannyas and was named Swami Satchidananda.

In 1951 Swami Satchidananda was requested by his guru Sri Swami Sivanandaji to undertake an "all-India tour," lecturing and teaching Yoga. In the following years, he began organizing branches of the Divine Life Society in many parts of India and Ceylon (now known as Sri Lanka). Swamiji made his first world tour in 1966, traveling to Europe and the United States, and founded the first Integral Yoga Institute (IYI) in New York City. From here, Swamiji's mission reads as a who's who, with regular world tours and meetings with other spiritual authorities, such as H. H. Pope John Paul II and H. H. the Dalai Lama.

Satchidananda became visible to most Westerners by opening the Woodstock Music and Peace Festival in 1969 to a gathering of over four hundred thousand. Today there are over forty Integral Yoga Institutes all over the world, offering classes in nutrition, yoga postures, and meditation. Satchidananda Ashram-Yogaville, in Buckingham, Virginia, encompasses almost 1,000 acres and is the international headquarters for Integral Yoga International.

Sri Swami Satchidananda has explained his perspective on God like this: "There are not many gods, there is only One. That One has no name, no form, no place. He is everywhere—in actuality, neither He, nor She, nor It. Unfortunately, such abstractions cannot be grasped by our limited minds. Only when the mind expands to a greater capacity can we understand infinite things. That is why, according to our capacity, the Infinite One reduces Himself to a lower level. God appears in different names and forms—to suit the taste, temperament and capacity of every individual." Swamiji teaches from an interdisciplinary perspective, recognizing that "although the paths are many, the Truth is One."

Swamiji has stated the goal of this path as follows: "The Goal of Integral Yoga, and the birthright of every individual, is to realize the spiritual unity behind all the diversities in the entire creation and to live harmoniously as members of one universal family. This goal is achieved by maintaining our natural condition of: a body of optimum health and strength, senses under total control, a mind well-disciplined, clear and calm, an intellect as sharp as a razor, a will as strong and pliable as steel, a heart full of unconditional love and compassion, an ego as pure as crystal, and a life filled with Supreme Peace and Joy."

Swamiji teaches that: "In reality each of us is peaceful and happy. This is our true nature." Since we are not usually in touch with this, he offers various methods for clearing away the toxins and other disturbances that made us diseased so we can regain our ease and realize our true Self. These methods include: Hatha Yoga (physical postures, breathing exercises, and relaxation techniques), Karma Yoga (selfless service), Raja Yoga (concentration and meditation, based on ethical perfection), Japa Yoga (repetition of a sound vibration), Bhakti Yoga (love and devotion to God) and Jnana Yoga (self-inquiry).

For further information contact: ███████████████

> Integral Yoga International
> Headquarters
> Satchidananda Ashram - Yogaville
> Buckingham, Virginia 23921
> Phone: (804) 969-3121

Recommended Reading:

> *To Know Your Self, the Essential Teachings of Swami Satchidananda*
> edited by Philip Mandelkorn
>
> *Sri Swami Satchidananda,*
> *Apostle of Peace*
> by Sita Bordow and others
>
> *Integral Yoga Hatha*
> by Yogiraj Sri Swami Satchidananda
>
> *The Golden Present: Daily Readings*
> by Sri Swami Satchidananda

GURUDEV AMRIT DESAI
(KRIPALU YOGA)

*K*RIPALU YOGA is a form of "meditation in motion" developed by Yogi Amrit Desai, who is known as Gurudev (Beloved Teacher) to his many followers. The teachings of Kripalu Yoga have their origins in the Pasupata Siva sect from India. Gurudev studied under the reclusive Yoga master Swami Kripalvananda—lovingly referred to as Bapuji— who maintained his meditation practice for twelve hours a day over thirty-three years. Under Bapuji's guidance, Gurudev's *kundalini* energy was awakened and he experienced heightened states of ecstasy and awareness. In 1969 Bapuji gave Gurudev both the title of Yogi and his blessings to teach yoga.

In America in 1961, Gurudev started out working from four o'clock to midnight in a paper-bag factory in Philadelphia, Pennsylvania. In addition to earning a paycheck and supporting a family, Gurudev would teach yoga to Western aspirants. By 1966 he had started the Yoga Society of Pennsylvania, and was teaching 150 classes a week.

Today Gurudev has the largest yoga ashram in the United States, the Kripalu Center for Yoga and Health, located on 350 acres in Lenox, Massachusetts. The ashram houses approximately 300 staff members and nearly 300 guests. It serves over 12,500 guests annually, and oversees 75 affiliate groups around the country and in Canada. Kripalu Yoga is one of the most popular and authentic forms of yoga in the United States (practiced most widely on the East Coast), and continues to grow under Gurudev's leadership.

Kripalu Yoga is based upon the utilization of *prana*, the life-force energy of the universe. According to Durudev: "This energy *(prana)* is further explained in Samkhya Yoga philosophy as not only differentiated Cosmic Spirit, God, or Purusha, but also what we recognize manifesting as the individual spirit, the spark of divine within us." Gurudev further describes how prana works in the Kripalu Yoga practice: " At the usual level, prana merely sustains life, whereas at the evolutionary level, awakened prana accelerates healing, rejuvenation, and purification of body, mind and emotions. The power of this secret science of awakening prana lies not just in accessing it, but in also knowing how to raise it for the unfolding of the higher consciousness."

Kripalu Yoga is practiced through a unique combination of disciplines: physical exercises *(asanas)*, meditation, devotion *(bhakti)*, and selfless service *(karma yoga)*. The intention of Kripalu Yoga is to establish conscious communication with the body wisdom, *prana*, and allow it to carry out automatically all the evolutionary purification processes of the body and mind at an accelerated rate. The technique involves moving through progressive stages of relaxation, absorption in sensation and movement, conscious attunement to experience, and free expression of released energy. This process is what Gurudev calls "meditation in motion." Kripalu Center is open year-round to support the transformational process of its guests and residents. Programs and workshops are offered on yoga, spiritual attunement, health and fitness, personal growth, and body work. Retreats at the ashram provide participants a chance for healing and integration of the body, mind, and spirit. Teacher training and intensive seminars are also available.

For more information:

Kripalu Center
P.O. Box 793
Lenox, MA 01240
Phone: (413) 637-3280

Recommended Reading:

Kripalu Yoga: Meditation-in-Motion
by Yogi Amrit Desai

Working Miracles of Love
by Yogi Amrit Desai

Premyatra: Pilgrimage of Love,
Books I, II and III
by Swami Kripalvanandaji

SWAMI RAMA OF THE HIMALAYAS (HIMALAYAN INSTITUTE)

SWAMI RAMA is the founder and spiritual head of the Himalayan International Institute of Yoga Science and Philosophy. Swamiji was born into a learned, wealthy Brahmin family in 1925, in the state of Uttar Pradesh, India. Orphaned at an early age, Rama was raised and instructed in the Himalayas by his Bengali teacher and surrogate father, Sri Madhavananda Bharati. Swami spent many years traveling throughout India and the Himalayas meeting with some of the world's great masters such as Neem Karoli Baba, Ramana Marharishi, Sri Aurobindo, Rabindranath Tagore, and Harikhan Baba. At the age of twenty-four, Swami Rama was initiated into the Order of Shankarachariya, and served as spiritual leader in Karvirpitham, South India, from 1949 to 1952. Rama then renounced his position and went back to the Himalayas to spend eleven months of solitary meditation in a cave. Swami was then directed by his spiritual master to head west, where he studied psychology and philosophy at Hamburg University (Germany), the University of Utrecht (Holland), and Oxford University (England).

In 1969 Swami Rama came to the United States at the instruction of his guru, who stated, "you have a mission to complete and a message to deliver." At the Menninger Foundation in Topeka, Kansas, Swami Rama astonished scientists with his abilities of yogic control over involuntary autonomic nervous system functions, such as his heartbeat, pulse rate, and skin temperature. In 1971 Swami Rama founded the Himalayan International Institute of Yoga Science and Philosophy in Glenview, Illinois. In 1978 he moved the entire operation to its present location in Honesdale, Pennsylvania. This 422-acre campus tucked away in the Poconos is comprised of devotees with M.D.'s and Ph.D.'s who are working to advance the science of Yoga. The institute holds annual conferences and teacher training courses in

Hatha Yoga. The facility accommodates 190 residents and guests, and oversees 21 branch centers around the world.

Swami's teachings are based upon the yogic sciences of personal experience. He is of the Smarta Sampradaya, a popular nonsectarian tradition of Hinduism that follows the Advaita Vedanta established by the famous *sannyasin* Adi Sankara. Rama asserts that "all the religions of the world have come out of one Truth," and that "if we follow religion without practicing the Truth, it is like the blind leading the blind. Those who belong to God love all. Love is the universal religion." Swami teaches that Truth is wisdom that is gained through deep meditation. His belief is that one must know Truth through his own personal experience.

Today, Swami Rama's work is being applied to methods of fighting high blood pressure, heart attack, headaches and other ills. His "holistic health" programs are gaining credibility among conventional Western medical practitioners, and the Institute now offers M.A. and Ph.D. level programs. His training seminars for health professionals include courses in biofeedback, diet and nutrition, Hatha Yoga, and meditation. Seminars, training programs, and retreats are also available to the general public.

For more information:

The Himalayan Institute of Yoga
Science and Philosophy.
RR 1, Box 400
Honesdale, PA 18431
Phone:(800) 822-4547

Recommended Reading:

Living with the Himalayan Masters
by Swami Rama

The Art of Joyful Living
by Swami Rama

*Perennial Psychology of the
Bhagavad Gita*
by Swami Rama

Exercise Without Movement
by Swami Rama

B. K. S. IYENGAR

B. K. S. IYENGAR is one of the best-known and respected yoga teachers in the Western world, with over fifty years' experience. B. K. Sunderaraja was born in Karnataka, India, in 1918. At the age of sixteen he went to Mysore to study with the yoga-adept Sri Krishnamacharya for several years during the 1930s. Iyengar became popular in the West when one of his students brought him from his home in Pune, India, to live and teach in Europe in 1954. He traveled to the United States for the first time in 1956. During the 1960s Iyengar trained many Western students throughout Europe and America; and in 1966, he published his first book *Light on Yoga*, which has become a classic Yoga text.

With San Francisco as a base, Iyengar founded the Iyengar Yoga Institute, which is currently one of the nation's largest and most visible yoga institutions. There are over 150 Iyengar centers around the world, with 100 centers in the United States, and over 500 Iyengar-trained teachers in the country. Over 500 students a week take courses at the San Francisco studio alone. Some of the West's most respected yoga teachers have been trained by Iyengar, and his books on yoga are considered by many to be the best.

Iyengar integrates both Hatha Yoga and Raja Yoga in his training courses, and draws upon the classics of Hindu teachings (Yoga Sutras and the Bhagavad Gita) to explain his philosophies. He describes Indian thought as "everything is permeated by the Supreme Universal Spirit (Paramatma, or God) of which the individual human spirit *(jivatma)* is a part. The system of Yoga is so called because it teaches the means by which the *jivatma* can be united to, or be in communion with, the Paramatma, and so secure liberation *(moksha)*. The practice of yoga is the uniting of the individual will to the Divine will, through discipline of the body, mind, and emotions. Hatha and Raja Yoga are the sciences through which this union, or communion, with God are made.

Iyengar's Yoga system is very popular in the West because it is very practical in its approach and applications, and is oriented to those who live "normal" householder lives. Emphasis is placed on maintaining health and well-being. The practice primarily involves yoga *asanas*, which consists of physical exercises, and *pranayama*, which is breathing exercises. These exercises develop physical, emotional, and mental strength and open up one's awareness of oneself at many levels. One develops a relationship and understanding of God through developing a greater awareness of the self.

For more information:

Iyengar Yoga Institute
2404 27th Avenue
San Francisco, CA 94116
Phone:(415) 753-0909

Recommended Reading:

The Concise Light on Yoga
by B.K.S. Iyengar

The Art of Yoga
by B.K.S. Iyengar

MAHARISHI MAHESH YOGI
(TRANSCENDENTAL MEDITATION)

*T*RANSCENDENTAL MEDITATION is a simple, natural mental technique based on the teachings of Maharishi Mahesh Yogi. Maharishi was trained as a physicist in college, but was not satisfied with the depth of knowledge he gained. Soon after graduation, he met the Shankaracharya of Jyotir Math, Shri Guru Dev Maha Yogiraj, and decided to study with him, spending the next thirteen years serving as his personal assistant. In 1953, Mahesh retired to the caves of the "Valley of the Saints" in Uttar Kashi, high in the Himalayas. After two years, he decided to take a pilgrimage to Rameshvaram, and then to the southern tip of India. It was here that Maharishi was first inspired to give the Vedic wisdom to the people. Although Maharishi did not actually speak his feelings, the people of Trivandrum spontaneously fulfilled the calling by asking him to give a series of lectures. Soon Maharishi was traveling all over Kerala, lecturing and instructing the people in Transcendental Meditation.

After Maharishi's six-month stay in Kerala, followers of Guru Dev and Maharishi formed the Spiritual Development Movement, and in 1955 organized the Spiritual Development Conference, attended by spiritual leaders of many disciplines. At the Seminar of Spiritual Luminaries in Madras in 1957, saints from all over India and over 10,000 seekers of Truth attended to hear Maharishi's message; and on January 1, 1958, Maharishi inaugurated the worldwide Spiritual Regeneration Movement "to bring the direct experience of pure consciousness to everyone in the world through the simple, natural, effortless technique of Transcendental Meditation." Since this time Maharishi has made numerous world tours, founded several universities, and established Transcendental Meditation centers in over 120 countries around the world. To date over 4 million people have been initiated into Transcendental Meditation, which makes it by far the largest meditation movement in the world today.

Transcendental Meditation is based on the timeless Vedic truth that there is a higher nature in man that is eternal and absolute, and that it is man's purpose and birthright to realize this state of "Being," or pure consciousness, within himself. Moreover, it is held that through this "realization," all suffering is alleviated. The process of attaining this realization and applying it to daily living is what the Maharishi calls "The Science of Being and the Art of Living." Through the process of Transcendental Meditation, the meditator is able to directly experience that eternal Being, the deepest level of his own consciousness, a field of pure creative intelligence—the source of all thought and creation. TM is not practiced as a religion, but rather as an effortless, natural practice for unfolding the full potential of human consciousness.

The actual practice of Transcendental Meditation consists of simply sitting for fifteen to twenty minutes twice daily in a comfortable position with eyes closed, and repeating a personal mantra (specially chosen sound) in a prescribed manner. During this simple meditation, the meditator's bodily functions and mental activity slow down, and the practitioner is able to experience deeper states of relaxation and awareness. Over 500 scientific research studies conducted at 200 independent universities around the world have shown that TM benefits an individual in terms of mental clarity and heightened awareness as well as significantly improving physical, emotional, and mental health.

For further information contact...

... the nearest Transcendental Meditation Center listed in the phone book, or:

Maharishi Continental Capital for
the Age of Enlightenment in
North America
1600 North Fourth Street
Fairfield, IA 52556
Phone: (202) 723-9111

Recommended Reading:

The TM Book
by Denisee Denniston &
Peter Mc Williams

Science of Being and the Art of Living
by Maharishi Mahesh Yogi

YOGIRAJ VETHATHIRI MAHARISHI

YOGIRAJ VETHATHIRI Maharishi (or Swamiji) is a *kundalini* Master from a line of Tamil Siddhas in South India. He was born in 1911 in Guduvancheri, a small village near Madras in South India. Vethathiri came from a family of weavers, and started weaving by the age of seven to help his family. From an early age Vethathiri sought after truth and served an apprenticeship for many years under his Master Vaidya Boopathi, Dr. Krishna Rao, who instructed him in the ways of ayurvedic healing and the spiritual science of *kundalini*. After many years of meditation practice, Swamiji evolved his consciousness to the realization of the self, and was called upon to share his insights and awareness with others. He quickly gained a large following, and today has hundreds of thousands of students, with centers throughout India and around the world.

In 1958 Swamiji founded the World Community Service Centre, which strives for world peace through individual peace by the practice of Simplified Kundalini Yoga. Since 1972, Yogiraj Vethathiri Maharishi has traveled around the world teaching Simplified Kundalini Yoga to many thousands, and is one of the few enlightened Masters who works individually with spiritual aspirants. He is a regular speaker at universities, explaining the theory of Unified Force, and has addressed the United Nations to announce a plan for world peace.

Swamiji explains the workings of the Universe, God, and the nature of man through a very scientific method involving the mechanics of "magnetism." The Divine Consciousness is the Absolute Space, or "Plenum," which is the latent potential within and beyond the Universe. From the static state, a fractionalized portion of consciousness creates fundamental energy particles with whirling motion. From this whirling motion of life-force energy particles, a spreading wave is generated, creating a field of magnetism with attractive and repulsive forces. Mass is created out of the joint functioning of energy particles. Whenever the magnetism in the Universe gets intensified, it evolves into physical transformations as six characters: pressure, sound, light, smell, taste and mind. Thus the world of our senses is created. To evolve the mind and awareness beyond limited perception, one must observe the life-force energy *(kundalini)* and merge the individual consciousness with the total consciousness.

Swamiji has developed the advanced practice of kundalini yoga so that it may be practical for householders and Westerners. He calls this practice Simplified Kundalini Yoga, or SKY, and has made it available for anyone regardless of age, religion, or culture. Through the initiation into Kundalini Yoga, the aspirant's life-force energy or "Kundalini Shakti" is awakened and brought up to, first, the *ajna chakra*, or "third eye" point, and then to the *sahasrara chakra*, or "crown center." After awakening these powerful centers of higher consciousness, the aspirant learns to ground the energy through the practice of Shanti Yoga and learns to integrate his or her higher awareness into daily living. Swamiji also teaches the ancient practice of Kaya Kalpa, which rejuvenates the body's life-force energy in order to withstand the aging process and optimize good health and well-being.

For information, contact:

World Community Service
Centre of California
926 La Rambla
Burbank, CA 91501
Phone:(818) 848-1509

Recommended Reading:

Yoga for Modern Age
by Yogiraj Vethathiri Maharishi

Karma Yoga
by Yogiraj Vethathiri Maharishi

World Peace
by Yogiraj Vethathiri Maharishi

THE RAMAKRISHNA ORDER

*T*HE RAMAKRISHNA Order is connected to the ancient Vedantic tradition and was inspired by the great Indian saint Sri Ramakrishna, and founded by the leader of his disciples, Swami Vivekananda. Ramakrishna was born in the Bengali village of Kamarpukur, northeast India, in 1836. As a young man, he went to Calcutta and became a priest at the Kali temple at Dakshineswar. While serving as a priest, Ramakrishna began intensive training *(sadhana)* in various Hindu spiritual traditions. He was unique among saints in that he had experienced "enlightenment" in both Shaivism (God as Shiva) and Vaishnavism (God as Vishnu) as well as in both dualist and nondualist modes of Vedanta. Ramakrishna serves as an archetypal figure who inspired a renaissance of Hindu spirituality at the end of the nineteenth century. His wife, Sarada, who was known as "the Holy Mother," also became recognized as a fully realized saint. A group of disciples formed around him, which became known as the Ramakrishna Mission, the leader of which, Swami Vivekenanda, became instrumental in bringing Hindu, and specifically Vedantic, teachings to Western civilization.

Swami Vivekenanda, whose original name was Narendranath Datta, was born in Calcutta in 1863. He was brought up in a Western-educated, middle-class family, and later studied at Calcutta University. In 1881, Narendranath met the great saint Sri Ramakrishna, and shortly thereafter set aside his plans for a legal career and became a *sannyasin* (renunciate of material life). Following Ramakrishna's *mahasamadhi* (final union with God) in 1886, Vivekenanda embarked on a pilgrimage across India, speaking on Vedanta and inspiring thousands. In 1893, Vivekenanda went to represent Hindus at the World's Parliament of Religions in Chicago, which opened the West to Vedanta and initiated a worldwide interest in Eastern philosophy. He later helped found the Ramakrishna Order in India and the first Vedanta centers in America and England. Today there are Vedanta centers throughout the United States and Europe, and the Ramakrishna Order is the largest spiritual organization in India.

The Ramakrishna Order teaches Vedanta, which is a philosophy taught by the Vedas, the most ancient scriptures of India. "Its basic teaching is that our real nature is divine. God, the underlying reality, exists in every being." The purpose of the religion is then to search for self-knowledge, a search for God within ourselves. The Vedantic view of God is that "it is not possible to define God as being only this or that. God is conceived according to our state of mind. God has form when called Christ, Buddha, or the Divine Mother, and again is without form when thought of as a Divine Force or Consciousness." Some of the main tenets of Vedanta are: (1) Brahman, or Existence-Consciousness-Bliss Absolute, is the ultimate reality. It is the unchanging Truth that is beyond name and form, and is devoid of qualities, without beginning or end. (2) The universe is perceived through space, time and causation, which begins when you receive a body and start thinking. But like water in a mirage, the limited perception of the tangible universe disappears when one enters the state of *samadhi*. (3) The real nature of the human being is the Atman, which is eternal, infinite, and identical with Brahman. The goal of human life is to free one's self from the limited illusion that we are separate from the Divine, and to become free in the Realization of God. (4) The divinity that lies within can be manifested through the practice of yoga, which signifies the union between the individualized soul and the universal soul. The four suggested yogas are: Karma Yoga (path of action), Jnana Yoga (path of knowledge), Raja Yoga (path of meditation), and Bhakti Yoga (path of devotion).

Vedanta is practiced in various ways, depending on the personal characteristics of the individual. It stresses self-effort and direct personal experience as a means for knowing Truth. The four yogas that are prescribed for realization are described by Vedanta as follows: "**Bhakti Yoga** is the cultivation of a devotional relationship with God through prayer, ritual, and worship. In this practice, the human emotions are given a 'Godward turn.' Their energy is used in the search for God within. **Jnana Yoga** is the approach to God through discrimination and reason. The goal is freedom. All of our miseries in life are caused by seeing differences, and so the jnana yogi tries to break through this delusion by seeing God everywhere. **Karma Yoga** is the path to God through selfless service to others. By working in this spirit, the God within each person is worshiped. **Raja Yoga** is sometimes called the yoga of meditation. It is the soul of all yogas. The emphasis here is on controlling the mind through concentration and meditation."

For more information... ████████████████

...on the Ramakrishna Order and Vedanta Societies, look in the directory of the nearest large city to you, under Vedanta, Ramakrishna or Vivekenanda, or contact:

The Vedanta Society of Southern California
1946 Vedanta Place
Hollywood, CA 900068

Recommended Reading:

Vedanta, Voice of Freedom
by Swami Vivekenanda
edited by Swami Chetanananda

The Gospel of Sri Ramakrishna
by Swami Nikhilananda

Vivekenanda: The Yogas and Other Works
by Swami Nikhilananda

KRISHNAMURTI

JIDDHU KRISHNAMURTI was a great spiritual philosopher of this century, who taught the pathless way. He was born in 1895 in Andhra Pradesh, south India, to a Brahmin family. At the age of twelve he was "discovered" by C. W. Leadbeater, Annie Besant, and other Theosophists, and was reared and educated by them in Adyar, outside Madras, to prepare him to become a vehicle for the Lord Maitreya, or World Teacher. A religion called the Order of the Star was organized around him to deliver his message; however, in 1929, Krishnamurti resigned as head of the Order after a series of psychic and physical experiences, and renounced all religions and philosophies regarding enlightenment.

After disassociating himself from the Theosophical Society, he began teaching through discussions and lectures held throughout India, Western Europe, and North America. He is believed to have achieved enlightenment in 1948, at the age of fifty-three, but he had already gathered a large following, even though he clearly stated that he wanted no "followers." Until his death in 1986 at the age of 91, J. Krishnamurti circled the globe giving lectures and discourses. His work is now known around the world, and several schools have been founded in India, Europe, and North America.

Krishnaji's philosophy was summed up by him as follows: "I maintain that truth is a pathless land, and you cannot approach it by any path whatsoever, by any religion, by any sect. That is my point of view and I adhere to that absolutely and unconditionally. Truth, being limitless, unconditioned, unapproachable by any path whatsoever, cannot be organized; nor should any organization be formed to lead or to coerce people along any particular path." The object of Krishnamurti's teaching was to set man free by experiencing truth unencumbered by dogma or mental concepts.

Krishnamurti taught the importance of being aware. To do this one is to give up his preconceived ideas, theories and beliefs, and investigate the source of our experience. The objective is to get out of the state of having experiences, and to remain in the state of experiencing; to veer away from the collection of thoughts and ideas, and to simply "be." As Krishnaji explains: "Truth is the understanding of *what is* from moment to moment without the burden or the residue of the past moment."

For more information contact: ▉▉▉▉▉▉▉▉▉▉▉▉

Krishnamurti Foundation
P.O. Box 1560
Ojai, CA 93023
Phone:(805) 646-2726

Recommended Reading:

The Future is Now:
Last Talks in India
by J. Krishnamurti

Commentaries on Living (Vols. I-III)
by J. Krishnamurti

The Awakening of Intelligence
by J. Krishnamurti

Freedom from the Known
by J. Krishnamurti

Think on These Things
by J. Krishnamurti

SHRI SHRI SHRI SHIVABALAYOGI MAHARAJ

SATHYARAJU WAS born on January 24, 1935, in the small village of Adivarapupeta in Andhra Pradesh, southeast India. When he was quite young his father died, and he was forced to work as a weaver to help support his family. On August 7, 1949, at the age of 14, an amazing thing happened to Sathyaraju. On his way home after playing with his friends, he passed under a tree, and a piece of fruit fell into his hands. He squeezed the fruit and began to tremble all over. As he gazed into his hands, he saw a *jyoti*, or bright light, shining from the fruit, followed by the *omkar dvani* (sound of Om) coming from his palm. Following this, a Shivalinga (a symbolic emblem of Lord Shiva) appeared in place of the fruit, and a *sadhu* (holy man) approached him and touched him between the eyebrows. With this, Sathyaraju lost outer consciousness and went into deep *samadhi* (the superconscious state).

Sathyaraju's experience prompted him to begin a period of deep and intense meditation known as tapas. The next twelve years were spent completing Yugas Tapas; which consisted of meditating for *twenty-three hours per day for eight years*, and then for *twelve hours per day for the next four years*. Then on August 7, 1961, at the age of twenty-six, Shivabalayogi (as he became known) emerged from his *samadhi* with extraordinary spiritual powers received through Self-Realization. In front of a crowd of over 300,000, Shivabalayogi appeared with a strange luster, exuding peace and grace, although his body was almost deformed by the rigors of tapas. For over thirty years Shivabalayogi has been guiding and healing people from all over the world, and to date he has initiated over 2 million into Dhyan meditation. He is now regarded as one of India's greatest living saints, and thousands of holy men and women come from all over the world to receive his *darshan* (blessings).

Shivabalayogi's message is "World Peace through Inner Peace." Although Shivabalayogi is of the Hindu tradition, he teaches no doctrine. In his own words: "Know Truth through meditation *(dhyan)*. Then you will yourself know who you are, your religion, your caste, and your nature. Do not believe what others say and become a slave to religious prejudices ..." Through Shivabalayogi's meditation techniques and spiritual guidance, willing aspirants will be led into ultimate union with God. All answers come through the individual's direct personal experience in meditation. Shivabalayogi is also renowned for his ability to heal, with numerous accounts of the lame walking, the blind seeing, and other ailments being miraculously healed.

The practices consists of regular Dhyan meditation after being initiated by Sri Swamiji. During the initiation aspirants are given Vibhuthi (Holy Ash), which has been consecrated by Sri Swamiji. The aspirants are then asked to concentrate their attention on that spot, and Swamiji will guide them from there. The initiation is solely for the deepening of meditation. Initiates may follow the spiritual path of their choice. Shivabalayogi has several ashrams in India, and he makes regular world tours. Sessions with Swamiji consist of singing of *bajans* (devotional songs), followed by meditation in Swamiji's presence, Prasad (partaking in food that has been blessed); then those who have personal questions or need healing may approach Swamiji for his help. Shivabalayogi does not typically give discourses or lectures, but rather encourages aspirants to learn the truth for themselves through inward-turned consciousness. There are no dogmas to follow, for all things can be known from within during deep meditation.

For additional information:

Shri Shivabalayogi Maharaj Trust
6770 N.W. Jackson School Road
Hillsboro, OR 97124
Phone: (503) 693-1582

or   National Organizer
Ninu Durgesh Kumari
816 S. Vermont Street
Smithfield, NC 27577
Phone:(919) 934-3534

Recommended Reading:

Darshan
by Thomas L. Palotas

Tapas Shakti
by Thomas L. Palotas

SRI RAMANA MAHARSHI

*B*HAGAVAN SRI Ramana Maharshi was the enlightened Master of Non-duality. Ramana Maharshi was born in the small village of Tiruchuzi near Madurai (southeast India) on December 30, 1878. He was born with the name Venkataraman, the second oldest son of a local pleader (legal profession), Sundaram Ayyar. In his family there was a history of one member of each generation becoming a person dedicated to spiritual pursuits. At the early age of seventeen, Venkataraman experienced a sudden profound introspection, which established him in the Realization of the Self, the Absolute. He left his home, leaving only a brief note and taking three rupees for train fare to Tiruvannamalai in the State of Madras.

At the Arunachala Temple in Tiruvannamalai, he gave up all his possessions and remained silently absorbed in the non-dual state, wherein the meditator is absorbed in unspeakable Absolute Union with Being. The young "Brahmana Swami," as he was called, would sit on a bare floor, in a dark pit, or under a tree for many hours, unaffected by external annoyances. He soon gained quite a reputation, and within a year received his first disciple, who would take care of him. The silent sage soon attracted quite a following, and by the early 1900s began teaching aspirants from all over the world. By 1935 his devotees rose to considerable numbers, and later an ashram was built at Arunachala Hill. By the time of Sri Ramana Maharshi's translation into Mahanirvana in 1950, his teachings on Non-duality were known throughout the world.

The Bhagawan taught that you are not separate from truth, from God. Sri Ramana Maharshi stated that "The self is pure knowledge, pure light where there is no duality." Duality implies ignorance. The Knowledge of the Self is beyond relative knowledge and ignorance; the Light of the Self is beyond ordinary light and darkness. The Self is all alone. His teachings focused on obtaining enlightenment, which he expressed as follows: "To know the truth of one's

Self as the True Reality and merge and become one with it is the only True Realization." God, or Brahman, is Perfect Bliss, and "Perfect Peace is the Self." That alone exists and is Consciousness. That which is called happiness is only the Nature of the Self; Self is not other than perfect Happiness.

The emphasis of his teachings is not on reading or on an intellectual processes, but rather on a constant process of introspection and abidance in identity with the Absolute. Inquiring within as to "who am I?" or following the I-thought back to its source, and the discovery of limitless Love or God through self-surrender (non-dual devotion) are also integral parts of the teaching.

For more information:

Ramana Publications
P.O. Box 1326
Sarasota, FL 34230
Phone: (813) 951-0431

You may also contact the Sage Nome, who is the great disciple of Sri Ramana Maharshi, who is carrying on the Teachings of Non-duality and is the enlightened Master of this lineage.

For more information on the Sage Nome, contact:

The Society of Abidance in Truth
P.O. Box 8080
Santa Cruz, CA 95061
Phone:(408) 425-7287

Recommended Reading:

Be As You Are
ed. by David Godman

Bhagavan Sri Ramana Maharshi
by Joan & Matthew Greenblatt

Talks with Ramana Maharshi
published by T. N. Venkataraman

Forty Verses on Reality
by Ramana Maharshi

SRI CHINMOY

*S*RI CHINMOY was born in Bengal, northeast India, in 1931. At the age of twelve he entered an ashram and remained there in intense spiritual practice for the next twenty years. While in the ashram he would write poetry, essays, and devotional songs, perform selfless service, and meditate up to fourteen hours a day. While still in his early teens, he had many profound inner experiences and attained self-realization. In 1964 the Supreme commanded him to come to New York to serve sincere seekers in their aspirations to achieve enlightenment. Currently, there are over eighty centers around the world, mostly in North America, Europe, and the Far East. Sri Chinmoy is very active in lecturing in universities and has written over 650 books, composed some 5,000 devotional songs, and painted over 140,000 mystical paintings. Sri Chinmoy also conducts peace meditations twice each week for ambassadors and staff at the United Nations headquarters in New York, and frequently for government officials at the United States Congress in Washington, D.C. He also meditates with his students regularly at his center in Jamaica, New York, and accepts students at all levels.

Sri Chinmoy teaches that "God is the Infinite Consciousness. He is also the Self-illuminating Light. There is no human being who does not have within him this infinite Consciousness and this Self-illuminating Light." Moreover, he states that "Consciousness is a spark that lets us enter into the Light. It is our consciousness that connects us with God. It is the link between God and man, between Heaven and earth." The human body is considered the temple, and the heart the shrine where the soul resides; and the soul works in and with the body in order to manifest and evolve consciousness. As Sri Chinmoy explains: "For the realization of the highest Truth, the body needs the soul; for the manifestation of the highest and deepest Truth, the soul needs the body."

The practice involved in this spiritual discipline is called the "Path of the Heart," in which love is the most direct way for the seeker to approach the Supreme. In this life-game "man fulfills himself in the Supreme by realizing that He is his own highest self. The Supreme reveals Himself through man, who serves as His instrument for world transformation and perfection." The path does not end with realization, however, as it is necessary to manifest this reality in the world around us. Meditation and selfless service are emphasized in this practice.

For information contact:

Sri Chinmoy Center
86-24 Parsons Blvd.
Jamaica, NY 11432
Phone:(718) 523-3471

or   The God-Adoring Song
P.O. Box 280934
San Francisco, CA 94128
Phone:(415) 584-1027

Recommended Reading:

Beyond Within
by Sri Chinmoy

Meditation, Man-Perfection God-Satisfaction
by Sri Chinmoy

Samadhi and Siddhi
by Sri Chinmoy

SRI AUROBINDO

AUROBINDO GHOSE was born in Calcutta, India, in 1872. He was the son of wealthy Bengali parents who sent him to a private grammar school in England, and then to Kings College, Cambridge, where he was awarded a number of scholarships for academic achievement. At the age of twenty he returned to India to begin a career of teaching at Baroda College, where he became politically active in India's nationalist movement against the British colonial regime. In January 1908, Aurobindo met Vishnu Bhaskar Lele, a Mahashtrian yogi, in Baroda, from whom he learned to silence his mind and experience the spaceless and timeless Brahman. In May 1908, Sri Aurobindo was imprisoned for one year on charges of sedition, whereupon he began an intensive study of the *Bhagavad Gita* and underwent a spiritual transformation.

After his release from prison, Sri Aurobindo went to the French colony of Pondicherry, in South India, where he devoted himself completely to the study and practice of Yoga. While in Pondicherry, his writings on "Integral Yoga" and philosophy became increasingly popular, and followers from all over the world flocked to his ashram. On November 24, 1926, Sri Aurobindo experienced "The Day of Siddhi," where the overmental consciousness *(Krishna)* descended into the physical, and he retired to concentrate on his *sadhana* (spiritual practice). Mira Alfassa, a French woman and his most devoted follower, who was known as "the Mother," assumed the running of the ashram and the spiritual studies. In 1950 Sri Aurobindo died, and The Mother acted as the temporal head of the ashram and the international spiritual community "Auroville" until her death in 1973. Today Sri Aurobindo's teachings are considered classic to spiritual seekers, and study centers are active throughout the United States and abroad. Moreover, Auroville, near Pondicherry in south India, is the sight of numerous reforestation and other community projects, and is one of the most popular stops for spiritual seekers traveling in India.

Sri Aurobindo's spiritual premise is that life is a field for the evolution of spirit involved in mind, life, and matter. Within this play:

> *"man has been evolving, now self-consciously, from the lowest to the highest levels of existence; his latest evolutionary stage will integrate the physical, vital, and mental in a synthesis made possible by the Supermind. Thus the Supermind is the bridge between the lower and higher hemispheres of existence, as follows:*
>
> *Existence (Sat)*
> *Consciousness-Force (Chit)*
> *Bliss (Ananda)*
> *Supermind (perfect unity in diversity)*
> *Mind (intellect and intuition)*
> *Life (vital, organic)*
> *Matter (physical, inconscient)*
>
> *Just as the lower levels of consciousness need to be transformed by the higher three, the Sat-Chit-Ananda is not fulfilled until it completely spiritualizes the entire realms of physical, vital, and mental existence."*

Sri Aurobindo does not offer any strict or prescribed set of spiritual disciplines. His "Integral Yoga" is a synthesis of the forms of yoga discussed in the Gita: Jnana (knowledge), Karma (action), Bhakti (devotion or love), and a fourth one, The Yoga of Self-Perfection, developed by Sri Aurobindo to focus on physical transformation. However, Aurobindo's emphasis does not lie only in striving for individual liberation; he states that one's spiritual aspiration should be to transform the "spiritual, mental, vital and physical orders of existence." Moreover, "The first necessity is the inner discovery by which one learns who one really is behind the social, moral, cultural, racial, and hereditary appearances." Emphasis is placed on directing one's attention on one's own divine nature, and devoting oneself to selfless service.

For more information:

Sri Aurobindo Associates
2550 9th Street Suite 206
Berkeley, CA 94710
Phone:(415) 848-1841

or   Matagiri
HC 1 Box 98
Mt. Tremper, NY 12457-9711
Phone:(914) 679-8322

Recommended Reading:

The Essential Aurobindo
edited by Robert Mc Dermott

Sri Aurobindo, A Brief Biography
by Peter Heehs

Sri Aurobindo, The Adventures of Consciousness
by Satprem

SWAMI HARIHARANANDA GIRI
(KRIYA YOGA)

*K*RIYA LITERALLY means "action," and Kriya occurs "when one acts to combine the action of the mind with breath, with the view to dissolving the mind at its Source." Kriya Yoga is then the science of Self-Realization. Kriya Yoga is a science that has been passed on through different ages by the ageless and ethereal Master of Master Yogis, Mahamuni Babaji. In recent history it was Babaji who drew the father of Kriya Yoga, Yogiraj Sri Shyama Charan Lahiri Mahasay, up to the Himalayas to reveal again the authentic Kriya Yoga. Lahiri Mahasay was born in the village of Ghurni on the bank of the Jalangi river in Krisna Nagar, India, on September 30, 1828. Raised in the Brahmin caste, Lahiri Mahasay was educated in the Vedic tradition, and received the sacred thread, becoming "Dwija," or "twice born," in 1836. Lahiri Mahasay was married in 1846, and fathered two sons who later became Kriya Masters. In 1851 Lahiri Baba joined the Bengali Military Engineering Service as a clerk. He traveled extensively and was eventually transferred to Ranikhet in the Himalayas. It was here at age thirty-three that Lahiri Mahasay at last followed his compulsion to climb into the mountains in search of his guru, and it was at the top of Dunagiri Hill that he was met by the great Mahamuni Babaji and initiated into Kriya Yoga.

After several weeks of training every day with Babaji, Lahiri Mahasay was instructed to give initiation to several disciples who had been waiting for him. Then, in 1865, Lahiri Mahasay's attainment of Realization was affirmed publicly by the famous saint Trailanga Swami, and many seekers started coming to see him. Lahiri Mahasay gathered fourteen disciples under him (Sriyukteswar being the best-known in the West), but he did not start any formal organization, as was Babaji's explicit instruction, since "those getting Kriya from the organizations and unpermitted persons are not getting initiation to the real spirit of Kriya but simply learning about the Kriya techniques." Many of Lahiri Mahasay's disciples developed a following of their own, most of whom remained within India with a small following of dedicated Kriyabans. Kriya Yoga is now one of the most widely known and respected yogic paths in the world, but there are very few people authorized to initiate in true Kriya, and they do not accept many students.

The underlying Truth in Kriya Yoga is this: "The Self is Absolute and One, there is nothing outside of It." All activities and manifestations are then a Divine Play of Consciousness. This Consciousness is much like a screen on which all of the world's happenings, activities, etc., are seen going on, but is not separate from the Self. The multiplicity of states that are perceived by the mind are simply transitional phases on the way to Pure Consciousness. The Awareness of this reality is grasped through vibrations. Vibrations are radiations of the Inner Light, which find dimension in various degrees and rhythms of radiation. Those vibrations, which are perceived through our physical senses, are merely a reflection of a range of vibrations we know as our physical world. The seer and the seen are in the same state, or level of vibration, as the object and its reflection. The mind is the object, and the world its reflection. However, those who are able to become established in higher levels of vibration, transcend the lower states of form and become one in Pure Consciousness. The object of Kriya Yoga is to attain this level of awareness, to Realize the Self, or make conscious union with the One Absolute.

In order to establish oneself in the Absolute, the aspirant must learn to look within and attune to frequencies of vibration that lie beyond physical perception. Meditation and introspection are the tools for focusing the attention within and attaining peace and harmony in your life. Kriya Yoga involves a meditation which "acts to combine the action of the mind with breath, with a view to dissolving the mind at the Source." Attaining the state of Pranayam, that is, the tranquil or still state of Breath, and thereby "eternal Tranquility" (Sthirattva), is the aim of Kriya science. Kriya Yoga is considered to be a more highly developed form of Raja Yoga, a synthesis of Karma, Bhakti, and Jnana Yogas.

For more information:

Kriya Yoga Ashram
4904 Cloister Drive
Rockville, MD 20852

There are also several institutions in the United States that teach Kriya Yoga, including Self-Revelation Church and the Kriya Yoga Center, both in Washington, D.C.; the Self-Realization Fellowship Church in Los Angeles (see following section); the Ananda Community in Nevada City, CA (see Donald Walters); and the Center for Spiritual Awareness in Lakemont, Georgia. Sanskrit Classics in San Diego, CA, publishes several books on Kriya Yoga.

Recommended Reading:

Kriya Yoga
by Swami Hariharananda Giri

PARAMAHANSA YOGANANDA
(THE SELF-REALIZATION FELLOWSHIP)

*T*HE SELF-REALIZATION Fellowship was founded in 1920 by Paramahansa Yogananda for the worldwide dissemination of Kriya Yoga—the universal science of Self-Realization for the development of physical, mental, and spiritual harmony. Paramahansa Yogananda was born on January 5, 1893, in Gorakhpur in northeastern India, near the Himalayas. His name at birth was Mukunda Lal Ghosh, and upon completion of his college studies, Mukunda was admitted to the ancient monastic Swami Order in 1915 by his Master, Swami Sri Yukteswar, and was given by him the monastic name Yogananda. In 1936, Swami Sri Yukteswar bestowed upon him the further spiritual title of Paramahansa.

Yogananda came to America in 1920 and was the first great spiritual master of India to live in the West for an extended period—over thirty years. In 1917 Paramahansa Yogananda founded the Yogoda Satsanga Society of India, and in 1920 established his institution in America, where it is known as the Self-Realization Fellowship and is headquartered in Los Angeles, California. Yogananda's classic book, *Autobiography of a Yogi*, has introduced many thousands of Westerners to the methods of Self-Realization and the science of Kriya Yoga. Today the Self-Realization Fellowship disseminates the teachings of Kriya Yoga through temples, centers, and meditation groups throughout the world and through a series of printed lessons for home study. Yogananda entered *mahasamadhi* (a yogi's final conscious exit from the body) in Los Angeles on March 7, 1952; and since then Sri Daya Mata is carrying on the work as president and spiritual leader of the Self-Realization Fellowship.

The aims of the Self-Realization Fellowship are to disseminate throughout the world the knowledge of scientific techniques for attaining direct personal experience of God. The Fellowship teaches that the purpose of life is the evolution, through self-effort, of man's limited mortal con-

241

sciousness into God-consciousness. Through daily, scientific, devotional meditation on God, man can be liberated from physical disease, mental inharmonies, and spiritual ignorance and demonstrate superiority over body, mind, and soul. An objective of the Self-Realization Fellowship is to serve mankind as one's larger self.

Kriya Yoga is "an advanced Raja Yoga technique that reinforces and revitalizes subtle currents of life energy in the body, enabling the normal activities of heart and lungs to slow down naturally. As a result, the consciousness is drawn to higher levels of perception, gradually bringing about an inner awakening more blissful and more deeply satisfying than any of the experiences that the mind or the senses of the ordinary human emotions can give." The initial techniques of the Self-Realization teachings are: (1) Energization—which enables one to draw energy consciously into the body from the Cosmic Source, (2) Concentration—to develop one's latent powers of concentration, and (3) Meditation—to use the power of concentration to discover and develop the divine qualities of one's own true Self.

For additional information:

Self-Realization Fellowship
3880 San Rafael Avenue
Los Angeles, CA 90065
Phone:(213) 225-2471

Recommended Reading:

Autobiography of a Yogi
by Paramahansa Yogananda

The Divine Romance
by Paramahansa Yogananda

Man's Eternal Quest
by Paramahansa Yogananda

Finding the Joy Within You
by Sri Daya Mata

The Holy Science
by Swami Sri Yukteswar

ANANDA CHURCH OF GOD REALIZATION (KRIYANANDA)

JAMES DONALD Walters was born of American parents in the Rumanian expatriate colony of Teleajen, on May 19, 1926. As his father worked for Esso Oil in Europe, he lived most of his childhood abroad, attending boarding schools in Switzerland and England. With the advent of World War II, his family moved back to the United States and he completed high school in Connecticut and New York. He then spent the next three and a half years at Haverford College and at Brown University, where his interests in the spiritual became the primary focus in his life. After leaving college, Donald began working as a playwright at the Dock Street Theater in Charleston. It was during this time that Don became interested in Eastern philosophy, and was inspired by reading first the Hindu classic *Bhagavad Gita* and then *Autobiography of a Yogi*, by Paramahansa Yogananda. After reading Yogananda's work, Don was compelled to come to California in 1948 and meet with the Master. Due to his "good karma" (spiritual merits), Don was soon accepted as a "Brother" and began to live and study at the Self-Realization Fellowship (SRF) ashram at Mt. Washington in Los Angeles.

Don was privileged to work closely with the Master, to whom he devoted his life, and was rapidly given more responsibilities and privileges in SRF. While working with the Master at their retreat at Twentynine Palms, in the California desert, Donald was asked to edit Paramahansa's Commentary on the Bhagavad Gita and write articles for their newsletter. He was also asked by the Master to lecture on his behalf, and to give Kriya initiations. On March 7, 1952, Paramahansa Yogananda entered *mahasamadhi* (a yogi's final conscious exit from the body). Donald spent the next few years reorganizing the SRF office of the SRF centers worldwide. In 1955 Donald was initiated into the Giri Swami Order and was given the spiritual name Kriyananda. From 1955 to 1958, Kriyananda was the main minister of the

Hollywood Church. He was elected to the board of the Self-Realization Fellowship in 1960. In 1962 Kriyananda was taken off the board of SRF due to personal differences, and began writing and lecturing on his own in San Francisco. It was during this period that he wrote his first book *Crises in Modern Thought.* In 1967, with the help of friends, he purchased some land in the Sierra Nevada foothills, and by 1968 began construction of the Ananda Cooperative Village. This spiritual community has set the example of a successful self-sustaining spiritual community, where thousands come to learn how to live harmoniously and to practice yoga.

Donald Walters was trained by the realized master Paramahansa Yogananda in the practice of Kriya Yoga, a more highly developed form of Raja Yoga. The objective of the practice is to realize the Self, which "is absolute and one; there is nothing outside of it." Moreover, "our egos are nothing but vortices of conscious energy that, within the vast ocean of consciousness, take on the appearance of a separate reality of their own." Through the practice of Kriya, these "separate vortices of consciousness are dissolved in infinite consciousness." The purpose of life is the evolution of man's consciousness from mortal to God consciousness.

Ananda fosters spiritual living and makes it easier for the seeker to go into "deep communion with God." Classes in Yoga and meditation are offered and vegetarian dining is provided. Kriya Yoga is the principal practice at Ananda. Kriya literally means "action," and Kriya occurs when "one acts to combine the action of the mind with breath, with the view to dissolve the mind at its source." So Kriya meditation involves the breath, it is a form of *pranayam*. Ananda's guest facility, The Expanding Light, is open every day of the year, and a "Spiritual Renewal Week" is held during the last week of August each year.

For more information...

...on Donald Walters and the Ananda community and guest retreat, contact:

Ananda's Expanding Light
14618 Tyler Road
Nevada City, California 95959
Phone:(800) 346-5350

Recommended Reading:

The Path, A Spiritual Autobiography
by J. Donald Walters

Crises in Modern Thought
by Swami Kriyananda

SIDDHA YOGA
(BABA MUKTANANDA & GURUMAYI CHIDVILASANANDA)

SIDDHA YOGA is a spiritual path based on the highest principles of life. It teaches us to identify and love the light, truth, and peace within every human being. Siddha Yoga endeavors to bring about oneness on the earth, knowledge, a search for the inner consciousness, and the attainment of one's own Self. The heart of Siddha Yoga is meditation on the Self. Gurumayi Chidvilasananda is the living Siddha master of Siddha Yoga, and the successor of a great unbroken lineage of spiritual masters. She was born into Siddha Yoga and grew up at the feet of her master, Swami Muktananda. At a very young age she dedicated herself entirely to her Guru and his teachings, and at the age of twenty-six she took the vows of monkhood. Before Swami Muktananda passed away in 1982, he empowered Gurumayi with the vast spiritual legacy that his own Guru, Bhagawan Nityananda, had left to him.

Baba was born in Mangalore, south India, in 1908. He came from a wealthy family, but became a renunciate as a teenager, whereupon he was given the name Muktananda. For the next twenty-five years he wandered throughout India on foot, learning from many of the great sages and saints of his day. In 1947, at age thirty-nine, Baba met Bhagawan Nityananda, one of the greatest saints of India in recent times and Master of the Siddha lineage. Baba studied under Nityananda for nine years and achieved self-realization under his guidance. Swami Muktananda introduced Siddha to the West, and initiated hundreds of thousands into the Siddha path. Since then Gurumayi has continued to evolve the teachings and makes regular world tours, initiating many thousands into Siddha Yoga. Today Siddha Yoga is one of the largest forms of yoga practiced in the West.

Through the pursuit of Siddha Yoga the inner conscious energy called *kundalini shakti* is awakened. *Kundalini shakti* is a great spiritual power that lies dormant within the body. Anyone who wishes to experience *kundalini* must do so with his own conscious body. He then tastes divine bliss and ecstasy. This is the secret of Siddha Yoga. The awakening of *kundalini* in the great initiation called Shaktipat occurs through the grace of the guru during a program of meditation called the Siddha Yoga Meditation Intensive. After initiation, a seeker is encouraged to practice Siddha meditation.

Siddha meditation is a very simple and easy process that consists of repeating a mantra given to the aspirant by the guru. With the practice of the mantra, the power of the *kundalini* unfolds in the seeker, which induces the state of meditation within the aspirant. In time the seeker goes deeper into his or her own being until the mind is purified, the emotions become clear, and eventually inner peace is attained. In the final stage of meditation the knowledge "I am complete and I am perfect" arises spontaneously within.

For additional information: ██████████████

> Guru Siddha Peeth
> PO Ganeshpuri (PIN 401206)
> District Thana, Maharashtra,
> India

or

> Centers Office
> SYDA Foundation
> P.O. Box 600
> South Fallsburg, NY 12779 U.S.A.
> Phone: (914) 434-2000

Recommended Reading:

Kindle My Heart
by Gurumayi Chidvilasananda

Where Are You Going?
by Swami Muktananda

Play of Consciousness
by Swami Muktananda

THE NITYANANDA INSTITUTE
(RUDI AND SWAMI CHETANANANDA)

RUDI WAS born Albert Rudolph in New York City in 1928. At an early age he showed signs of psychic development, and was exposed to Buddhist, Hindu, and Western mysticism. Rudi studied under several spiritual teachers, the most notable of them being Sri Shankaracharya of Puri (one of the Jagadgurus of the Swami Order of Shankaracharya) and Bhagwan Nityananda of Ganeshpuri. After many trips to India, studying and practicing spiritual exercises with his teachers, he was recognized as a Swami (one of the first Westerners to be recognized as such). Rudi became a well-known spiritual leader, with thousands of followers in the United States and Europe, teaching the secrets of the East in a way that was more easily relatable to Westerners. Rudi died in a plane crash in 1973, but his teachings are still being carried out in the ashrams he established through his students, one of the most notable being Swami Chetanananda at the Nityananda Institute.

Rudi's teachings involved coming to an understanding that "everything is a part of perfection and must be taken in a state of surrender; it must be digested and transcended." Thus all experiences become spiritual exercises; and difficult experiences in our lives force us to change the patterns in our life that keep us from complete realization. Rudi emphasizes the role of the teacher, or guru, to serve as a role model and catalyst for spiritual development. His spiritual disciplines included both sitting meditations, yoga, and awareness of the energies affecting us all the time during any activity. Moreover, all barriers must be broken down and all energies must be utilized for spiritual unfoldment; thereby, all experience becomes our teacher.

For additional information:

Nityananda Institute
P.O. Box 1973
Cambridge, MA 02238
Phone:(617) 497-6263

Recommended Reading:

Spiritual Cannibalism
by Rudi (Swami Rudrananda)

Divine Presence
by M.U. Hatengdi

Nitya Sutras
by M.U. Hatengdi and
Swami Chetanananda

The Breath of God
by Swami Chetanananda

DA AVABHASA
(HEART MASTER DA LOVE-ANANDA, DA FREE JOHN)

*D*A AVABHASA (the "Bright") is a God-Realized Master whose teachings are called "the Way of the Heart." He was born already Awake on Long Island, New York, in 1939. His name at birth was Franklin Jones. He entered Columbia College at seventeen and studied Western philosophy. He did graduate work in English at Stanford University. Later he studied at three Christian seminaries.

But from the beginning of his college years, Da Avabhasa immersed himself in a spiritual quest. His primary break-throughs in understanding occurred before he met his human spiritual teachers, Albert Rudolph (Swami Rudrananda, known as Rudi), and Rudi's own teachers, Swami Muktananda and Swami Nityananda of India. He received the spiritual transmissions of each of these great yogis and was blessed by them to enter into an esoteric devotional relationship with the Divine Goddess, or Shakti. After an extraordinarily rapid spiritual evolution, which included three sacred pilgrimages to India, Da Avabhasa passed into the most radical or absolute Realization of the Divine Self in a temple of the Vedanta Society in Los Angeles, California, on September 10, 1970.

Since then he has been involved in a remarkable demonstration of the nature and work of a Divine Incarnation. He has provided a thoroughly new sacred literature of revealed wisdom for modern men and women, established and empowered three meditation and retreat sanctuaries (two in America, one in Fiji), and has many thousands of appreciative readers and over a thousand dedicated followers of his Way of the Heart all over the world. His devotees and many others regard Da Avabhasa as the Divine World-Teacher or our epoch.

Da Avabhasa's "Teaching Message" revolves around two principal revelations. The first is that "every ego-"I" is an addict," chronically locked in the adventure of self-created separation, suffering, and fruitless seeking for relief, union, or consolidation. The second principle is that Da Avabhasa is himself the Source of Divine Grace that makes our freedom from egotism possible. Practice of Da Avabhasa's "Way of the Heart" thus proceeds along two lines. It involves increasingly deep understanding of how we create the sense of egoic separation and why all our searches are futile. But even this is a joyous and in many ways miraculous ordeal, because the core of it is increasingly deep communion with Da Avabhasa as the agent of very tangible grace in one's life.

Speaking ecstatically in oneness with the divine, Da Avabhasa writes in his simplest and most popular scripture, *The Love-Ananda Gita*: "Separation is the first gesture made by anyone who has a problem, or who is seeking, or who is trying to account for anything whatsoever. Perfect understanding is the capability to directly (immediately) transcend dilemma, all problems, and all seeking. Perfect understanding is the capability inherent in Love-Bliss itself. I have ... thoroughly elaborated the great process wherein and whereby Love-Bliss-Unity is (ultimately) perfectly realized. Contemplation of my bodily (human) form, my spiritual (and always blessing) presence, and my very (and inherently perfect) state is the principle wherein and whereby the great process of the Way of the Heart is accomplished."

For more information:

Free Daist Communion
P.O. Box 3680
Clearlake, CA 95422
Phone: (707) 928-4936

Recommended Reading:

The Love Ananda Gita
by Da Avabhasa

Feeling Without Limitation
by Da Avabhasa

*The Divine Emergence of the
World-Teacher*
by Saniel Bonder

Divine Distraction
by James Steinberg

GURDJIEFF

*G*EORGES IVANOVITCH Gurdjieff was born in Russian Georgia on January 13, 1877. He was a mysterious man who managed to cover his tracks during his years of searching for Truth; however, he apparently traveled a great deal throughout the Middle East and ventured into Tibet. During this quest, he had studied with several spiritual masters of various backgrounds and disciplines, and developed a unique style and process of learning, which is now referred to as the "Fourth Way." He returned to Russia before the war in 1914, and met his most noted disciple, P. D. Ouspensky, in 1915. It was Ouspensky who wrote the first book on Gurdjieff's philosophy, and who contributed to making Gurdjieff's teachings known the world over. Gurdjieff later fled from Russia with a number of his disciples and settled in France in 1922. While in France, he created the "Institute for the Harmonious Development of Man," at Prieure of Avon. At Prieure he developed "sacred dances," which he began teaching in France, England, and the United States in 1924, and on several subsequent trips. After this touring, he returned to France to write his three major works of the "All and Everything" series. G. I. Gurdjieff is responsible for changing the direction of Western thought. He died in 1949, and the teachings were carried on by Ouspensky and other disciples of the Fourth Way path, and are still practiced at Gurdjieff/Ouspensky Centers around the world. There are over forty Gurdjieff/Ouspensky Centers throughout the United States alone.

Gurdjieff held that "every man is a three brained being." These centers are identified as: The **physical center**—which is functional, instinctual, and sexual in nature; the **emotional center**—which focuses on one's feelings and emotions; and the **intellectual center**—which is the source of the mind. Gurdjieff's premise is that it is our fate to be unbalanced and out of touch with these centers, which keeps us living under a "false personality." Moreover, most of us are operating primarily under the control of one of these centers, and he classified the whole of mankind as being one of three types depending on which center was most predominant in one's character. The first kind of individual is controlled by his instincts and desires, and basically copies others' behavior patterns as a means of survival. The second type of person is a slave to his or her emotions, and is caught up in achieving immediate emotional gratification. The third kind of being is preoccupied with mental concepts and ideas, and is limited by theories and idle speculation. In order to make the transformation into the more highly evolved fourth kind of being, the mechanical patterns associated with each respective type of person must be broken. This process is referred to as the **Fourth Way**.

The Fourth Way is an interactive process, rather than a philosophy or faith. The process not only involves the evolution of man's consciousness, but also the involution of consciousness within man. In a letter to P. D. Ouspensky in 1916, Gurdjieff wrote: "In speaking of evolution it is necessary to understand from the outset that no mechanical evolution is possible. The evolution of man is the evolution of consciousness and 'consciousness' cannot evolve unconsciously. The evolution of man is the evolution of his will and 'will' cannot evolve involuntarily. The evolution of man is the evolution of his power of doing, and 'doing' cannot be the result of things which 'happen.'" The Fourth Way is a way of living, and to understand the process is to participate in the process; and Fourth Way centers and trainers provide the tools to undergo the transformation.

For more information: ▉▉▉▉▉▉▉▉▉▉▉▉▉▉▉▉▉▉▉▉▉

The Fellowship of Friends
P.O. Box 500
Renaissance, CA 95962
Phone: (916) 692-2244

Recommended Reading:

Harmonious Circle
by James Webb

The Psychology of Man's Possible Evolution
by P. D. Ouspensky

Beelzebub's Tales to His Grandson
by G. I. Gurdjieff

In Search of the Miraculous
by P. D. Ouspensky

Periodicals: *In The Work* —
the newsletter of the Gurdjieff work.
Fourth Way Books
P.O. Box 2045
Madison Square Station
New York, NY 10159
(write for a free copy)

THE RADHASOAMI MOVEMENT
(SANT MAT)

*T*HE RADHASOAMI movement was started in 1861 in Agra, north India, by Shiv Dayal Singh, a retired money lender and mystic. Shiv Dayal introduced the spiritual discipline of Surat Shabdah Yoga, which connects the soul of the spiritual aspirant to the primal word or the "sound current," which is heard through the inner senses once awakened by the meditation techniques prescribed by the Living Master, or Sant Guru. By being initiated by the Living Master and practicing the spiritual exercises, the aspirant is able to transcend the "lower worlds," which are ruled by a negative force known as the Kal, and connect with an indescribable Godhead known as Radhasoami.

By his translation, Shiv Dayal Singh had initiated between eight and ten thousand devotees. Today there are estimated to be over 1.2 million devotees, divided into several major sects, which are represented around the world. The Radhasoami Movement is split into two major divisions, one in **Agra** and the other in **Beas**: The Agra Radhaswamis, which comprises the parent branch, known as Swami Bagh, which has been Guruless since 1949; and the Dayal Bagh sect, which was established in 1907 and later formed the Dayalbagh colony in 1915. The Beas branch is referred to as Sant Mat (Faith of Holy Men), and the movement is known as Satsang Beas. The Sant Mat sect was founded in Beas, Punjab, by Baba Jaimal Singh, a Sikh soldier who died in 1903. Sawan Singh then became the Living Master of the Sat Mat group in Beas.

The Satsang Beas movement was further split into other factions. One faction being the Satsang Beas Living Guru, better known as Radhasoami Satsang Beas, which was started in 1951 by Maharaj Jagat Singh Ji. Jagat Singh was succeeded by Maharaj Charon Singh who passed on in 1990 and proclaimed Maharaj Gurinder Singh the spiritual head and living guru. Another faction was the Ruhani

Satsang Delhi, which was founded in New Delhi by Sant Kirpal Singh. Upon Kirpal Singh's death in 1974 three devotees emerged as Spiritual Masters and founded new orders although Ruhani Satsang presently has no incarnate masters. Sant Thakar Singh founded the Kirpal Light Satsang. Sant Darshan Singh, Kirpal Singh's son, founded the Sawan-Kirpal Ruhani Mission, and then passed it on to his son Rajinder Singh. Sant Ajaib Singh founded the Sant Bani Ashram which also has a following in the United States.

The similarities between the sects lie principally in the practice of Surat Shabdah Yoga, which involves connecting with the Audible Life Stream, or the inner light and sound. Radhasoamis also practice vegetarianism, abstain from drugs and alcohol, uphold prescribed high moral values, work for a living (no renunciation of the world) and hold allegiance to the Sant Guru (Spiritual Master). The initiations are secret and the spiritual experiences one has during the spiritual exercises are not to be shared with others. The sects utilize various forms of chanting of the names of God, referred to as *sumiran*, or *simran*, and listening to the sound current, which is referred to as *bhajan*. Generally, the Agra Radhaswamis consider Shiv Dayal Singh as an avatar of the Supreme Being Radhasoami and founder of a new world order, while the Sant Mat sect see him as a revivalist master in the line of saints such as Kabir and Nanak. The Delhi faction see Shiv Dayal as a great successor to the tenth Guru of the Sikhs, Gobind Singh. The spiritual practices and beliefs among the various Radhasoami factions are similar. The primary differences concern who the true Sat Gurus, or Living Masters, are.

For more information:

Radhasoami Dayalbagh
AGRA, Uttar Pradesh, India

or (in USA) Radhasoami Satsang Association
of North America
PB. Nam Prasad Bhatia
5166, Down West Ride
Columbia, MD 21044

Radhasoami Satsang Colony
Radha Soami Satsang Beas
P.O. Dera Baba Jaimal Singh
Beas District
Via Amritsar, Punjab, India
Phone: Amritsar exchange: RAYYA 50

or (in USA) Radhasoami Society
Beas - America
10901 Mill Spring Drive
Nevada City, CA 95959
Phone: (916) 265-3990

Ruhani Satsang
(Founder Sant Kirpal Singh)
2618 Skywood Place
Anaheim, CA 92804
Phone: (714) 995-8181

Kirpal Light Satsang
(Founder Sant Thakar Singh)
R.R 1 Box 125
Kinderhook, NY 12106-9720
Phone: (518) 758-1906

Recommended Reading:

Sarbachan (or *Sar Bachan*)
by Soami Ji Maharaj

Discourses on Radhasoami Faith
by Param Guru Maharaj Sahab

Spiritual Letters
by Baba Jaimal Singh

Spiritual Gems
by Huzur Maharaj Sawan Singh

The Science of the Soul
by Maharaj Sardar Bahadur
Jagat Singh

Divine Light
by Maharaj Charan Singh

Spirituality —What It Is
by Kirpal Singh

Five Interviews
by Sant Thakar Singh

YOGI BHAJAN
(THE HEALTHY, HAPPY, HOLY
ORGANIZATION, OR 3HO)

Y OGI BHAJAN was born in Punjab, north India, in an area that is now a part of Pakistan. He was raised as a devout Sikh, and introduced early to yoga and meditation. At an early age he mastered Kundalini Yoga, and went on to study White Tantric Yoga. After receiving a degree in economics, he began working for the government, married and raised three children while maintaining his yogic discipline. At age thirty-nine he left India for the United States, and began teaching Kundalini and White Tantric yoga. He is founder of the Healthy, Happy, Holy Organization (3HO), which offers courses in Kundalini Yoga and a vegetarian diet. The 3HO has expanded rapidly, with ashrams throughout the United States, Canada, Mexico, Europe, Israel, and Japan. Yogi Bhajan is also the spiritual leader of the Sikh Dharma in the West.

Yogi Bhajan teaches that one should look inward to find God, and that in order to find the divine within, one must purify oneself through conscious living and regular meditation. The universe is described as being in "a constant state of vibration manifested to us as light, sound, and energy," and "the Word" mentioned in the Bible is actually the totality of vibration that underlies and sustains all creation." Moreover, although our external senses only perceive a fraction of this eternal vibration, one can "tune into" this universal essence of creation through meditation, using a mantra. This mantra is that given by Guru Nanak, the first of the ten Sikh Gurus, namely, Sa Ta Na Ma, which comes from Sat Nam, which means "truth manifested."

The Kundalini practice as taught by Yogi Bhajan involves physical postures *(asanas)*, breath control exercises *(pranayams)*, and various meditations, including the chanting of mantras. He teaches methods in conscious living and encourages a vegetarian diet.

For more information:

Healthy, Happy, Holy
Organization
House of Guru Ram Das
1620 Preuss Road
Los Angeles, CA 90035
Phone:(213) 275-7769

Recommended Reading:

The Teachings of Yogi Bhajan
by Yogi Bhajan

OSHO RAJNEESH
(BHAGWAN SHREE RAJNEESH)

*B*ORN RAJNEESH Chandra Mohan in central India in 1931, Osho Rajneesh was raised by his grandparents until the age of seven. He lived a simple childhood, and by the age of fourteen, he experienced his first satori, and for the next seven years he experimented with various forms of meditation. In 1952 he experienced his second satori. He then went on to college, where he was an excellent student and was awarded the All India University Debating Trophy. At the age of twenty-one, he entered into the natural state of enlightenment. After completing his studies, he went on to become a professor of philosophy at Jabalpur and traveled all over India lecturing. In 1966 he resigned his professorship and devoted all his energies to his spiritual work, holding his first meditation camp in Rajasthan.

First settling in Bombay, he would give controversial lectures to audiences of over 50,000. In 1974 he established the Shree Rajneesh Ashram in Poona (Pune), India. This ashram has become the largest "humanistic therapy" center in the world and attracts people from all around the world. Over the past fifteen years, Rajneesh has had over 540 books on his teachings published, and thousands of audio and video cassettes are available on his daily discourses. Meditation centers have been established all over the world, and his followers number over half a million. Osho Rajneesh is one of the world's best-known and most controversial spiritual masters of this century. Osho left his body in 1990, and an appointed council runs the ongoing practical affairs of the ashram and activities.

Osho Rajneesh does not teach a belief system or philosophy, his message is to give total commitment to life itself and celebrate each and every moment. Although raised in a Hindu culture, Rajneesh draws upon the eternal truths from all the world's great teachings. His views often run contrary to traditional interpretations, and his approach to teaching is iconoclastic. The structure of his teaching is dynamic, and designed so that the aspirant sees the reality, not from a concept, but from a continuous exchange with life—a living reality. Life is considered a "divine play," and God is something you experience. His credo is "love, life, and laughter."

Rajneesh employs many spiritual practices for his *sannyasins*. (Typically this word refers to a renunciate, but here it refers to one who has entered into a deep acceptance of life). Loving and laughing are an important part of the spiritual practice, but cathartic meditation is also encouraged. Typically, high-energy movements, such as deep breathing, shaking, compulsive dancing, and whirling, are followed by a quiet period of silent witnessing. Other meditation techniques include laughing and crying, chakra sounds and chakra breathing, and the "no-mind" meditation. Group meditations and workshops are held at the various meditation centers as well as at the ashram in Poona.

For more information:

Chidvilas
P.O. Box 17550
Boulder, CO 80308
Phone:(800) 777-7743

Major Osho Centers in the USA:

New York City, NY	(212) 725-6337
Mill Valley, CA	(415) 381-9861
Yorba Linda, CA	(714) 692-8044
Austin, TX	(512) 327-5900
Seattle, WA	(206) 322-9288

Recommended Reading:

With over 540 books in print, it would be a good idea to review the booklist from Chidvilas. Some of the classics for beginners would be: *The Orange Book, Sex,* and *The Book.* Other great books are *Glimpses of a Golden Childhood, The Book of Secrets,* and *Meditation, the First and Last Freedom.*

BABA HARI DASS

*B*ABA HARI Dass is a silent monk who has been teaching Ashtanga Yoga to the West since 1971. Babaji was born in 1923 in the Almora District of north India. At the age of eight he went to a brahmacharya school for spiritual instruction, and later went off to practice his *sadhana* (spiritual practice) on his own. During this time, he had the several experiences with several Indian saints, though he doesn't discuss his personal instruction or association with other spiritual teachers. Since 1952, Babaji has been a *mauna*, or silent *saddhu*, and communicates with others either through inner communication or by a chalkboard that he carries around with him.

Several American aspirants traveling in India discovered Baba Hari Dass, and persuaded him to come to the United States to teach. In 1971 Babaji arrived in America and began teaching the classical "eight-limbed" path of Patanjali known as Ashtanga Yoga. In 1974 a group of his students founded the Hanuman Fellowship to foster the teachings inspired by Babaji. In 1978 the Mount Madonna Center for the Creative Arts and Sciences was established as a spiritual community and a seminar and retreat facility to "nurture the creative arts and health sciences within the context of spiritual growth." This center comprises 355 acres in the redwoods overlooking Monterey Bay. There are over 100 residents at the facility, which includes a children's boarding school, a bookshop and a library, as well as the retreat and seminar facility. There are also centers in British Columbia and Ontario, Canada, and in Mexico City, Mexico.

Babaji teaches the classical form of Yoga from Patanjali's Yoga Sutras, known as Ashtanga Yoga. Babaji describes God as: "the creator of the world. We don't see his form. We don't know how he came into existence. His creation is He—But God is beyond name and form. Our desires have created the form and we worship our desire. It's a good method, but after reaching a higher stage the name and form disappear." Babaji states that our sole purpose in life is to find God, and to find God you must "open your heart in front of God and He will listen to your prayer. A yogi searches for God in the world and says, 'This is not God ... this is not God ... this is not God,' and he rejects everything. As soon as he finds God he says, 'This is God ... this is God ... this is God.' He begins to see God in everything and accepts everything.

Babaji's practice of Ashtanga Yoga consists of eight parts: (1) Yama—the restraints of nonviolence, truthfulness, nonstealing, continence, and nonpossessiveness; (2) Niyama—the observances of purity, contentment, austerity, scriptural study, and surrender to God; (3) Asana—the physical exercises (postures) of well-being; (4) Pranayama—the control of the breath; (5) Pratyahara—withdrawing the mind from sense perception; (6) Dharana—concentration; (7) Dhyana—meditation; and (8) Samadhi—Superconsciousness. Ashram life also consists of a vegetarian diet, kirtan (devotional singing), and Karma Yoga, or selfless service. Three-week teacher-training courses and retreats are available to the public.

For additional information:

Mount Madonna Center
445 Summit Road
Watsonville, CA 95076
Phone: (408) 722-7175

Recommended Reading:

Ashtanga Yoga Primer
by Baba Hari Dass

Silence Speaks
by Baba Hari Dass

Fire Without Fuel
by Baba Hari Dass

RAM DASS

*R*AM DASS, formerly known as Dr. Richard Alpert, Ph.D., was a psychology professor at various universities such as Harvard, Stanford, and the University of California until 1961. It was during this time that Dr. Alpert met Timothy Leary (another psychology professor at Harvard University at the time) and began experimenting with psilocybin mushrooms and, later, with other psychedelic drugs such as LSD (lysergic acid diethylamide). These experiences expanded Dr. Alpert's awareness of himself, and of life in general, and served as an impetus for focusing his attention on finding the answers to the purpose and meaning of life.

In 1967, Dr. Alpert went to India in search of Truth. There he met an American who had studied various Eastern spiritual disciplines such as Yoga and Buddhism, and who began teaching him various yogic techniques. This Westerner, who had taken the name Bhagwan Dass, eventually took Dr. Alpert to his guru, Neem Karoli Baba, whom the Western devotees called Maharajji. Dr. Alpert stayed with Maharajji for several months, and during this time he was also instructed in methods of Raja Yoga and later given the spiritual name Ram Dass, which means "servant of God." The daily routines consisted of observing a vegetarian diet, practicing yoga postures and breathing exercises, and meditation. One day Maharajji came up and touched Ram Dass on the forehead in such a way as to open up his spiritual awareness. Shortly thereafter Maharajji instructed Ram Dass to go back to the West to share what he had learned, and he has since become one of the best-known lecturers and writers in the field of spiritual development.

The gist of his teachings is summed up in the saying "Be Here Now," which is also the title of his very successful book, outlining his experiences and philosophies. Ram Dass suggests that one should look within for the answers—go beyond an analytical understanding of things and develop an awareness based on personal experience. Ram Dass draws upon many Western and Eastern teachings to illustrate his points, which emphasize learning by doing and being, rather than intellectual speculation. The teachings are designed to make the aspirant his own teacher and to follow his own unique spiritual path, though other spiritual teachers may be invaluable in one's endeavors toward self-realization. Emphasis is placed on learning by doing selflessly for others.

For additional information:

Hanuman Foundation
524 San Anselmo Avenue,
Suite #201
San Anselmo, CA 94960
Phone:(415) 457-8570

Recommended Reading:

Be Here Now
by Ram Dass

Grist for the Mill
by Ram Dass

*Miracle of Love, Stories about
Neem Karoli Baba*
by Ram Dass

How Can I Help?
by Ram Dass with Paul Gorman

SATYA SAI BABA

SAI BABA is an avatar—"a descent of deity to earth in incarnate form." Satya Sai Baba had previously incarnated and lived as an itinerant fakir, settling in the (then) Bombay State in India, around 1872. He was known to have performed astounding miracles and gave spiritual instruction to those who gathered around him in Shirdi, where he was known as Shirdi Sai Baba. Before leaving his body in 1918, he told one of his devotees that he would return as a boy in eight years.

In 1926, eight years after the death of Sai Baba of Shirdi, a boy was born in the remote village of Puttaparti named Satyanarayana, or "Satya." At an early age the child demonstrated supernormal powers, such as materializations, and later quoted long passages in Sanskrit—an ancient language that he ostensibly never learned. Puzzled by such phenomena, his father asked Satya who he really was. Satya answered "I am Sai Baba," but no one in the village knew what that meant. As word spread about the advent of Sai Baba, devotees, who knew of the previously incarnate Sai Baba, began to gather around the young teacher. In 1957 Satya Sai Baba first began giving discourses, publicly, and thousands of people flocked to hear him. Today, hundreds of thousands come to see him during religious festivals in India. He is known the world over, and he has a following of millions. Several colleges have been founded by Satya Sai Baba in India, and centers have been established in many countries over the world.

Satya Sai Baba is perhaps best known for the many miracles he performs, such as materializing objects and "vibhuti" (holy ash), curing people of various "incurable" diseases, foreseeing the future, and bringing things (events, etc.) about. All these miracles are Baba's way of illustrating the power of Divine Love that he has for us. The demonstrations are not meant to inspire us to perform miracles, but rather to illustrate that the divine is within us and to inspire us to seek the God within.

Baba teaches the path of love and devotion. He teaches that inward contentment, peace and bliss is found by liberation from the bondage of the trivial and temporary through daily contemplation on the Highest Self. Constant dwelling on the name (any name) of the Lord, cultivating love and giving up hatred, envy, anger, cynicism and falsehood is Baba's prescription for spiritual development.

For additional information...

...on Satya Sai Baba look up Sathya Sai Baba centers in the phone book, or contact:

> Sathya Sai Book Center
> of America
> P.O. Box 278
> Tustin, CA 92681-0278
> Phone: (714) 669-0522

Recommended Reading:

Sai Baba Avatar - A New Journey Into Power and Glory
by Howard Murphet

Sathya Sai Speaks (Vols. 1-11)
by Bhagavan Sri Sathya Sai Baba

MEHER BABA

MERWAN SHERIAR Irani was born in Poona, India, on February 25, 1894. His parents were of the Zoroastrian religion, but had sent him to a Catholic high school in Poona, and later to Deccan College, where he excelled in academics and sports. On his way home from college, Merwan would regularly stop to visit a woman saint known as Hazrat Babajan, who was his first spiritual master. It was Babajan who awakened Merwan to his realization of the Self through a kiss on the forehead, and who made him aware of his high spiritual destiny. Over the next seven years, Merwan visited with several perfect masters, the last of which was Upasni Maharaj who gave Merwan the experience of gnosis, or Divine Knowledge. Having thus attained spiritual perfection in 1921, Merwan began drawing together a group of disciples, who then gave him the name Meher Baba, which means "Compassionate Father."

After years of intensive training under Meher Baba, his disciples established a colony near Ahmednagar called "Meherbad," which embraced a free school of spiritual training, a free hospital and dispensary, and shelters for the poor. Baba welcomes people of every caste and creed, and would travel throughout the country feeding and clothing the poor and demonstrating such selfless acts as cleaning the latrines of untouchables (the lowest caste in India) and bathing lepers. Baba also spent a time seeking out "advanced souls" to assist them in the completion of their spiritual evolution. On July 10, 1925, Meher Baba began to observe silence, which lasted for the next forty-four years of his life. To communicate with his students he used an alphabet board, and later just hand gestures. His following quickly grew, and sometimes as many as 100,000 people would come to be with him on a single day. Beginning in 1931, Baba began the first of six trips to the West, visiting such regions as Europe, North America, and Australia. On January 31, 1969, Baba left his body, and in keeping with his request, no formal organization was created to perpetuate his teachings, but informally students continue to gather in centers around the world to discuss his teachings and express through music, poetry, dance, or drama their reflections on his life.

Meher Baba was the avatar of this age; an avatar being the periodic incarnation of God in human form. He had come "not to teach but to awaken" mankind to the revelation of all religions of "that One Reality which is God." Baba taught that "the goal of all life is to realize the absolute oneness of God, from whom the universe emanated as a result of the whim of conscious divinity to know itself as conscious divinity." Moreover, "to gain this realization the individual must traverse an inward spiritual path, eliminating all false impressions of individuality and eventuating in the knowledge of the 'real self' as God." Baba saw his work as awakening the world through love to a new consciousness of the oneness of all life.

Baba's teachings emphasized practicing love and compassion, the elimination of the selfish ego, and the potential of realizing God within oneself. Meher Baba has no dogma, and does not place any importance on religious ceremonies or rites. He directs his students to an understanding of the Seven Realities, as follows: "1. The only REAL EXISTENCE is that of the One and Only God, who is the Self in every (finite) self. 2. The only REAL LOVE is the love for this Infinity (God), which arouses an intense longing to see, know, and become one with its Truth (God). 3. The only REAL SACRIFICE is that in which, in pursuance of this Love, all things, body, mind, position, welfare, and even life itself are sacrificed. 4. The only REAL RENUNCIATION is that which abandons, even in the midst of worldly duties, all selfish thoughts and desires. 5. The only REAL KNOWLEDGE is the Knowledge that God is the inner dweller in good people and so-called bad, in saint and so-called sinner. This Knowledge requires you to help all equally as circumstances demand, without expectation of reward, and when compelled to take part in a dispute, to act without the slightest trace of enmity or hatred; to try to make others happy with brotherly or sisterly feeling for each one; to harm no one in thought, word, or deed, not even those who harm you. 6. The only REAL CONTROL is the discipline of the senses from the indulgence in low desires, which alone ensures absolute purity of character. 7. The only REAL SURRENDER is that in which the poise is undisturbed by any adverse circumstance, and the individual, amidst every kind of hardship, is resigned with perfect calm to the will of God.

For more information...

...on the teachings of Meher Baba, look up the local center in your phone book or contact either of the following:

Meher Spiritual Center, Inc.
P.O. Box 487
Myrtle Beach, South Carolina

or Avatar Meher Baba Center of So. Calif.
10808 Santa Monica Boulevard
Los Angeles, Ca 90025
Phone:(213) 474-9454

Recommended Reading:

God to Man and Man to God
edited by C. B. Purdom
(a compilation of Baba's work)

God Speaks
by Meher Baba

The Everything and the Nothing
by Meher Baba

MATA AMRITANANDAMAYI

AMMACHI WAS born on September 27, 1953, on a small island in Kerala, south India. She was born with an unusual dark-blue complexion reminiscent of the Hindu gods Lord Krishna and Divine Mother Kali, and demonstrated an inborn devotion to the Lord by constantly thinking about the Lord and repeating his name. By the age of seven, Ammachi was composing and singing devotional songs, which were known by the whole village. A few years later she began a rigorous and austere penance, living only on tulasi leaves and water, being absorbed in meditation on the Divine Mother throughout the day and night.

During her penance, the Divine Mother appeared to her and became a "mass of effulgence, merged in her." From this day on, Ammachi describes: "Nothing could be seen as different from my own formless Self wherein the entire universe exists as a tiny bubble." From here on, Ammachi was recognized as being one with the Divine Mother, and upon attaining this "Divine Realization," she has been known as Mata Amritanandamayi. Henceforth, Ammachi has been receiving thousands from all over the world who come to learn or be healed, and imbibe her compassion, blessings, and grace. Mata Amritanandamayi is now recognized as one of India's greatest living saints, and makes regular tours to Western countries.

Ammachi's teachings are basically *bhakti*, or devotional, and come from the heart. The learning is not just a mental process, but an experience that is felt in the heart. Although the context from which her teachings are imparted is that of an Indian culture, her message is universal: Love God with all your heart, and love your fellow man. God can be worshiped as a male form such as Krishna or Christ, or as a Devi (Divine Mother), but the essence of the divine dwells within you. Establishing contact with, and merging into, this Divine Realization is the focus of her teachings. The gist is in opening up your heart to God.

The practices involve primarily devotional singing and the chanting of holy mantras (empowered names of God). Devotees practice various meditation techniques, and carry out devotional service. Although the Divine Mother does impart oral teachings, answer questions, and give spiritual advice, the power of her teachings comes from the heart and is felt while in her presence. Sessions are provided in which Ammachi will see every individual who comes to see her, and she will give a hug to the aspirants and impart her love directly to them.

For more information:

Mata Amritanandamayi Centers
P.O. Box 613
San Ramon, CA 94583-0613
Phone:(415) 537-9417

Recommended Reading:

Awaken, Children! I-III
by Mata Amritanandamayi

For My Children
by Mata Amritanandamayi

On the Road to Freedom
by Mata Amritanandamayi

HARE KRISHNA MOVEMENT (THE INTERNATIONAL SOCIETY FOR KRISHNA CONSCIOUSNESS, OR ISKCON)

*T*HE HARE Krishna movement is dedicated to spreading the science of Krishna (KRSNA, or God) consciousness throughout the world for the good of all suffering humanity. The founder of this movement was His Divine Grace A. C. Bhaktivedanta Swami Prabhupada. Swami was born in 1896 in Calcutta, India, and was initiated by his spiritual master, Srila Bhaktisiddhanta Sarasvati Gasvami in 1933. In 1950, at the age of fifty-four, Prabhupada retired from married life, and in 1959 accepted the renounced order of life (Samyasa). Srila Prabhupada came to the United States in 1965 to fulfill the mission of his spiritual master—to spread the teachings of Krishna to the Western world. In July 1966 he established the International Society for Krishna Consciousness, and before his passing away on November 14, 1977, he had established the ISKCON movement through over one hundred ashrams, schools, temples, institutes, and farm communities all over the world.

Swami Prabhupada has written more than sixty volumes of authoritative translations and commentaries of the philosophical and religious classics of India. His writings have been translated into twenty-eight languages, and the Bhaktivedanta Book Trust (which publishes his works) has become the world's largest publisher of books in the field of Indian religion and philosophy. He is perhaps best known for his translations of the eighteen-thousand-verse *Srimad - Bhagavatam* and the *Bhagavad Gita- As It Is*. The ISKCON movement today is well established in centers around the world, and his message is carried through "devotees," or "Sanyasans," and through his writings.

In the Hare Krishna faith, Lord Krishna (KRSNA) is recognized as the Supreme Personality of Godhead, and as the highest form of God, is within all life and substance. Lord

Krishna is the object of devotion and is the absolute truth, the highest there is to seek. Sri Krishna is seen as the creator of the universe, and the destroyer. Periodically, the Lord incarnates into human form in order to teach humanity how to live right. Some of the best-known incarnations are known as Hari, Rama, Buddha, and in the modern age (Kali Yoga) Lord Caitanza Mahaprabhu. The Gods Brahma and Vishnu are believed to have been created by Lord Krishna.

In the Hare Krishna movement, the devotees (those devoted to Lord Krishna) practice a form of Bhakti Yoga—devotional discipline—where one places all his attention on God (Krishna) and thinks, acts and speaks in the name of Krishna. Moreover, this is achieved by chanting the holy names of God either silently during meditation or out loud in a congregation. The classical mantra is as follows:

Hare Krsna, Hare Krsna, Krsna Krsna, Hare Hare

Hare Rama, Hare Rama, Rama Rama, Hare Hare.

By chanting this mantra (which means "that which delivers the mind"), the mind is purified and the devotee develops greater mental control, attains a heightened sense of awareness, and awakens to the pure love of God. The aim is to reach the highest state of consciousness, or understanding of truth, which is Krsna Consciousness (God consciousness). When the devotee achieves this higher awareness, he is delivered from the perpetual cycle of reincarnation and will reside in eternal ecstasy with Lord Krishna. The Hare Krishna movement also promotes the vegetarian diet and advocates refraining from the killing of animals through its numerous vegetarian restaurants and books on the subject.

For additional information contact...

...a local ashram or restaurant (in most major cities around the world) in the phone book under International Society for Krishna Consciousness. Or write to:

International Society for Krishna
Consciousness
3764 Watseka Avenue
Los Angeles, California 90034
Phone: (213) 836-2676

Recommended Reading:

The Science of Self Realization
by A. C. Bhaktivedanta Swami
Prabhupada

The Srimad Bhgavatam, First Canto
by A. C. Bhaktivedanta Swami
Prabhupada

The Bhagavad-Gita As It Is
by A. C. Bhaktivedanta Swami
Prabhupada

GURUDEVA SIVAYA SUBRAMUNIYASWAMI
(THE SAIVA SIDDHANTA CHURCH)

GURUDEVA SIVAYA Subramuniyaswami is the foremost exponent and teacher of Saiva Siddhanta in the west—a self-realized Western spiritual master of an age-old Saivite tradition. Gurudeva was born on January 5, 1927, in Oakland, California, and grew up near Lake Tahoe. He began studying yoga and meditation as a youth, and spent many hours in meditation daily. In 1947, at the age of twenty, he traveled to Sri Lanka, renounced all worldly possessions, and trekked to remote caves to practice yogic disciplines until he attained the enlightenment of Self-Realization. Two months later he met Siva Yogaswami at his ashram in Columbuthurai, who initiated him into the Saivite Hindu religion (Siddhar line) and gave him his spiritual name Subramuniya. It was Siva Yogaswami who gave him instructions for his life mission as a spiritual teacher to the West.

After returning to America, Gurudeva spent seven years in continued spiritual practice in Denver, Colorado, where he had a series of *kundalini* experiences, which brought about many *siddhis* such as clairvoyance and clairaudience. In 1957, at the age of thirty, Gurudeva established in California a branch of the Saiva Siddhanta Church, which had begun in 1949. He also opened the Palani Swami Temple in San Francisco that year, and founded the Himalayan Academy to foster in the West a greater understanding of ancient Hindu culture and spirituality. In 1970 Gurudeva established the Kauai Aadheenam ashram and temple on the Hawaiian island of Kauai, where he lives and guides the advanced disciples of his yoga order. In 1975 he founded a ten-acre spiritual sanctuary on Kauai called the San Marga Sanctuary, and in 1979 Gurudeva founded the international newspaper *Hinduism Today*, which is published in five countries and reaches hundreds of thousands around the world. Gurudeva lectures around the world, initiating thousands into Saivite Hinduism.

Saiva Siddhanta is the path of personal experience of Siva consciousness and self-realization. Gurudeva explains the Self as follows: "The Self, you can't explain it. You can sense its existence through the refined state of your senses, but you cannot explain it. To know it, you have to experience it. And the best you can say about it is that it is the depth of your Being, the very core of you. It is you. If you visualize above you nothing; below you nothing; to the right of you nothing; to the left of you nothing; in front of you nothing; in back of you nothing; and dissolve yourself into that nothingness, that would be the best way you could explain the realization of the Self. And yet that nothingness would not be the absence of something, like the nothingness inside an empty box which would be a void. That nothingness is the fullness of everything: the power, the sustaining power, of the existence of what appears to be everything."

Saiva Siddhanta is a path that places stress on the all-embracing nature of human spirituality, that is, it seeks to reveal that every dimension of life is sacred. It teaches seekers to see God everywhere, and in everyone, inside and outside ourselves. It is a tolerant path, accepting whole-heartedly the many ways of seeking God, and denying emphatically that any path is the one or only path. A traditional manual of this ideal is found in Gurudeva's book, *Living with Siva*. Some of the practices found in Saiva Siddhanta, are a synthesis of Vedic and Agamic insight. Some of the practices include: Bhakti Yoga—devotion to God, Siva, through acts of worship and observing certain acts of moral conduct. Karma Yoga—serving God selflessly through your thoughts, words, and actions. Raja Yoga—involving yogic exercises and meditation. Jnana Yoga—the path of intense mysticism and wisdom, which comes from the direct knowledge of the divine as personal experience transcending all other knowledge. A catechism for Saiva Siddhanta called *Dancing with Siva* is available through the Himalayan Academy.

For information contact:

Himalayan Academy
1819 Second Street
Concord, CA 94519
Phone:(415) 827-0127

Recommended Reading:

Living with Siva
by Sivaya Subramuniyaswami

Hindu Catechism
by Sivaya Subramuniyaswami

Raja Yoga
by Sivaya Subramuniyaswami

THE INTERNATIONAL SUFI ORDER FOUNDED IN 1910

*T*HE SUFI Order is "an interfaith approach to spiritual growth." The Order was founded by Pir-O-Murshid Inayat Khan, in order to "spread the message of unity and promote the awakening of humanity to the divinity in all." Hazrat Inayat Khan was born in Baroda, India, on July 5, 1882. He was born into a family of musicians and became a master musician himself. Later in his career, he was initiated by his Sufi teacher, Abu Hashim Madani, and trained in the four main schools of Sufism in India. Upon completing his training in 1910, he was instructed to spread the Sufi message to the West. For seventeen years he traveled and taught throughout Europe and the United states, inspiring the West with the message of spiritual liberty and world unity.

Before his passing in 1927, Inayat Khan initiated his eldest son, Vilayat Inayat Khan (who was only ten years old at the time), as his spiritual successor. Vilayat Inayat Khan was educated in psychology, philosophy, and music, in both the East and West. He holds an undergraduate degree from the University of Paris, and did postgraduate work at Oxford University in England. He has also undergone extensive training in meditation and contemplation. Pir Vilayat has since successfully taken the Sufi message worldwide, and integrated the principles of the teachings into practical applications, such as counseling and therapy. Pir Vilayat is a recognized speaker, and holds seminars, camps, and retreats throughout the United States and abroad. The "International Sufi Order Founded in 1910" (previously known as the Sufi Order of the West) now has a network that spans the United States and Europe, and has members from around the world.

A brochure on the Sufi Order describes it as "a community of seekers who are drawn to the same ideals of service to God and to humanity. Its purpose is to work toward unity, bringing humanity closer together in the deeper understanding of life. It seeks to bring the world that natural religion which has always been the religion of humanity: to respect one another's belief, scripture and teacher. Its message is an awakening of humanity to its inherent divinity." Sufism is not so much a religion or doctrine, but rather constitutes practices that immerse one into life, bringing one's highest ideals into everyday practice. They often refer to themselves as the "Religion of the Heart," which seeks to see God in the heart of mankind.

The Sufi Order describes its approach as "a school for personal transformation and a preparation for service to humanity. Its esoteric teachings deepen a philosophical understanding of life; the personal guidance which is given provides help in the problems of both outer and inner life; retreats which are made available strengthen the effect of the teachings in one's being." The Sufi Order operates as an umbrella organization for a number of different activities that it sponsors, such as: (1) an esoteric school; (2) the Healing Order; (3) the Universal Workshop, uniting the themes underlying all the world's religions; (4) the Ziraat, an application of Sufi principles to planetary consciousness; and (5) the Brother/Sister Work, which is dedicated to serving humanity.

For more information contact:

Sufi Order North American
Secretariat
P.O. Box 85569
Seattle, WA 98145
Phone:(206) 323-2944

or　　The Abode of the Message and
AEgis Programs
RD 1 Box 1030D
New Lebanon, NY 12125
Phone:(518) 794-8090

Recommended Reading:

The Call of the Dervish
by Pir Vilayat Inayat Khan

Spiritual Dimensions of Psychology
by Pir Vilayat Inayat Khan

The Sufi Message, Volumes I-XIII
by Hazrat Inayat Khan

WHERE TO GO FROM HERE

WHERE TO GO FROM HERE

SO WHERE do you go from here? There are so many paths to choose from, and so many people that are sure that their path is THE ONLY way or THE BEST path to follow. It seems that the less people know from their own personal experience, the more they try to convince others to believe what they believe as a way of convincing themselves. Each teaching has something beautiful to offer the aspirant, but unfortunately many individuals have taken it upon themselves to narrowly define the interpretation of their teachings to suit their own personal convictions, biases, and beliefs. Consequently, many spiritual teachings often get fragmented and/or distorted, and it can be very difficult to discern the Truth.

Each individual is capable of discovering the Truth for themselves. Be suspicious of people and organizations that do not encourage you to think for yourself or to question their doctrines and beliefs. The Truth should always stand on its own. Be cautious of teachings that make you dependent upon outside authority figures, or who have secret knowledge or powers that only their leaders possess to control your way of thinking. Ask yourself: Does this group encourage people to follow their inner guidance, or do they undermine the individuals' integrity in making their own decisions? Ultimately each individual forges his or her own path, your relationship with the divine is unique and personal. Questioning is what leads you to the Truth. Be leery of people who want to control your way of thinking. Trust what you feel inside. Find your own Truth.

Generally, people depend on external input to learn about things: Reading, talking and listening, watching and observing things with our physical senses. We are bombarded by external stimulation, and rarely make the time to just be with ourselves. How can you learn about yourself without spending quality time alone with yourself? We fill our world with distractions, and rarely get a chance to get to know ourselves. In the beginning it is sometimes difficult to be alone with ourselves without something to do; the mind is conditioned to seek activities that stimulate it. But it is in that time of quiet introspection that we can learn the most about our Self.

Try simply sitting quietly or walking with nature, no music, no TV, no attention to outside activity; just listening and observing yourself. It takes discipline, but so does any endeavor that you excel in. Moreover, everyone has time to be alone with themselves, it's a matter of priorities and efficient management of time. When you are sincere about your spiritual development, then you will adjust your priorities and make the time. Even fifteen minutes a day can do wonders for you. Try taking a day off to just be alone with yourself, and you are assured to learn a great deal about yourself and may discover your own best friend.

As each reader will have a unique cognitive understanding about the creator, and will hold a different set of spiritual beliefs, no one form of relating or communing with God will apply to all people. However, there are some forms of contemplation, meditation, and prayer that can be used regardless of your particular religion or spiritual path. Techniques that quiet the mind and withdraw the senses have been practiced throughout recorded time. Every great spiritual master, prophet, or saint took the time to look within, so some form of introspective discipline is apparently required to learn about the Self and God. In other words, spiritual development requires some form of spiritual discipline.

CONTEMPLATION, MEDITATION, AND PRAYER

One of the simplest yet most profound forms of contemplation is simply to observe yourself: To become the observer or witness of your physical, mental, and emotional activity. Thoughts pass by in the mind like clouds passing by overhead; watch the passing thoughts from a distance, and let them go. Detach yourself from the activity. Sometimes it is helpful to picture yourself sitting as if you were watching from the other end of the room, or from some point overhead. Detach yourself (the Witness) from your body, your thoughts and feelings. This will increase your objectivity and will heighten your awareness. Then, from outside yourself, observe yourself as the witness of the self (observe the observer). Another approach is to follow your thoughts back to their source. Find the source where your thoughts originate; be conscious of your consciousness; or with steadfast determination, ask yourself: "Who am I." Go beyond the concept, and feel your way back to the source. Have you ever thought about where your thoughts come from? Most of the time we don't consciously decide what we are going to think. Thoughts just come. When you trace your thoughts back to the source, you learn a great secret about the self. Try to re-connect with your essence, soul or spirit.

As it is hard to concentrate in the beginning, start by sitting quietly and concentrate on your breath. Simply follow your breath in and out. Don't try to control it, just flow with it: in and out, over and over. Soon you will find mental activity slowing down, and you will become quite relaxed. As your mind becomes clear of excessive thoughts, you will become increasingly receptive to a more subtle awareness. As thoughts come up, just let them go. Don't try to stop or repress them, simply follow the breath in and out. Focus on the breath. You can practice this exercise with eyes open or closed. If you do this exercise with your eyes open, focus on one point at eye level across the room in order to maintain your focus of attention. This practice will also develop your ability to concentrate and relax.

One of the most popular forms of meditation is the repetition of holy words or sounds. Typically these words are names for God, or are sounds that activate subtle energies in the body and your consciousness. For instance Jews might contemplate the ancient Hebrew name for God, "Yahweh" (YHWH), or on one of the sound vibrations of the Hebrew alphabet, whereas a Christian could contemplate the name "Jehovah," or "Jesus Christ," or the spiritually charged sound vibration "Amen." By the repetition of the name of the God being worshiped, the mind and emotions are able to focus on the spiritual concept or feeling. It's a form of communing with the Creator. This meditation can be done by either chanting the sound out loud over and over with each outgoing breath, or by repeating the word silently to yourself.

In the east it is very common to chant "spiritually charged" sounds called "mantras." The mantras are usually words from the ancient Indian Sanskrit language, which have tonal qualities that, when pronounced correctly, can raise the subtle frequencies of energy in your body and open up centers of awareness within you. The mantra is particularly powerful if it is given to you by a spiritual master during an initiation. Some common Eastern mantras are Om (or Aum), Shanti, and Hu. It may look or sound funny to you, but try this: Simply place the palm of your hand over the top of your head, but not touching the head, and repeat the sound Om, pronounced "Oooooommmmmmmmmmmmmmmm." You will feel the vibrations from this mantra in the palm of your hand. This exercise raises the life-force energy to the top of your head, and you will feel bliss as the mind turns inward.

Other common mantras are various names of Hindu gods, reflecting the different aspects of God, such as: Krishna, Radha, Rama, Brahma, Vishnu, Shiva, and Durga, or Kali. These mantras are popular with devotional (Bhakti) types of individuals, because when they are chanted with love they create a feeling of communion with God and make their relationship with God more personal. It's like singing to God. Typically, mantras are repeated as a chain of vibrations or sounds, such as "Om Namah Shivaya," or "Om Mani Padme Hum." Often an image or symbol of the God or deity is placed in a prominent position during the chant, and the devotee may burn incense or a candle to get into the right mood.

Contemplation on holy scripture is also a very effective form of contemplation. Deep reflection upon a verse from the Torah, the Holy Bible, the Koran, the *Bhagavad Gita*, or any of the many splendid Sutras from the Eastern teachings can open you up to greater awareness and love for the Creator. The eternal Truths appear to be alluded to in all of the world's great teachings. Passages from sermons, spiritual discourses, and discussions can also provide insights and inspiration for spiritual unfoldment. One of the greatest forms of spiritual discipline is to simply meditate on God. Whether you perceive God with form or formless, placing your attention on the highest aspect of your reality is very powerful. Seeing God through a living example or physical incarnation, such as Jesus Christ, the Buddha, or a guru, has proven to be an effective spiritual path for many people for thousands of years. If you feel drawn to one of the great exemplars, whether currently physically incarnate or alive in spirit, open your heart and surrender your love unconditionally, and miracles can occur.

Communicating with the divine through prayer is perhaps the most popular and successful form of spiritual exercise in the world today. Simply acknowledging God and expressing gratitude to God, opens up a personal communication with the Creator and through this channel, spiritual guidance is provided. The greater your faith, the greater the effectiveness of this practice. One of the most effective forms of prayer is to offer to serve God. Allow the Divine, or The Holy Spirit, to use you as a vehicle or channel to do good works and evolve the consciousness in the world. To simply serve or help your fellow man, animals, or the earth through selfless acts is to live a spiritual life. To perform services in the name of God without seeking recognition or reward is saintly. Moreover, to see the divine in all people, places and things, is to bring out the divine in you. The more you look, the more you will find; both in the world around you and within you.

THE MIND—AFFIRMATIONS AND VISUALIZATIONS

The mind is a powerful tool for spiritual development. As you direct your thoughts, so go your actions. Things that you think about create the reality in your existence. You have a choice to be happy or sad, wealthy or poor, conscious or asleep. Much of the metaphysical and New Age teachings delve heavily into the power of the mind and creative intelligence. The scientific breakthroughs of the twentieth century were considered fanciful before being proven. Such accomplishments as landing on the moon, splitting the atom, or even discovering the atom, were a direct consequence of the power of the mind. Imagine the possibilities if thoughts were directed toward learning about yourself. How better could you spend your time and energy?

There are two very effective tools for directing the mind's attention toward your goals of spiritual development: Affirmations and visualizations. By repeating a statement that expresses those things you wish to manifest in your life, so that your subconscious mind will receive and record clearly, you can effect changes in how you automatically express your thoughts, words, and actions that will affect those desired changes. The imprints that you reinforce through autosuggestion will draw upon the creative energies of your higher self, which attract the energies from the environment to manifest the stated desire. Simply identify the concept or goal, write out a statement that expresses it, and then repeat the affirmation either out loud or to yourself after your meditation or before going to sleep (while you are in a twilight or alpha state). Typically, affirmations are used to focus your attention on a stated goal, or to help bring about changes in behavior, attitudes and thoughts (similar to self-hypnotic techniques).

Visualization techniques work similar to affirmations in that they focus your attention on the object of meditation, and utilize the creative energy to effect the change. When we can clearly picture in our mind a situation that we wish to create in our life, and imagine it as already manifested, then this image and feeling is imprinted in our subconscious mind and draws the necessary energies from within us to effect that change. Most of us realize that we have not fully developed the faculties of the mind, and yet we are still leery of believing in the power of it. But believing in its power provides the power necessary to make use of it. This is for you, the reader, to discover for yourself. Sometimes visualizations are used to make a connection with God or a deity, a spiritual master or entity, or with a manifestation of higher consciousness. By focusing attention on an image or symbol of that higher expression, one can make a connection with the higher energies of that manifestation, often reflected in the form of a vision, an inner sound, or an "out-of-body" experience.

In applying the mind and the will, it is important that you are sure that you are working in concert with "Divine Will," or under the direction of your higher consciousness.

The ego is an insidious aspect of our nature, which lulls us into believing that we "need" so many things. In your soul's effort to evolve itself, it must contend with the ego and its self-centered nature. If we listen to our inner guidance, we will be directed through the experiences in life that will help us evolve the most spiritually. The ego has a tendency to become attached to material possessions, circumstances, and opinions, which limits our spiritual perspective and growth. When we look within and harmonize our personal will with Divine Will (Soul or Spirit), then life's lessons are learned more easily, and we live happier lives.

THE PROCESS OF MEDITATION

During meditation several things occur: Your breathing and heart rate slow down; your body, emotions, and mind start to relax; and you become more aware of yourself. In the beginning of each meditation, many thoughts and feelings stored within you work their way out, as you focus your attention and relax. Everyday living consists of problem solving, and energy is created in the mind in order to find solutions. When the solutions and acts don't keep up with our expectation and demands, excess energy as stress is created and stored in the body, while the mind continues to process the energy in order to find the desired solutions. This excess energy, or "thought momentum," clouds our thinking and inhibits our faculties of higher awareness. The meditation process actually releases the excess energy from the body and mind, like opening a valve. As the mind and body become clear of the old energy, which has lost its vitality, fresh energy is able to flow through you. As you calm the mind and body, the brain-wave frequencies in you head slow down (as do your other biological functions), and your awareness is drawn inward.

In the normal waking state, the mind is typically functioning at a brain-wave frequency of fourteen cycles per second (cps) or higher. This is known as the Beta range of frequencies. As you go into meditation, the frequency of brain activity slows down, and the wavelength expands (more frequency = smaller wavelengths; less frequency =

higher wavelengths). Typically, when we are asleep and dreaming, we have lowered our brain-wave frequencies, involuntarily, to from eight to thirteen cps, which is referred to as the Alpha state. Here the body is able to restore itself, and energy in the subconscious mind plays itself out in what we refer to as dreams. When we are asleep we are not usually aware of this state, but when we are in meditation we are fully conscious. As you develop the ability to concentrate and relax, your brain-wave frequency will drop to a range of from four to seven cps, the Theta range. In Theta, the body is in deep relaxation, and you become aware of the subtle energies within you. You may experience manifestations of energy, such as forms of light and sound, which are new to you. Through deep meditation, the mind will enter the Delta state. The Delta range is between zero to three cps. While in Delta, you become only vaguely aware of your physical body and open yourself to a higher consciousness. A whole new range of experiences open up to you as you go deeper into these levels of expanded awareness, and you may experience profound states of peace and bliss.

As the senses turn from the outer to the inner, you become increasingly aware of activities occurring within you. Just as your physical senses provide for your experiences in the external physical world, your subtle inner senses provide for experiences at other levels of your awareness. As a consequence of heightened awareness, your intuitive or psychic faculties develop and your perception of creation is expanded. It's a natural progression of becoming more aware of who and what you are, and of the very essence of creation. As you start tuning into these different levels of awareness, various energies manifest within you. Various lights and sounds may occur, feelings of energies moving or that you are moving. A vision of God or a deity could occur, or different-colored lights could form in your inner vision, you may see various symbols or images of different places. You may witness events of the past, the future, or see things of other worlds. Spiritual masters, saviors, and saints may appear before you to impart knowledge or answer your questions. You may hear different sounds: the buzzing of bees, the sound of water, or a high-pitched ringing sound. Tuning into these sounds can be a source of ecstasy, and can heighten awareness. You may feel heat in your body, or the sense of energy rising within you. You could feel tingly sensations on certain parts of your body such as between the eyebrows or on top of the head; or you may not even be able to feel your body at all. The phenomenon is merely a consequence of the development, and it is the experience of getting in direct contact with your higher self that is the real accomplishment.

ACTUALIZING AWARENESS

Spiritual development is facilitated by meditation, but it is actualized by the practice of daily living. All the sitting and being with, or within, yourself is all for naught, if you are not able to make use of it. You are the walking example of your own state of consciousness. It's easy to be "spiritual" when you live in a cave or monastery, and isolate yourself from the "real world." But we were born into this world with a purpose, and into a society that is suited to provide the life lessons that we need to unfold spiritually. The real test is in how you deal with your home and work life, with handling monetary and love affairs, and even with driving on the freeway during heavy traffic. Each and every experience provides a lesson, a vehicle for learning about yourself. Adversities occur in our life to test our faith and demonstrate our understanding of spiritual principles. When we don't pass the test, we can see the next one coming. How often do we ponder why certain situations in our life keep recurring? If we really took the time to see the lesson in the experience, then we would not have to go through the trial again. Seeing the underlying cause, and living in harmony and balance with your surroundings, is a true sign of spiritual development.

By becoming aware of the interrelationships with our surroundings, we become more aware of ourselves and of the divine. Look at how you are influenced by your environment, and how external energies affect your state of mind. As you set goals as to what direction you want to take regarding your spiritual development, observe what energies are providing the proper guidance and impetus for that unfoldment and which are holding you back. What kind of life-style do you live? How do you spend your free time? What themes and concepts are presented in the entertainment you watch, and what is the meaning of the words in the songs you listen to? Do they reflect the concepts and virtues you wish to uphold? What do your friends like to do and talk about? Do they encourage you to further yourself, or do they pull you down to a level that you know you've already outgrown? Little by little you can effect the change you desire by simply observing your thoughts, words, and actions. Associate yourself with people, places, and things that reflect your state of mind. This may appear obvious, but we are often held back by simply being too lazy to observe, and change, our program.

Raising the consciousness and expanding your awareness involves being in the "here and now." It is so easy for us to get tricked into becoming attached to what has already occurred, or to become preoccupied with some future turn of events. When we dwell in the past, we limit our state of consciousness in the present. Why carry around our past experiences like a suitcase of old socks? Identify what you have learned from your past life lessons, and get on with seeing what is transpiring with every moment. Similarly, we can get so caught up in what is going to happen that we limit what can be realized right here and now. Even as you are reading this, be aware of what is occurring. As this concept and its experience is occurring, your awareness is expanding. You are not the experiencer, you are the experiencing. Observe yourself: When you catch yourself speaking in past or future tenses, or allowing your mind to cling to the past or the future, then simply bring the conversation or thought process back to the present and become aware of what you are experiencing right here and now. Go deep within that feeling. Of course you reference the past and plan for the future, but you must learn to live in the now to be conscious. Moreover, your true nature, your higher self, is always peaceful and happy; if you find yourself in any other state, simply go within and find your indwelling spirit. The state of consciousness you are in is completely up to you. Why allow yourself to be in any lesser state? When you are not at peace or happy, you simply need to go within and find yourself.

THE SPIRITUAL NOTEBOOK

In order to better be able to observe your state of mind, and the changes that are occurring in your consciousness, keep a spiritual notebook, or journal. The act of sitting down and expressing on paper the various aspects of your development, brings out more of what is occurring within you and enables you to clarify subconscious thoughts and feelings. Moreover, keeping a spiritual notebook will assist you in organizing your path of development and in keeping track of the subtle changes occurring within you. All you need to get started is a three-ring binder, tab dividers for five sections, college-ruled paper, and a pen. Your journal should be set up to reflect your own personal interests; however, I am going to suggest a format that you can modify as you please.

The first section in your Spiritual Notebook you can label **Dreams**. Keep this notebook and a pen near your bed, and as soon as you wake up in the morning pick up the pen and just start writing all you can remember about your dreams. Sometimes in the beginning it is difficult to remember much of what you had been dreaming, but with practice it gets easier. Just before falling asleep at night, tell yourself that you're going to remember your dreams and picture yourself remembering and writing it all down. You will find that the suggestion will help you remember. Even if you only recall portions of your dreams, it's good to jot down what you can. Your dreams can tell you a lot about what is occurring in your subconscious mind, and will help you get in touch with hidden thoughts and feelings. Dreams are often symbolic representations of subconscious mental activity. By analyzing your dreams, you can discover a lot about activity within your psyche, and identify areas that you may need to work on but that may have been repressed from your awakened consciousness. Left undealt with, these subconscious fears or mental attachments can stifle your spiritual progress. Don't rely on others to interpret your dreams either, as each individual thinks with a different cognitive understanding, and the same symbol will represent different things to different people. Eventually you will recognize the meaning of your dreams; sometimes only in retrospect many days later. You may also have some spectacular experiences while in your dream state, and learn some very valuable things that would be good to remember. Once you get in the practice, it's easy.

The next section in your journal you can use to write about your **spiritual experiences**. During times of quiet introspection or meditation, you will become aware of things that would be handy to write down for future reference. These experiences could include various phenomena that occur during your meditation (which is a sign that you are accessing higher states of awareness), or it could include a "realization" you had. During your spiritual discipline, regardless of the particular form you adopt, you will become aware of things you previously may never have thought about. It's as if you've always known them to be true, but you were previously not conscious of it. The "knowing" was innate within you, but you hadn't accessed it yet. Emotions and feelings may also surface that would be valuable to jot down and contemplate. Moreover, through daily living you are learning valuable lessons that will help you unfold. By writing down what you have learned you will be better prepared for the next test that comes your way. As you learn to work in harmony with spirit and follow your inner guidance, you will gain mastery over your life and enjoy living more fully.

In the third section you can include **reminders** of things that you are going to keep track of. It would be handy to write down the goals and objectives of your spiritual development, and your strategy for getting there. If you would like to use affirmations and visualizations to assist you in your practice, then you could write them down here and keep to a schedule for going over them. As you come across things you've read or heard that really strike a chord with you, jot them down for future reference and inspiration. If you hear about a good group or teacher you would like to see, jot down their name and how to contact them. If someone refers to a good book or resource for you, get the information you need and write it down, so you can look it up when you have the time. Here you can plan and organize your custom-designed path, and keep track of what you got out of your studies.

The fifth section is set aside for writing out your thoughts and feelings—a **journal**. Through creative expression you can learn a lot about yourself. By simply writing about your ideas and beliefs, you can develop a conceptual framework about yourself and the world you live in, and identify the areas that you have not thought about and may want to explore. Try writing yourself a short essay about your concept of what God is, about what the purpose of creation is, and who you are. Write out your ideas about love and relationships, what your concept of success is, and what your religious convictions are, and you will learn a great deal about yourself. Try contemplating on the purpose of your existence, and then sit down and start writing. You may be surprised at what you will learn. If you are still unsure, ask within for guidance and direction and see what things materialize in your life to inspire you. Finally, if you catch yourself reacting to something or saying something without thinking, write out the thoughts and feelings you have about that subject. By developing such an understanding of yourself, you will be able to cope with situations easier and will feel better about yourself.

The last section is for what I call a **tool box** for spiritual development. In this section, write down helpful tools for learning, such as spiritual contemplative techniques, meditation practices, physical and mental exercises, and prayers. You can also write down concepts that help you adjust your attitude or inspire you, answers to questions that keep coming up in your life, and the names of people, places, and things that help you through certain trials or challenges. Here you write out the "how to's" of spiritual development.

PERSPECTIVE

With our busy schedules, it takes a concerted effort to make time to write in a journal or to meditate, but then what's the purpose in our existence anyway? Is the goal to accumulate as much wealth as we can, and is our free time best spent entertaining ourselves, or is there a greater reason for our existence? If you've read this far, you must know that there is a little more to life than merely sense gratification. The question is, what are you willing to contribute toward your own development? This, of course, is a decision you must make for yourself, and the answers lie within you. Spiritual development is the greatest source of happiness for those who have made the effort. What else of any importance is there? Imagine finding real meaning in your life, a purpose for your existence, a real reason for living. There is a whole quality or dimension to life that most people are missing. It is the difference between just existing and really living. Life is an adventure, and if you don't feel the thrill of just being alive, then you haven't spent enough time getting to know yourself and learning about why you were born.

To know the Self is the highest fulfillment. To be in conscious contact with your Creator is sheer bliss. Look around you, how many people are really happy? Some people mask their unhappiness by constantly entertaining themselves or by covering their real feelings with stimulants or depressants. But when you look in the eyes of one who has discovered that which lies deepest within, you will see a profound peace that is unlike that of other people. When you make conscious contact with your higher self, you don't have to do anything to be happy because complete contentment and happiness is your natural state. Whenever you are not oozing in joy, you're not in touch with your Self. It's that simple. To know the Self is to be, to be is total freedom, and total freedom is ecstasy. There is really no word for the peace within yourself, it defies sense perception and intellectual grasp. You owe it to yourself to know yourself.

READER RESPONSE

*C*OMMENTS ABOUT the book or submissions for the next edition of *The Spiritual Seeker's Guide* can be sent to the following address(with a self-addressed stamped envelope). Due to the number of responses I cannot guarantee inclusion in the next edition or a personal reply to any correspondence:

Steven S. Sadleir
Self Awareness Institute
219 Broadway, Suite 417-S
Laguna Beach, CA 92651
Phone: (714) 491-3356

The Self Awareness Institute is a college for evolving your conscious awareness. SAI provides tools to help you reactivate your higher mind and fully evolve your latent potential as a human being. We are non-sectarian, our teaching methods are based on three principles: (1) think for yourself, (2) learn through your personal experience, and (3) fulfill your life purpose.

We offer meditation intensives, retreats, training seminars for developing higher awareness and weekend workshops in Kaya Kalpa — a scientific method of regenerating your life force energy to slow down the aging process and develop mental acuity. For an information packet, contact the Self Awareness Institute.

Please tell your friends about this book.

VEDIC RELIGION

*T*HE VEDIC religion is based on the Eternal Truths, or Sanatana Dharma, as recorded in the Vedas. The Vedas refer generally to an entire corpus of literature extending from the *Rig Veda* to the Upanishads, and include in the broadest definitions the Sutras and Vedanta, which were developed much later. The *Rig Veda* is the oldest scripture in the world, dating back to (approximately) 1400 B.C. The "collections" of the Vedas comprise four principal texts: the *Rig Veda*, the *Yajur Veda*, the *Sama Veda*, and the *Atharva Veda*.

The Vedas were written in the ancient language of Sanskrit. The Sanskrit word *Veda* denotes "knowledge." The Vedic literature came to be considered the divinely revealed work that contains the truth of all existence and all time. The religion of the Vedas is primarily one of sacrifice to many gods who are conceived as powers in the heavens and earth, and divine counterparts to humanity. The Vedas explain the proper structure of existence and of society, and the truths as to the purpose and meaning of existence. The *Rig Veda* contains verses of praise, and is famed for its descriptions of the ritual use of *Soma*, the divine elixir that provides visions of God. The *Yajur Veda* explains the sacrificial formulas to be used by priests. The *Sama Veda* contains verses or chants for priests at the time of sacrifices. And the *Atharva Veda* is a collection of spells and magical means of obtaining human desires in this world.

Much later, these works were expanded into a collection of diverse speculations regarding liberation, metaphysics, and epistemology, which is known as the Upanishads. These compilations probably date back to the first millennium B.C., but the only systematic summary of the Upanishads appears in the eighth century A.D. The Upanishads generally refer to a collection of 108 texts on secret doctrine, but more specifically refer to the thirteen classical texts that are the authoritative source of Vedic Wisdom. These texts include the *Isa, Kena, Katha, Maitri,*

303

Prasna, Mundaka, Aitareya, Mandukya, Kausitaki, Chandogya, Taittiriya, Svetasvatara, and *Brihadaranyaka* Upanishads.

The Sanskrit word *upanishad* means "knowledge," or *vidya*, which, when received from a competent teacher, totally loosens the bondage of the world and enables the pupil to realize the Self. The contents and symbolism of each Upanishad are as separate as the history, traditions, and texts of the Vedic schools from which they came. They generally agree on problems of the human condition and the solutions, the superiority of the spiritual to the physical, that knowledge is preferable to ignorance, and that one must be disciplined to attain true spiritual wisdom. The Upanishads do explain methods of attaining spiritual freedom and spiritual wisdom, including specific techniques and practices. The Upanishads, with the Vedanta Sutras and the *Bhagavad Gita*, constitute the authoritative sources of the Vedanta schools of thought.

VEDANTA

*E*ARLY SCHOOLS of Vedanta include the *Vedantasutras* (or Brahma Sutras), which are attributed to Badarayana, and the *Mimamsasutras*, of Jaimini, both of which were written in the first or second century B.C. The *Vedantasutras* places emphasis on the Upanishads and convey information about liberation and the way to it, in other words, knowledge (jnana). The *Mimamsasutras* views the entire corpus of Vedic scripture as essentially composed of injunctions to perform ritual actions to various gods and emphasizes the scripture found in the earlier sections of the Vedas (e.g. Brahmanas) which have to do with *karma*, action. (See also The Ramakrishna Order in the section in "Masters and Movements".)

The *Advaita Vedanta* is the most widely known of classical Vedanta systems. The earliest texts were written around A.D. 600 and attributed to Gaudapada. This system is referred to as "nondualism," since it argues that all distinctions are illusion and the only reality is Brahman (the supreme spirit, or god). Closely associated with Advaita is the *Brahmasutrabhasya*, which is probably the most widely studied text of classical philosophy in India today. Its writing is attributed to Sankara (eighth century), whose students developed and proliferated its teachings. The essence of the teaching is to point the way to the liberation of the true self, soul or Brahman, from the bondage of rebirth *(samsara)*, or reincarnation. This bondage is due to ignorance (*Avidya* or *Maya*), which is removed with knowledge *(vidya)* via reasoning, study, and meditation.

Visista Advaita Vedanta was developed by philosophers of the Sri Vaisnava sect (devotees of Vishnu) in south India during the first millennium A.D. This interpretation of the Upanishads stresses theism and devotion. In Visista Advaita Vedanta, Brahman (or Vishnu) is considered awareness, trust, or reality as substance with modes of being conscious selves (*jiva* or *cit*) and unconscious matter *(acit)*, as opposed to objectless pure consciousness as in Advita Vedanta. Moreover, Brahman is considered the ruler and redeemer, whose creation provides a stage for the individual's quest for realization through karmic activity. The aim is to give oneself to god (Brahman), which is the totality of all selves. To reach Brahman, one must practice desireless action (Karma Yoga), and devotion (Bhakti Yoga), which leads to a direct awareness of Brahman (Jnana Yoga).

Dvaita Vedanta was started by Madhva (Anandatirtha) around 1300 A.D. This system is referred to as "dualistic" because it emphasizes the distinctions between god, self, and things in the material world. This belief is in direct contrast to Advaita Vedanta. In Dvaita Vedanta, Brahman is that principle which controls the evolution into various forms of material nature. To free the self from the bondage of the material existence, one must think and meditate on scriptural statements. This practice is nondevotional; however, liberation is achieved only through God's grace.

BRAHMANIC RELIGION

THE FUNDAMENTAL aspects of the Brahmanic religion developed around the first millennium B.C., from a series of priestly commentaries on the original four Vedas, commonly known as the Brahmanas. Brahmanas is a Sanskrit word meaning "explanations of Brahman" ("holy power" or "word," "supreme spirit"), or the "sacred word." Each of the four Vedas acquired Brahmanas; for the *Rig Veda*, the *Aitareya* and *Kausitaki (Sankhayana)*; for the *Yajur Veda*, the *Kathaka*, *Taittiriya*; and *Satapatha*; for the *Sama Veda*, the *Pancavimsa* *(Tandyamaha)* and its appendix, the *Sanvimas* and *Jaiminiya* *(Talavakara)*; and for the *Atharva Veda*, the *Gopatha*. These extensive ritual and theological discourses served as guides for the priests (Brahmins) in performing rituals and sacrifices, and as explanations of the nature of Brahman and Brahma.

The perception of understanding of *Brahma* varies within differing schools of the Brahmanic religion, and with time. Brahma is a Sanskrit work meaning "swelling, growth, expansion" or "to grow great, strong, increase." Brahma is also perceived as the personification of Brahman (holy power or eternal word). Brahma is often called the first among gods (replacing Prajapati), the maker of the universe, and protector of the worlds. Brahma is often referred to as "the creator" (of the universe), and is frequently considered the source of all knowledge. Brahma shows a marked transition from Vedic to Bhakti Hinduism, as Brahma's role as god takes a secondary role to those of Vishnu and Shiva.

The Brahmanic religion places an emphasis on the role of society and the individual in maintaining the cosmic *rta*. *Rta* is the proper structure of existence, the right order, in which there is a uniformity and symmetry to all existence, which is strengthened and maintained by strict observance of the proper sacrifices. Later this concept was broadened to include all human activity as having a proper cosmological pattern to follow, known as *dharma*. The *Rig Veda* refers to *tapas* (heat) as the basic element of power in creation. *Tapas* was originally considered a possession of the Brahmin and the sacrifice he performed as a creative force sustaining the cosmos. This belief evolved into the idea that an individual could perform the sacrifice within himself by way of his knowledge of its essence, and be in possession of a unique *tapas* that could raise him above human limitations. Thus sacrifice, primarily to the great gods or powers of the universe, and a conviction that intellectual reflection upon Vedic truth can endow humans with the *tapas* that enables them to rise above human limitations are the foundations of the Brahmanic religion.

Another primary concept in Brahmanic Hinduism is *karma-samsara*, rebirth-redeath. This belief is that individual souls exist from beginningless time, passing on from one form of existence to another in continuous rebirth-redeath (reincarnation). The conditions or circumstances of each new existence are determined by the merits or demerits of the actions *(karma)* that have taken place in previous lives. The aim is then to liberate the soul from bondage to the suffering of this existence and to attainment of bliss by way of knowledge and through the ritual sacrifices explained in the Brahmanas.

Later, an emphasis was placed on the utilization of yogic techniques and meditation, and a concern with the unity of the universe and the acquisition of spiritually potent knowledge *(vidya)*. Although theistic devotionalism took on new forms, such as Shaivism and Vaishnavism, the quest centered upon achieving Atman (the spiritual essence of man) as a means of providing direct and unequivocal access to knowledge of Brahman, and thus to achieve spiritual liberation and bliss. This approach to Brahman developed around the seventh to eighth century A.D., and was taken from the Upanishads. Thus knowledge *(vidya)*, asceticism *(tapas)* and meditation *(dhyana)* became the thrust of the Brahmanic religion (see also "Yoga").

BHAKTI HINDUISM

*T*HE ELEMENT of devotion *(bhakti)* to a personal god appears early in Indian religious history. The Non-Vedic Buddhist movement provides some of the earliest evidence of popular religious devotional practices (see "Buddhism"). Early in the second century B.C. the Maurya Emperor Asoka made several pilgrimages to Buddhist sacred places and erected commemorative columns at these sites. Coins issued by the Bactrian rulers of northwest India in the second and first centuries B.C. and the Kushan rulers of northern India in the first three centuries A.D., depict images of Hindu deities and that of a lingam (symbol of Lord Shiva). Vasudeva and Shiva appear most frequently.

In early Vedic Brahmanism, the ultimate divine, Brahman, was held to be without qualities *(nirguna)* and therefore beyond human thought and unapproachable in a personal devotional manner. However, in one of the later Upanishads, the *Svetasvatara*, a direct connection was made between a personified *(saguna)* Brahman and the Vedic god Rudra, later known as Rudra-Shiva and today as Shiva. Later, Vasudeva was merged with Krishna and identified with the Vedic god Vishnu. Thus Brahman (the "creator"), Vishnu (the "sustainer") and Shiva (the "destroyer") are identified as the preeminent of the gods and goddesses (devis) worshiped in early Bhakti Hinduism, and a foundation was laid for the development of theistic devotional worship within the Vedic-Brahmanic tradition.

The Epics and Puranas serve as the foremost accounts of the great adventures of divine beings. The *Mahabharata* epic, written sometime before A.D. 200, reflects the popular religious Bhakti movement while preserving the continuity of the Vedic tradition. One of the most influential works of popular devotional Hinduism is a section of the *Mahabharata* known as the *Bhagavad Gita*. The Gita, through the teachings of the Lord Krishna, explains that devotion is the fulfillment of social duty, Upanishadic knowledge and Vedic ritual obligations, and serves as the preferred means of salvation.

Bhakti Hinduism gained wide acceptance among the populace, for while not everyone can become a priest (which was traditionally reserved for the Brahman caste in India) or a learned seer, everyone can know the lord through devotion, and can perform duties or acts of devotion to him (or her). *Puja*, the offering of gifts and services to the deity via an image of the deity, is a traditional means of Bhakti worship, along with pilgrimages to sacred places, fasting, and the chanting of devotional songs.

Individual gods and goddesses and their various forms within Hinduism are too numerous to mention in this work, and there is no definitive number of them. Many of the deities are regional, and many of them have changed names and forms through history. Brahma is still generally considered the supreme god, but is not typically depicted as a personal god, and is not often worshiped, as such, in Bhakti Hinduism. Shiva is one of the principal gods and was the first of the Hindu deities with a clear set of personal characteristics. The most prevalent images of Shiva are the lingam, represented as an eternally erect phallus (symbolizing his generative potency and his yogic powers of self-control), and as Nataraja, lord of cosmic dance. Shiva goes by many names (at least 1,008), and is given many different attributes. Generally, Shiva is considered the destroyer, and is worshiped as being the destroyer of *maya*, the illusion of the physical existence.

Vishnu, the other principal god along with Shiva, is generally referred to as the maintainer and protector of the world, and combines a range of qualities and characteristics by appearing in the world in a series of incarnations as avatars. In the Bhagavad Gita, Vishnu appears as Krishna to teach Arjuna (his disciple) the path of Bhakti Yoga through devotion to Krishna (himself). In the Ramayana, Vishnu appears as Rama, who epitomizes the virtues of self-denial and dedication as a model king. In the Puranas, Vishnu takes on numerous other forms as well.

Sectarian traditions have evolved around most major deities, with distinctive forms of worship and religious practices. It is common in Bhakti Hinduism to worship more than one god, or goddess; each community typically has its own deity, as do most families. New devotional movements have periodically arisen to stimulate and evolve the Bhakti faiths. Various saints and poets have revitalized their religions and traditions in the various languages and images familiar to the people of the time throughout the history of Hinduism.

VAISHNAVISM

*T*HE BEGINNING and end of Vaishnavism is bhakti, itself. Bhakti is the reciprocal love which exists between humans and the Divine, and it is the highest and purest form of love possible. Deep within the human heart burns the desire to love and be loved. Bhakti provides the vehicle to cultivate and know this love and to develop a personal relationship with the personality of God, or Godhead. Historically, the most intense form of Bhakti has been associated with the worship of Vishnu (from which the word *Vaishnavism* is derived) or his incarnation as Lord Krishna. The origins of Vaishnavism predate historical records, and the presence of Bhakti is prevalent throughout all schools of Hindu theology; however, the forms of Vaishnavism that are represented today were developed during the "Bhakti renaissance" from the twelfth to sixteenth centuries.

Some of the earliest proponents of Vaishnavism include the Alvars (poets and devotional mystics) and the Pancharatras of south India, as well as the Bhagavatas and the followers of Vasudeva-Krishna in north India. During this time a vast literary heritage was developing, including such classics as the *Ramayana*, the *Bhagavata Purana*, and the *Mahabharata*. Within the *Mahabharata*, which is the world's longest poem, lies the veritable bible of the Bhakti faith, the *Bhagavad Gita*. Within the Gita lies the essence of all Bhakti theology and practice, total devotion and service to the Lord as Krishna.

The *Bhagavad Gita* consists of a conversation between Krishna, the supreme incarnation of God (Vishnu), and Arjuna, a great army general who is Krishna's devotee and friend. In the moments preceding a battle, Lord Krishna explains to Arjuna his threefold theistic identity: Krishna is the very foundation of all spiritual and material existence, Brahma; Krishna is the supreme soul that enters into the hearts of all living creatures, Purushottama; and Krishna is the original, eternal Supreme Personality, or Godhead. Krishna further explains to Arjuna that his own soul is an eternal spiritual portion of himself, and that the best way to reconnect the soul with himself is through Bhakti Yoga.

Although all Vaishnava traditions advocate bhakti, as described in the *Bhagavad Gita*, differences arise in the descriptions of the personal nature of God, the relationship between God and the world, and the relationship between God and the individual soul. Most of the modern schools of Vaishnavism arose from theoretical differences with the interpretation of key scriptures by Adi Sankara. Sri Sankara (A.D. 788-820) formalized the monastic system that became the standard for most religious sects in India. Sankara espoused the doctrine of unqualified monism *(kevaladvaita)*, generally known as Advaita Vedanta, which purports that all distinctions or variations in this world are false and that only Brahma, or the Absolute Spirit, is real. The five primary schools of Vaishnavism argued this cosmology, and formed independent movements. The five schools that comprise the bulk of mainstream Vaishnavism evolved over hundreds of years, and adapted to the cultural differences that characterized the different areas and times when these movements were initiated. These five schools are summarized as follows:

The *Ramanuja School* was established during the twelfth century in south India. Ramanuja established the first formal theology of Vaishnavism, and wrote many important Vedantic texts. He also developed a form of worship that is the basis of most systems of worship in India today. Ramanuja states that although everything is indeed united with God, there are real differences between God and souls and the world. The liberated soul realizes and communes with God (Vishnu), but never actually merges with God. Moreover, liberation is a result of God's grace, and the individual must completely submit to God to realize the self. This school is most prevalent in southeast and northern India.

The *Madhva School* was established by Madhva during the thirteenth century in western India. Madhva was educated in the Sankara impersonalist school of thought, but he became dissatisfied with it and left it. He gained widespread recognition through his debates and discourses on "personalist" theology. Madhva completely contradicts Sankara and ignores the concept of oneness, believing that not all souls will attain liberation and that some may even suffer eternal

313

damnation (unique in Hindu philosophy). Madhva stresses the differences between God and man, and emphasizes the worship of Lord Krishna for salvation.

The *Nimbarka School* developed around the fourteenth century in north India. Nimbarka initiated the widespread worship of Krishna and Radha (Krishna's consort), but now has a relatively small following in India. Nimbarka identified the Supreme Brahma as the divine couple Radha-Krishna, and considers both concepts of dualism and nondualism as equally true, given God's power. Emphasis is placed on worshiping the sweetness of God's qualities.

The *Vallabha School* originated in the north and northwest portion of India during the fifteenth century. Vallabha identifies everything in the world as one with a personal god, similar to Ramanuja, but sees everything as Krishna (rather than Vishnu). Vallabha taught that the way to liberation is through God's grace gained by devotion to Krishna.

The *Chaitanya School* developed in northeast India during the sixteenth century. Chaitanya taught that everything in this world is simultaneously inconceivably one and yet different from God. Krishna's mystical powers enable him to be both immanent and transcendent. Krishna, with his lover Radha, is worshiped as the Divine Lover, and liberation is seen as eternal enjoyment of this love in heaven. Chaitanya emphasizes chanting the Lord's name, and the school developed great popularity with the masses that glorify his name. (See also the Hare Krishna Movement—ISKCON.)

For information:

Various teachers of the Vaishnavite tradition are frequently listed in the *Hinduism Today* newspaper.

Recommended Reading:

The Bhagavad Gita (various translations)

The Ramayana (various translations)

SHAIVISM

SHAIVISM IS both the worship of the God Shiva, or Siva, and the practice of evolving the soul to liberation and union with Shiva (transcendent consciousness). Shiva is one of the principal gods recognized in Hinduism, with millions of followers. He is known by at least 1,008 names, and is often called "the Destroyer," referring to his ability to destroy illusion, delusion, and error, which are the obstacles to realization of Self and God. The worship of Shiva can be traced back to the figure of Rudra in the *Rig Veda* (1200 B.C.) and extends to every part of India, Hindu sections of Southeast Asia, and recently to isolated parts of Europe and North America. Shiva is also represented by the lingam (a phallic symbol), as the creative life force and the energy that is utilized for attaining union with God (*not* typically representing the worship of the sex act or the penis, as it is often mistakenly thought to in the West).

Shaivism is primarily theistic and monistic, and is often characterized by various forms of asceticism. For most Shaivites, Shaivism is not a philosophy, but is life itself. Temples are erected and holy sacraments are performed. Shiva is viewed as both immanent and transcendent. Forms of worship and practice include pilgrimages, daily prayer, singing hymns, and reciting scripture, by devotional followers and by daily meditations and yogic disciplines by yogis.

There are six primary schools of Shaivism, though not all devotees of Shiva will consider themselves as belonging to any one of these schools. These schools are: Pasupata Shaivism, Vira Shaivism, Kashmir Shaivism, Shaiva Siddhanta, Gorakhnath Shaivism, and Shiva Advaita. The differences are philosophic, geographic and linguistic in character. The similarities include the desire to liberate the mind or soul from its binding attachments to the body and the physical world. Some of the common features that distinguish Shaivas in general, and yogis in particular, are: covering the body with ashes or making three horizontal ash marks across the forehead. Some sects of Shaivites wear their hair long and matted and many sects wear a necklace, or rosary, of *rudraksha* berries, representing their "austerities." Isolated sects of Shaivas may also practice self-mortifying vows such as: never lying down, inserting needles into their body, lying on a bed of nails, walking on a bed of hot coals, and long periods of fasting or sleep deprivation.

For more information... ████████████

... see the section "Masters and Movements."

Recommended Reading:

Siva Sutras
Ed. by Jaideva Singh

Gathas, 97-98
gatherings, informal, Meher Baba, 273
Gaudapada, 305
Gautama, Siddhartha (The Buddha), 23
Gelugpa (merit system ones), 32
Gem Elixers and Vibrational Healing, 186
gems and minerals, 185
Genesis, book of, 51
Gentiles, 60
Gentleman, The (Chuntzu), 41
genuflection, 80
Germain, Saint, 161
Ghotb (Sufi Master), 117
Giri Swami Order, 244
giving up, 38
gnosis: (knowledge), 106, 107; (spiritual
  awareness), 89, 117; individual, 107
Gnosticism: 85, 106-107; defined, 106;
  history, 106; writings destroyed, 107
Gnostics (knowers of Truth), 86
goals and objectives, 297
Gobi Desert, 161
Gobind Singh, 259
God's chosen people: Ethiopians, or Black
  race, 139; Jews, 56
God: (Allah), unity of, 79; absolute sovreignty
  of, 69; almighty, 51; belief in, 181; Black,
  139; channeling, 187; conceived according
  to our state of mind, 223; concept of, 298;
  consciousness, 7, 12; dependence on, 181;
  devotion to, 207; emotions, 51; essence, 168;
  everything, 132; everywhere, 51, 267, 281;
  experiencing, 265; faith in, 117; father, 66,
  166; fear of, 97; female and male aspects,
  94, 132; form, 267; friend to all, 97;
  genderless, 94, 206; grace, 66, 306; harmony
  with, 101; highest form of, 277; in all, 281;
  incarnation, 6, 270; infinite consciousness,
  233; infinite good, 74; inner light, 107; in
  the heart of mankind, 284; laws, disobeying,
  52; love for, 61, 117; many-faceted, 94;
  meditation on, 289-90; mystical union with,
  63; nature of, 6; obedience to, 55, 61, 91;
  oneness of, 126, 273; opening heart to, 275;
  Paramatma, 214; patriarchal, 55; personal,
  51, 73, 153; personal, devotion to, 309-11;
  personal experience with, 71; personality of,
  or Godhead, 312, 313; personal relationship
  with, 6, 313; realization, 7, 107, 173, 223,
  252, 273; relationship with world, 313;

spirit of, 171; submission to, complete, 313;
  sweetness, 314; total attention on, 278;
  uniting with, 101, 117, 228; Western perspective, 51; within us, 271; word of, 18
God-Adoring Song, 234
God and man, differences between, 314
Goddess, Divine (Shakti), 252
God-Goddess-All That Is, 193
Godhead, Supreme Personality of, 277
Godhood, realizing our, 192
"God is man", 114
gods, no other but God, 54
gods: family, 311; idols of, 54; images of,
  289; local, 311
gods and goddesses, individual Hindu, 310
good and evil: 61; contest between, 98, 104
goodness: initially, of humans, 41; of life to
  all, 153
Gorakhnath Shaivism, 315
Gospel, the: 80; preaching the, 60
gospels, Gnostic, 106
govi, 136
Graham Potentializer, 178-79
Grand Lodge, 119
Granth Sahib (Adi Granth), 17, 18
greater power, 182
Great Learning school of Confucianism, 41
Great White Brotherhood, 122, 160
greed, uprooting of, 27
Greek Orthodox Church, 111
Gregory Palamas, Saint, 111
grove, 95
Gurdjieff, Georges Ivanovitch, 255-57;
  mysterious, 255; Russian Georgian, 255
Gurdjieff/Ouspensky Centers, 255
Gurdjieff work, 257
guru: contemplation of, 253; seeing God
  through, 290; (spiritual teacher), 13;
  (truth teacher), 200

Hadith, 81
hair: long and matted, 316; unshorn, 18
hair. *see also* dreadlocks, 138-139
Haiti, 135
Hajj (pilgrimage), 80-81
Halloween (All Hallows Sabbath), 90, 91
hallucinogenic plants, 129
handfasting (marriage), 95
handparting (divorce), 95
Hanukkah (dedication), 57

Satanism: belief in Satan, 94; not witch-
craft, 94
Sa Ta Na Ma, mantra, 262
Satchidananda (name defined), 201
Satchidananda, Swami, 202
Sat-Chit- Ananda, 236
Sat Nam (truth manifested), 262
Satori, 35, 264
Satsang Beas, 258
Sawan-Kirpal Ruhani Mission, 259
scholasticism, 65-66
School of Elders (Theras), 25
School of Mind (Hsin-Hsueh), 41
School of Principal (Li-Hsueh), 41
Schucman, Helen, 190
science, religion and philosophy corre-
lated, 150, 152
Science and Health, 74
Science of Being and the Art of Living, 217-18
Science of Mentalphysics, 157, 158
Science of Mind, 152, 154
Science of Mind, 152-54
Scientology, 155-56
*Scientology, the Fundamentals of
Thought,* 156
scriptural interpretation, freedom of, 70
scripture: apocalyptic, 74; reading, 70;
reciting, 315; reliance on, 68
seax (knife), 95
secrecy, 90, 95, 100, 104, 259
Secret Doctrine, 150, 151
secret doctrine, *Upanishads,* 303
secret knowledge or powers, 286
Selassie, Haile: 138, 139; Messiah, 138, 139
Selene, Goddess, 95
Seleucid Empire, 97
self (atman):14, 223; absolute, 245; all
alone, 230; defined, 281; giving up the,
117; impermanence, 26; knowledge, 299;
fulfillment, 299; one, 239; perfect
happiness and peace, 231; real, as God,
273; real (soul body, jiva), 21
self-analysis, 166
self and nature identical, 38
self-awareness: 147, 148, 156, 215; during
meditation, 292
Self-Awareness Institute, 300, 343
self-defense with T'ai Chi, 44
self-discipline, 80
self-image, 193

selfish desires, 24
selfish thoughts, eradication of, 26
selfless service. *see* Karma Yoga
self-mortification, 316
self-observation, 295
Self-perfection, Yoga of, 236
self-realization: 157, 227, 238, 239, 281;
obstacles to, 315
Self-Realization Fellowship: 241-42, 244-
45; aims, 241; Church, 240
Self-Revelation Church, 240
self-surrender, 231
self-understanding, 298
semen, retention of, 15, 39
sensation, 26
sensation and movement, absorption in, 209
sense control, 206
senses, subtle inner, 293
Sensory Enhancement Environment, 179
separation: illusion of, 223: self-created, 253
service: to God's creations, 98, 290; to
mankind, 91, 98, 125
service, selfless. *see* Karma Yoga
Seth channeled by Jane Roberts, 189-90
Seven Realities, 273
Seventh-Day Adventists, 73-74
sexual acts, sacred, 142
sexual restraint, Taoist, 38-39
Shahadah, 80
Shaiva Siddhanta, 315
Shaivism: 4, 7, 8, 308, 315-16; schools of, 315
shakti: 11, 13; energy, 14; God's power, 13
Shaktipat, 248
shamanism: 4, 128-131; in Central Asia,
128; in Hawaii, 87, 132; in Siberia, 87,
128; in Tibet, 31
Shamanism (Native American Spiritual
Traditions), 128-131
shamans, use of: crystals, 185; mind-
altering plants, 141, 142
Shamballa, 161
Shankaracharya, of Puri, Sri, 250
Shanti (mantra), 289
Shi'ite Muslims, 80, 117, 167
Shinto (way of the Kami, or gods), 46;
ancient & modern, 47; shamanistic
elements, 4, 47; shrines, 47;
Shrine Shinto, 46; State Shinto, 46
Shintoism, 46-47

wisdom, 281, 304
witchcraft: 85-86, 94-96; repression of, 94
Witchcraft Act, English, repeal of, 94
witches, black and white, 94
witness, 288
Won-li Kang Mon (Lectures of Principle), 76
Woodstock Music and Peace Festival, 206
working for a living, 259
World's Parliament of Religions, 222
world: as mental representation of
  "ideation", 29; as reflection of mind, 239
World Community Service Centre, 219
world order, new, 259
World Teacher (Maitreya), 225
World-Teacher, Divine, 252
worldview, limited, 193
worship: personal freedom of, 70;
  polytheistic, 310-11
writing, 298
Wycliffe, John, 68, 69

yag-disk (knife), 95
Yahweh (God, Jewish): 51, 103; covenant
  with Abraham, 54, 55
Yajur Veda: 303; *Kathaka, Taittiriya,* and
  Satapatha Brahmanas, 307
yama (moral restraints), 10, 267
Yasodhara, 23
Yeshua ben Joseph (Jesus), 59
YHWH (I am that I am), 55
Yin and Yang, 41, 42, 44
Yoga: 4, 10-12, 250; age of, 10; defined,
  214, 223; limbs of, 10; teacher training,
  203, 209, 211-12, 214, 267; union with
  Divine Consciousness, 10, 11; *see also*
  specific types of Yoga; e.g., Hatha Yoga
Yoga, Shanti, 220
Yoga Journal, 12
Yogananda, Paramahansa, 241-42
Yoga of Self-Perfection (physical
  transformation), 236
yoga postures. *see* asana
Yoga Sutras, 10, 214, 266
"Yoga Teachers Directory", 12
yogi (self-realized person; yoga practitioner or teacher), 201
Yogi Bhajan, 262-63
yogic disciplines, 315
yogini (female yogi), 201
yogiraj (highest yogi), 201

Yogoda Satsanga Society of India, 241
Yomi-no-Kuni (Japanese underworld), 46
Yom Kippur, 57
Yoruba, 136
Young, Brigham, 73
Yukteswar, Sri, 238, 241, 243

Zarathustra,97-98; philosophy, 98
za-zen (seated meditation), 35
Zealots, 103
zekr (spiritual word, mantra), 117
Zen (Ch'an): 34-36; aim of
  enlightenment, 34; Buddhism; 25, 29;
  defined, 34; direct personal experience
  of enlightenment, 35; history, 34; in
  China, 34; in Japan, 34-35; in the West,
  35; meditation, 34; school of Mahayana
  Buddhism, 35; sects, 35; synthesis of
  two schools of Mahayana Buddhism, 34;
  see also Rinzai Zen sect, or Soto Zen sect
zendo (meditation hall), 35
Ziraat, 284
Zohar (Book of Splendor), 56, 100
Zoroaster, 97
Zoroastrianism: 4, 97-99; history, 97; in
  India, 86, 97; in Persia, 86, 97
Zoroastrians: conversion to Islam, 97;
  number and location, 97
Zwingli, Huldrych, 68

Steven S. Sadleir

A NATIVE of Southern California, Steve was born with a longing to know God. While other kids were playing kickball, Steve was off meditating. Innately obsessed with self discovery, he has spent over seventeen years actively investigating virtually every major spiritual path in the world. He traveled throughout the globe to meet the world's great spiritual leaders, and to actively participate in the rituals and rites of the world's religions and esoteric teachings. Over five years were spent writing this book.

Academically Steve holds a Bachelor's in Business from Menlo College and a Master's in Economics from the University of Wales, United Kingdom. He was a Rotary Foundation Scholar in 1981. Steve had his own financial consulting firm for many years, and now devotes himself entirely to spiritual work. Steve has personally studied with some of the world's most illustrious saints and master's, and has been trained as a spiritual teacher and meditation instructor in several different disciplines. He is founder of the Self Awareness Institute in Laguna Beach, California, which provides workshops and training courses in developing greater awareness and peace. He is also a Director of the Kaya Kalpa Institute, founded by Vethathiri Maharishi of Madras, India, and has a spiritual counseling and healing practice in Laguna Beach.

*T*o order contact:

**National Book Network
4720 Boston Way
Lanham, MD 20706**

1-800-462-6420

Visa and Master card accepted

*Pure Wisdom: Insights for Those Seeking
Happiness and Peace of Mind. $10.95*

*The Spiritual Seeker's Guide: The Complete
Source for Religions and Spiritual Groups of
the World. $12.95*

*Straight from the Heart: Authors, Celebrities
and Others Share Their Philosophies on
Making a Difference in the World. $10.95*

2000	1500	1250	1000	750

← ~4000 B.C.
Adam & Eve
1st Man & Woman
(Traditional Geneology)

• 2000 B.C.
Abraham goes
to promised land

• 1325 B.C.
Moses leads
Isrealites in Exodus
from Egypt

• 1000 B.C.
King David

• 975 B.C.
Temple of Solomon
Contructed

Prehistoric
Druid/Celtic
culture in Europe

• 1850 B.C.
Stonehenge III

• Hittite civilization
at its peack

• Mycenaean period

Shamans inNorth America
& Siberia

• 1700 B.C
Zoroaster
(tradional date)

← 2,600 B.C.
Egyptian Old Kingdom
great pyramids built

• Egyptian Empire
at its peak

• 1200 B.C.
Trojan War

← 8,000 B.C.
Dravidian Culture
in India Worships
"An" or "Shiva" (Hindu)

• 1500 B.C.
1st Aryan Invasion

• 1300 B.C.
Aryans Migrate to
Ganges River Basin

• 1000 B.C.
Brahmanas written
(Explanation of Brahman)

• 1400 B.C.
Rig Veda in Written Form

← 3,200 B.C.
Lord Krishna
(Traditional Geneology)

(Oldest Spiritual Text)

← Rishi's (Great Seers) →
Expound Wishdom of
Sanatana Dharma
"Eternal Truths"

Tantric Yoga practiced in India

• 1800 B.C
Harappan culture (India).
Builds sophisticated cities

Prehistoric
Shamans in China & Tibet

Shinto in Japan

← Hsia Culture (China)

Shang Period

APPROXIMATE DATES ROUNDED